Clientelism, Interests, and Democratic Representation

This book charts the evolution of clientelist practices in several Western European countries. Through the historical and comparative analysis of countries as diverse as Sweden and Greece, England and Spain, France and Italy, Iceland and the Netherlands, the authors study both the "supply side" – the institutional context in which party leaders devise and implement their political strategies – and the "demand side" – the degree of empowerment of civil society – of clientelism. This approach contends that clientelism is a particular mix of particularism and universalism, in which interests are aggregated at the level of the individual and his family (particularism), but in which all interests can potentially find expression and accommodation (universalism). In contrast, consociationalism and corporatism are systems of interest representation in which interests are aggregated at the level of "social pillar" or functional association (universalism), but in which not all interests can find representation and accommodation (particularism).

Simona Piattoni is Associate Professor of Political Science at the University of Trento, Italy. Her doctoral dissertation studied the impact of local politics on economic development in two southern Italian regions. She has published articles and essays on clientelism and regional development.

Cambridge Studies in Comparative Politics

General Editor

Margaret Levi   *University of Washington, Seattle*

Associate Editors

Robert H. Bates   *Harvard University*
Peter Hall   *Harvard University*
Stephen Hanson   *University of Washington, Seattle*
Peter Lange   *Duke University*
Helen Milner   *Columbia University*
Frances Rosenbluth   *Yale University*
Susan Stokes   *University of Chicago*
Sidney Tarrow   *Cornell University*

Other Books in the Series

Stefano Bartolini, *The Political Mobilization of the European Left, 1860–1980:*
   The Class Cleavage
Carles Boix, *Political Parties, Growth and Equality: Conservative and Social*
   Democratic Economic Strategies in the World Economy
Catherine Boone, *Merchant Capital and the Roots of State Power in Senegal,*
   1930–1985
Michael Bratton and Nicolas van de Walle, *Democratic Experiments in Africa:*
   Regime Transitions in Comparative Perspective
Valerie Bunce, *Leaving Socialism and Leaving the State: The End of Yugoslavia, the*
   Soviet Union and Czechoslovakia
Ruth Berins Collier, *Paths Toward Democracy: The Working Class and Elites in*
   Western Europe and South America
Donatella della Porta, *Social Movements, Political Violence, and the State*
Gerald Easter, *Reconstructing the State: Personal Networks and Elite Identity*
Roberto Franzosi, *The Puzzle of Strikes: Class and State Strategies in Postwar Italy*
Geoffrey Garrett, *Partisan Politics in the Global Economy*
Miriam Golden, *Heroic Defeats: The Politics of Job Loss*
Merilee Serrill Grindle, *Changing the State*
Frances Hagopian, *Traditional Politics and Regime Change in Brazil*
J. Rogers Hollingsworth and Robert Boyer, eds., *Contemporary Capitalism:*
   The Embeddedness of Institutions

Series list continues on the page following the Index.

Clientelism, Interests, and Democratic Representation

THE EUROPEAN EXPERIENCE IN HISTORICAL AND COMPARATIVE PERSPECTIVE

Edited by

SIMONA PIATTONI

University of Trento

CAMBRIDGE UNIVERSITY PRESS

PUBLISHED BY THE PRESS SYNDICATE OF THE UNIVERSITY OF CAMBRIDGE
The Pitt Building, Trumpington Street, Cambridge, United Kingdom

CAMBRIDGE UNIVERSITY PRESS
The Edinburgh Building, Cambridge CB2 2RU, UK
40 West 20th Street, New York, NY 10011-4211, USA
10 Stamford Road, Oakleigh, VIC 3166, Australia
Ruiz de Alarcón 13, 28014 Madrid, Spain
Dock House, The Waterfront, Cape Town 8001, South Africa

http://www.cambridge.org

First published 2001

Printed in the United States of America

Typeface Janson Text 10/13pt.   *System* QuarkXPress [BTS]

A catalog record for this book is available from the British Library.

Library of Congress Cataloging in Publication Data

Clientelism, interests, and democratic representation : the European experience in
historical and comparative perspective / edited by Simona Piattoni.
        p.   cm. – (Cambridge studies in comparative politics)
    Includes bibliographical references and index.
    ISBN 0-521-80033-1 – ISBN 0-521-80477-9 (pb.)
      1. Patronage, Political – Europe – History.   2. Patronage, Political –
Europe – Cross-cultural studies.   I. Piattoni, Simona, 1960–   II. Series.
JN94.A69 A63   2001
306.2'094 – dc21   2001018429

ISBN   0 521 80033 1   hardback
ISBN   0 521 80477 9   paperback

Contents

Contributors

Georgina Blakeley
Department of Politics
University of Huddersfield
Queensgate, Huddersfield,
United Kingdom

Jonathan Hopkin
Department of Political Science
and International Studies
University of Birmingham
Edgbaston, Birmingham, United
Kingdom

Gunnar H. Kristinsson
Department of Government
University of Iceland
Reykjavik, Iceland

Alfio Mastropaolo
Dipartimento di Studi Politici
Università di Torino
Torino, Italy

Frank O'Gorman
Department of History
University of Manchester
Manchester, United Kingdom

Apostolis Papakostas
Stockholm Center for
    Organization Research
Stockholm University and School
    of Economics
Stockholm, Sweden

Simona Piattoni
Faculty of Sociology
University of Trento, Italy

Nico Randeraad
Nederlands Centrum voor
    Contemporaine
    Geschiendenis
Groningen, The Netherlands

Carolyn M. Warner
Department of Political Science
Arizona State University
Tempe, Arizona

Dirk Jan Wolffram
Nederlands Centrum voor
    Contemporaine
    Geschiendenis
Groningen, The Netherlands

Preface

At a time when the transformation of the European political space profoundly affects the way in which interests are democratically represented, it might be useful to revisit a political phenomenon – clientelism – that has been mostly studied as a corruption of representation rather than one of its legitimate forms. Because it provides preferential access to state-administered jobs, services, and decisions through small groups of insiders, upon which the influence of strategically positioned bureaucrats and political leaders is strong, clientelism is frequently mentioned as an apt description of some of the mechanisms at work also within the European Union. And because clientelist exchanges occur between restricted groups and individuals, on the one hand, and individual bureaucrats and representatives, on the other, clientelism captures that element of personalism which characterizes the demand and supply of representation in today's Europe. Once considered a marginal phenomenon, clientelism may again become salient.

This book traces the roots of clientelism in the period in which democratic representation was introduced and perfected in most European countries – a period occupying approximately two centuries, from the late eighteenth to the late twentieth century. The relative timing of the extension of the franchise, the social composition of the active and passive electorate, the general structure of society at the time of mass political mobilization, and, not least, the structure of the state, in particular of the public administration, are the key dynamics that explain the character of democratic representation, in general, and the space, if any, occupied by clientelism within it. The same broad dynamics explain also whether such space subsequently contracted or expanded, and which traits clientelism acquired in each country. A deeper understanding of the circumstances present during the expansion or contraction of clientelism should prove of interest for this period of institutional and social transformations.

I became interested in clientelism while studying economic development of two southern Italian regions in the 1970s and 1980s. What attracted my attention was the different role played by the local political classes in the promotion of economic development of these regions. Although both local political systems were generally considered clientelistic, their practical workings were very different. While in one region, Abruzzo, politics, although clientelistic, managed to provide the material and immaterial public goods – mainly infrastructure and impartial enforcement of cooperative enterprises – that sustain development; in the other, Puglia, clientelism distributed divisible benefits to selected individuals and groups, and economic growth flagged. In other words, clientelism exerted a different effect on development because it worked at different levels of aggregation – the regional community versus selected groups and individuals (Piattoni 1996). This finding ran against the conventional wisdom and prompted further study.

The more immediate impulse for embarking upon a historical and comparative reflection of clientelism came from the workshop on "Clientelist Politics and Interest Intermediation in Southern Europe" organized by Kostas Lavdas, José Magone, and Ilias Nicolacopoulos at the European Consortium for Political Research Joint Sessions of Bern in 1997. The workshop brought together junior and senior scholars who, for days, engaged in an extremely stimulating debate on southern European clientelism. What was missing from that debate, however, was systematic reflection of whether clientelism is truly exclusively or even mainly a southern European phenomenon. Hence my decision to expand the scope for analysis and take a fresh look at the record of other Western European countries. Some of the participants in that workshop ended up writing chapters for this volume.

Thanks to three generous funds, one from the Norwegian Research Council (grant no. 121783/530) and two from the Faculty of the Social Sciences of the University of Tromsø (for Internasjonale symposier and for Internasjonalt samarbeid), I was able to organize two meetings, one in Tromsø in June and the other in London in November 1998, during which the contributors and I sought to develop a common vocabulary and a common approach to the study of clientelism. This was particularly important, as we came from different countries and different social disciplines – history, sociology, and political science – and began with not immediately compatible conceptual apparatuses. The first meeting was further enriched by the presence of four distinguished scholars – Professors Mario Caciagli, Richard Katz, Yannis Papadopoulos, and Luis Roniger – who answered our request to travel to the 70th parallel north (under rather difficult contingent conditions) to discuss our draft papers and help us in the discussion and search for a common framework. The London meeting gave us the possibility of expressing all remaining doubts and deepening our common understanding.

In the process, we have become not only an intellectual community but also a group of friends. It has been this spirit which has sustained our determination to write a volume which would not haphazardly assemble disparate think-pieces, but probe as thoroughly as possible a consistent set of propositions. These we drew, first and foremost, from Martin Shefter's 1994 book, *Political Parties and the State*. It is a tribute to Professor Shefter's scholarship that we found his approach to clientelism so compelling that we felt, at times, that we were only marginally improving on it. We hope, of course, to have done more than that.

The insightful comments of two anonymous reviewers and those of Paola Cesarini, who kindly commented on a handful of chapters at the 2000 Chicago Conference of Europeanists in the panel on "Spoiling Democracy with the Spoils: Patronage and Clientelism in Modern Europe," prodded us to further refine our argument and to make this book as cohesive as we could. At the end of this approximately three-year-long enterprise, I express my warmest thanks and personal feelings to the contributors to this volume, who have been willing to write and rewrite their pieces to clarify most ambiguous points. It is safe to say that without their knowledge, availability, and determination this book would have never been written. Finally, I also thank the Faculty of the Social Sciences of the University of Tromsø for its generous financial and organizational support and my ex-colleagues of the Institute of Political Science for their collegial friendship.

1

Clientelism in Historical and Comparative Perspective

SIMONA PIATTONI

Clientelism as Strategy

Political clientelism and patronage are widely diffused phenomena spanning across time and space and touching virtually all political systems in which votes count for something. In Europe, political clientelism and patronage are commonly considered as phenomena typical of only some countries, normally the Latin or Mediterranean countries.[1] The ascription of clientelism and patronage to given geographical areas goes hand in hand with their attribution to the cultural traits that supposedly uniquely characterize these countries, such as familism, tribalism, clannism, "orientalism." Political clientelism and patronage are, thus, generally understood as cultural phenomena: as the reflection onto the political sphere of a generalized way of conceiving interpersonal relations, particularly those between the powerful and the powerless. Alternatively, they are blamed on the distorted or incomplete development of given political systems. According to this second view, lasting marks were impressed early on onto the system of political representation of these countries – an imprint which even today affects the way in which interests are represented and promoted in these polities. For both the *culturalist* and the *developmentalist* approach, then, clientelism and patronage are *structural features* of given polities,

---

[1] In reality, patronage and clientelism are ubiquitous phenomena and an exceptionally vast literature supports this contention; see Roniger (1981, 1994) for extensive bibliographies. Yet for a long time and even today, they have been considered typical of the Mediterranean-Latin world. It suffices to take a look at the table of contents of Gellner and Waterbury (1977) or Eisenstadt and Lemarchand (1981) to confirm the bias. Later volumes, such as Schmidt et al. (1977), Clapham (1982), Eisenstadt and Roniger (1984), Roniger and Güneş-Ayata (1994), and Briquet and Sawicki (1998), considerably expanded the scope of analysis, including countries from Asia, Africa, America, and non-Mediterranean Europe.

which therefore explains their resilience even in the face of momentous social and political transformations.

This book, rather, starts from the assumption that clientelism and patronage are strategies for the acquisition, maintenance, and aggrandizement of political power, on the part of the patrons, and strategies for the protection and promotion of their interests, on the part of the clients, and that their deployment is driven by given sets of incentives and disincentives. As such, their relative diffusion is connected with, yet not determined by, the emergence, transformation, and demise of constellations of institutional and historical circumstances which make these strategies politically more or less viable and socially more or less acceptable. It should not be surprising, then, to find these phenomena in a variety of political systems characterized by allegedly rather different (political) cultures and social structures, and to observe their ebb and flow within the same political system in connection with the transformation of the set of incentives which make them viable and acceptable.

As political strategies, clientelism and patronage have the capacity to adapt to the existing circumstances as well as to alter them. Although they more or less likely depend on the sets of circumstances – generally conceivable as costs and benefits – in which patrons and clients happen to make their choices, their adoption is ultimately always a question of choice. Hence, while the study of the contextual circumstances in which clientelism and patronage are adopted may allow us to reach general statements – of limited spatial and temporal validity, to be sure – about the greater or lesser likelihood with which these particular strategies will be adopted, we still allow for the strategic choices of individual actors to prove these expectations wrong. In other words, while the logic of the argument made by this book is macro, it allows for micro-decisions both to supersede the contextual circumstances and to alter them.

The approach to clientelism and patronage as political strategies is as timely as it has important theoretical consequences. Several authors (e.g., Fantozzi 1993, Moss 1995, Vitali 1996) have recently lamented the lack of an approach to clientelism and patronage which is capable of accounting for the wide variety of clientelist and patronage systems while explaining their resilience under changing contextual circumstances. The challenge, then, is to account at the same time for adaptability and resilience or, better, for *resilience through adaptability*. The goal of this book, then, is to identify the sets of incentives that make political clientelism and patronage into viable and acceptable strategies or, conversely, make them impractical and unacceptable within the West European context, while also pointing to the real maneuvering room left to individual and collective choice.

A subsidiary goal is to challenge the dichotomous view, recently propounded by Robert Putnam (1993) in his study of Italian regions' institutional performance, that polities can be neatly divided into two groups: those in which particular interests are promoted at the expense of the general interest – the clientelist polities – and those in which particular interests manage to be expressed as particular cases of broader categorical interests – the civic polities.[2] By arguing that *politics is inherently particularistic* and that what makes the difference is how particular interests are presented, promoted, and aggregated, this volume wants to substitute a multivariate vision of politics for this dichotomous view. "Constituency service," "brokerage politics," "pork-barrel politics," to name just a few, are some of the expressions which denote the promotion of particularistic interests without regard for, and even at the expense of, "the general interest" in otherwise "civic" polities.[3] Existing democracies strike different compromises between the protection of particular interests and the promotion of the general interest, hence represent different mixes of particularism and universalism. Each of these compromises includes certain interests and excludes others, with different consequences for the policies that are enacted and the political culture which gets promoted.[4]

This introductory chapter presents the theoretical approach which informs this volume and proposes a critical overview of the classical literature on clientelism. The evidence which will illustrate and support the theoretical argument is drawn from past and present West European politics and takes up the remainder of the volume. By limiting the analysis to Western Europe, we certainly do not wish to suggest that political clientelism is a phenomenon characteristic of this part of the world in particular. The geographical delimitation, rather, is suggested by analytical

---

[2] Admittedly, Putnam (1993) builds continuous or interval variables to measure the institutional performance (dependent variable) and the degree of civicness (independent variable) of the Italian regions. However, when plotted against one another, these two variables give rise to two rather distinct blocs of regions, which are then labeled "civic" and "clientelist," respectively (p. 98ff). The historical account of how the two blocs got formed further polarizes the analysis (pp. 121–62), creating two ideal-typical modes of political regulation.

[3] The question of whether anything like the "general interest" exists is obviously a contentious one, which is discussed in greater depth in the concluding chapter.

[4] A more detailed comparative discussion of these different systems of interest representation is developed in the concluding chapter.

considerations. By focusing on an area which shared the fundamental processes of state-building and political mobilization, on the one hand, and whose citizenry shares a similar cultural heritage (Christianity, Roman law, feudalism, etc.) and a similar social structure (grounded in the historical subdivision in estates), on the other, and yet appears to encompass large differences among the predominant kinds of particularistic politics, we wish to determine which sets of circumstances underlie the relative diffusion of and the nature of particularistic politics – clientelism and patronage included.

Before discussing in greater detail the theoretical approach espoused by this volume and contrasting it to the conventional approaches, it is necessary to tackle some definition issues. While clientelism and patronage amount fundamentally to the same type of exchange, they evoke different mental images, which need to be described and discussed if we are to use these terms with precision.

Some Issues of Definition

Determining what causes the presence or absence of clientelism and patronage and their relative diffusion is a difficult task, which is further complicated by the confusion which surrounds their definition. It seems, therefore, appropriate to put forth a few definitions that are used consistently throughout the volume and that, if analytically fruitful, may further the development of this field of inquiry. In proposing rather minimal definitions of patronage and clientelism, my aim is to establish the genus from which species – variants of patronage and clientelism – may be derived by adding connotating elements to the definitional few. Replacement of definitional traits will instead denote cognate, but different phenomena.[5]

To begin with, we need to discuss the relationship between *clientelism* and *patronage*. So far we have used them together, as denoting largely the same phenomenon, that is, *the trade of votes and other types of partisan support in exchange for public decisions with divisible benefits*. And, in fact, the two terms are commonly used interchangeably, patronage being more diffused in the English-speaking world and clientelism stemming from the Roman lexical tradition. However, patronage seems to have plural meanings, in part coinciding with the British and American uses of the term. We must

---

[5] My debt, here and elsewhere, to Sartori (1970, 1984) should be clear. See also Kitschelt (2000: 853).

therefore begin by discussing these two terms and the mental images that they elicit.

Sometimes *patronage* is used to denote the public resources – jobs, goods, and public decisions – which constitute *the object of the exchange* between patrons and clients. But even when used to describe *the exchange itself*, patronage acquires different connotations depending on which side of the Atlantic it is used. In the British scholarly tradition, patronage serves to indicate mostly the distribution of posts in the administration to people from a given constituency in return for electoral support. The distribution of governmental largesse, which normally comes with such a slanted assignment of administrative posts, takes backstage and is generally considered as an inevitable consequence of the former.[6] This kind of patronage then suggests the existence of strong "organic" ties between representatives and public officials, on the one hand, and the constituency, on the other. Although it imparts a class, local, or ethnic bias to public decision-making, it does not systematically bend public decision-making to favor selected individuals and is, therefore, not perceived as wrong or immoral as long as the representatives manage to channel back to the community of reference – the constituency – resources from the state.

This type of patronage characterized mostly the early phases of the political development of many European countries, at a time when political mobilization was still low and the parties were still largely "electioneering committees." When represented and representatives largely belonged to the same social strata, election in a district could be obtained with just a handful of votes, and the public administration was limited in size and not fully professionalized, it was appealing and possible to distribute appointments in the public administration to members of the same constituency in exchange for electoral support.[7]

---

[6] In the Anglo-American tradition, this phenomenon would be called more precisely the "spoils system."

[7] What connection is there between patronage, thus defined, and *patrimonialism*? In patrimonial systems, public offices are owned and treated as private possessions: the office-holders are entitled to drawing an economic profit from the discharge of their public duties and can bequeath their job to their descendants. Under patronage the jobs cannot be passed down to offspring (even though there are cases of offices passed on from father to son, cf., Briquet 1997) nor does the officeholder normally draw extra profits from the discharge of his duties, but rather a fixed salary. However, as the prestige attached to such offices can be great, the officeholder does indeed enjoy additional benefits. For example, he is uniquely positioned to know about public policies that could affect his revenues and can act in a timely fashion and through preferential channels to protect his wealth. In this way, social

Whereas in nineteenth-century Britain, patronage truly reflected the "organic" ties between representatives and constituencies, in continental Europe[8] patronage often showed a less benign face and was less the expression of constituency ties than sheer instrument of repressive rule. Here, patronage would serve less the interests of the communities than those of the ruling classes, delivering governmental majorities that had no connection with the socioeconomic composition, the real interests, and the actual needs of the represented. In continental Europe, then, patronage came to indicate a phenomenon closer to that denoted by the American use of the term: the instrumental use of positions of power to distribute jobs, goods, and other public decisions to partisan supporters in order to maintain and strengthen positions of political power. This kind of patronage, then, is closely related to clientelism, which needs to be defined in its turn.

While denoting fundamentally the same type of political exchange as patronage, *clientelism* is a phenomenon typical of fully mobilized polities, in which the distribution of jobs in the public administration no longer suffices to secure any fundamental advantage to the incumbents. The expansion of the public administration and the increasing extension of state responsibilities into areas of social concern formerly within the private sphere multiply the jobs that can be distributed in view of their electoral return and explains why an overinflated form of patronage can be found also in many fully mobilized polities. However, in order to truly reach the masses, methods other than the handing out of public jobs in exchange for partisan support are needed. With clientelism, all public decision-making may become a token of exchange: from a birth certificate to a building permit, from a disability pension to public housing, from a development project to a tax exemption.[9]

and economic status, on the one hand, and political activity, on the other, feed onto each other, reinforcing each other and creating veritable socioeconomic and political dynasties. As for the connection between patronage and *nepotism*, this latter could be considered as a particular form of the former, in which only family members and close friends get the plum jobs in return for support and loyalty. On the likely resurgence of patrimonialism in contemporary societies, see Theobald (1992).

[8] This distinction between insular and continental Europe is suggestive and must not be understood rigidly. On the continent, for example, the Dutch provinces came very close to the British situation (see Chapter 5 below).

[9] The most striking feature of mass clientelism is that, in an effort to truly reach the masses, it often works through fairly impersonal means, such as the passage of laws or implementation of measures that favor entire categories of persons. This impersonalism constitutes a problem for those who analyze clientelism in terms of the structure of the clientelistic relationship, as we see below.

Patronage and clientelism, then, are largely the same phenomenon, with the latter being more penetrating and all-encompassing than the former. According to the above characterization, then, clientelism "implies" patronage: in order to bend the administrative decision-making process to particularistic criteria, in view of the electoral return that this would yield, the elected officials need to be able to put pressure on career officials, hence to control (albeit informally) their hiring, firing, and advancement. The close link between elected and career officials is commonplace in many so-called clientelist polities, even those in which hiring, firing, and advancement are nominally regulated by impersonal rules.

With clientelism, the emphasis is clearly put on the clients: how to win their vote, retain their support, command their allegiance. This alone shows that the balance of power between patron and clients has shifted in time: democratization and the extension of citizenship rights, on the one hand, and the bureaucratization of political leadership, on the other, have redefined the balance of power between patrons and clients. The clients are no longer "forced" to enter the clientelist deal, if they do not wish to, but rather choose to do so in order to gain privileged access to public resources. Moreover, they increasingly do so as members of broader categories of individuals with grounds for claiming publicly allocated resources. The patrons, in turn, are no longer secure of their power basis, as this depends on the political consensus that they muster. Nor can they be sure that the "clientelist deal" will be honored, as no legal enforcement mechanism can be devised. Once these trends are taken into account – that clientelism is becoming more and more bureaucratized and impersonal and tends to involve entire categories of persons in the role of both patrons and clients, and that enforcement becomes more and more difficult – it becomes increasingly clear that clientelism is but a variant of particularistic politics – "politics as usual," we would be tempted to say – and that singling it out as cultural pathology and developmental distortion is wrong.

Corruption, which is often likened to both patronage and clientelism on the rather weak ground that these two constitute a "corruption" (in a common language sense) of the democratic ideal, is rather *the exchange of money (or monetizable goods) for decisions on the part of career or elected officials that favor economically particular individuals or groups*. Whether or not votes are contextually exchanged is irrelevant. This, too, is a case of privatization of public decision-making, but it remains a phenomenon very different from either patronage or clientelism. While it may be argued that clientelism may lead to corruption, these two phenomena are not necessarily linked nor do they necessarily have a common root.[10] Indeed, it would seem that corruption is an even more ubiquitous phenomenon than either patronage or clientelism, spanning across geographical areas, political cultures, and levels of development (Della Porta and Mény 1997).

To conclude this definitional overview, a word should be spent also on *organized crime* as it, too, has been often closely associated with the previous phenomena (Blok 1974, Walston 1988) and blamed on the particular ethos or developmental path of certain political systems (Caciagli 1996). *Organized crime seeks to control illegal markets and to enforce certain types of illegal exchanges* (Gambetta 1993). However, organized crime shows the tendency to become involved in and distort public decision-making processes. First, as organized crime fatally clashes against the official structures of the state in its operations, it has to deal with it either by fighting it or, possibly more effectively, by trying to influence it. Second, organized crime finds in the market for public contracts one instance of those types of markets – characterized by restricted access, large sums of money, and the possibility to single out the "buyers" and apply threats to bend their decisions – which it is uniquely equipped to overtake and regulate. In this case, too, what matters is how vulnerable the state is to the attempted inroads of organized crime. And in this case, as well as in the previous cases, political development has something to say in this regard: a weak ruling class and a corruptible administration may invite the expansion of organized crime into the market for votes and for public works. By infiltrating these markets and by corrupting the rules that should regulate them – as when votes are delivered under the threat of violence or contracts are obtained by bribing public officials – organized crime widens its sphere of operation. However, organized crime is primarily an economic phenomenon which, out of necessity or convenience, spills into the political sphere.

Conventional Approaches to Clientelism

Scholars of patronage and clientelism have produced a rich and fascinating literature covering the many embodiments of these phenomena in

---

[10] It is sometimes argued that when an entrepreneur offers to employ a politician's supporters in exchange for a public contract, this is a form of clientelism practically indistinguishable from corruption. I would propose to see this as a double exchange: the first, between the entrepreneur and the politician involving the trade of the availability of jobs for public contract, is a *corrupt* exchange; the second, between the politician and the clients involving the trade of jobs for votes, is a *clientelist* exchange.

different times and different places. A less felicitous result has been conceptual stretching. To reach some common ground on which to base a meaningful discussion, scholars have sought to distill a definition of the patron–client relation. Yet, starting from largely ethnographic research material, they ended up hypostatizing an archetype of the patron–client relation closely resembling the landlord–peasant relation most common in traditional agrarian societies.[11] For example, Sydel Silverman defines patronage as "an informal contractual relationship between persons of unequal status and power, which imposes reciprocal obligations of a different kind on each of the parties" (Silverman 1977a: 296).

Drawing from the possibly most authoritative and exhaustive definition of patron–client relation by Eisenstadt and Roniger (1984: 48–49), which summarizes the work of many other authors, the main elements of the patron–client relation appear to be: (1) the dyadic, personal nature of the relation, (2) the simultaneous exchange of unspecified bundles of resources, (3) the sense of obligation inherent in the relation, often verging on emotional attachment, and (4) the informal, semilegal character of the relation. Of these traits, it is particularly the personal, dyadic nature of the patron–client relation and the emotional attachment, which is supposedly engendered by it, that need to be called into question, as their insertion among the definitional traits of the patron–client relation has rooted in the public imagery the idea of patronage and clientelism as characteristic of traditional societies. According to this view, the contamination of the public sphere of interaction with a type of relationship that should rule only private dealings "reveals" the traditional nature of these societies, in which private and public role structures and spheres of interaction are not yet completely separate and autonomous. As we argued above, such an understanding of clientelism is *culturalist* because it blames on the particular culture of certain societies the presence in the public sphere of modes of interaction characteristic of the private domain. It is also *developmentalist* because it argues that only in polities marred by a defective process of development could such a confusion between private and public modes

---

[11] Although rarely found in contemporary societies, such an archetype still serves as a benchmark against which deviations and developments are measured. To denote the more contemporary variants, which point to mutations in the more established concepts of "clientelism," "patronage," and "machine politics," many new categories have been created, such as "clientelism of the notables" and "clientelism of the bureaucracy" (Tarrow 1967), "bureaucratic clientelism" (Lyrintzis 1984), "semi-clientelism" (Fox 1994), and "low-level" and "high-level" clientelism (Papadopoulos 1997), to name but a few.

of interaction persist, sometimes because of the willful action of the ruling classes.[12]

Personalism and dyadicity may indeed have characterized traditional clientelism in subsistence (particularly agrarian) societies, but they are hardly typical of political clientelism in contemporary societies. How can the patron–client relationship, which according to this view is *by definition* personal and dyadic, become impersonal and categorical and still remain clientelist? Some scholars (Boissevain 1974) have attempted to solve this paradox by invoking the existence of long and sometimes obscure chains of friends of friends, so that, even though the system functions rather impersonally and involves great numbers of people, personalism and dyadicity are retained at each step of the chain.[13] And, indeed, Eisenstadt and Roniger insert among the definitional traits of the patron–client relation that (5) "these relations are undertaken between individuals or networks of individuals in a vertical fashion" (1984: 48).[14] Yet, as we know from, for example, Tarrow (1967), Weingrod (1968), Caciagli et al. (1977), Silverman (1977b), and Mavrogordatos (1997), clientelism can involve also entire corporate groups, such as producers' associations, trade unions, and political parties.[15] How can these cases be subsumed under the definition of patron–client relation given above if not by shedding at least person-

---

[12] Historically, accusations of clientelism have been used in the struggles between opposed political formations, with the ruling elites trying to maintain control of political representation by labeling the political opponents, and representatives of different social interests, as "opportunists" or "transformists" (Briquet 1997). In those countries where the functional cleavage (primary vs. secondary sector) coincided with a territorial (center vs. periphery) or a constitutional cleavage (monarchy vs. republic), the political discourse tended to generate a specific "geography of clientelism," with areas criticized as "backward and clientelist" (e.g., the Italian south) and areas celebrated as "modern and civic" (e.g., the Italian north and center) simply because they happened to be the strongholds, respectively, of the governing and opposition parties. Social scientists have sometimes consciously or unconsciously ended up bestowing scientific legitimacy upon such political operations (e.g., Banfield 1958; Putnam 1993). The classical reference to cleavages is Lipset and Rokkan (1967).

[13] This has in turn led to the elaboration of the concept of "broker" as someone whose career is built on his capacity to establish a contact between clients and patrons (Boissevain 1974).

[14] This is the trait of clientelism that most disheartens liberal scholars like Putnam (1993).

[15] And, even before them, Boissevain (1966: 23) argued, "The present-day Sicilian has more than one patron and works through the one that he deems most useful in a given situation. As relations become progressively specialized and the Sicilian moves out of his relatively isolated community to deal with increasingly diverse decision-makers – thus requiring functionally specialized patrons – the danger of an encounter between two patrons operating in the same social field diminishes."

alism and dyadicity from it and possibly also the emotional attachment supposedly engendered by them?

Another element of the definition of patron–client relation supplied by Eisenstadt and Roniger (1984: 49) – (6) "the strong element of inequality and difference in power resources between patron and client" – has earned clientelism the qualification of exploitation in disguise.[16] And yet, according to the same authors, (7) "patron–client relations are entered into, at least in principle, voluntarily and can, officially at least, be abandoned voluntarily" (ibid.: 48). As Eisenstadt and Roniger acknowledge, "the combination of these characteristics . . . creates several paradoxical contradictions," one of which is "a combination of potential coercion and exploitation with voluntary relations and mutual obligation" (ibid.: 49).

The way out of this paradox, I believe, is to follow the lead of Luigi Graziano (1976, 1980)[17] and interpret patron–client relations strictly as exchange relations. Patronage and clientelism are quid pro quo relations, ruled by economic principles. The real nature of this relation is somewhat obscured by its being projected externally as a personal and almost affective relationship with the usual protestations of loyalty, appreciation, and affection from both sides, but there is evidence to show that it is a relationship ruled by the pure economic goal of benefit-maximization. This *economistic* approach resolves the contradiction inherent in the *culturalist* and *developmentalist* approaches and allows us to subsume under the concept of clientelism *both* personal *and* group relations.

---

[16] This trait elicits the normative reaction of Marxist thinkers like Graziano (1976).

[17] Yet Graziano, too, thinks that while the exchange may take place between groups, the nature of the exchange is still personalistic. Graziano's terminology is a little confusing, but the substance of his analysis is clear. Even though clientelism may involve groups, he states, the incentives exchanged remain *direct*, as in purely dyadic relations, and never become *indirect*, as in true group relations. Participation in a dyadic relation is dictated only by the direct and selective, often material, incentives that can be drawn from it, while participation in group relations is induced by indirect incentives, such as the intrinsic satisfaction of contributing to the welfare of the group and of upholding an ethical code (Graziano 1976: 166). So, according to Graziano, even though clients may come in groups, they do not constitute anything more than a collection of single individuals and do not share anything more than their disjointed, direct convenience in engaging in a dyadic relation with the patron. However, Graziano acknowledges that it is possible in practice to cross the theoretically insurmountable threshold between group as disjointed collection of individuals and group as community when he talks of the transformation of the patron's "influence" into "authority" (ibid.: 167). See Abers (1998) and Piattoni (1998) for a discussion of how such a transformation might occur.

Unevenness of power resources between two contracting parties does not per se indicate the existence of an exploitative relation.[18] The real question is whether the parties are equally free to enter and exit the deal. In traditional clientelist systems, in effect, the freedom of the clients to enter the relation or not, and on which terms, was severely constrained. The patron usually held virtual monopoly over the means of livelihood of his clients, so that not entering or exiting the relation was often prohibitively costly. In many societies, this situation of de facto coercion and exploitation was tempered by the existence of customary norms imposing on the patron specific duties of assistance and support vis-à-vis the clients (cf. White 1980 on Abruzzo, Roniger 1983 on ancient Rome, Briquet 1995 on Sicily and Corsica). It is therefore understandable that a sense of obligation and even affection could color the patron–client relation.

The modernization of society and the marketization of the economy stripped the clients of these customary protections and left them vulnerable to unmitigated exploitation. At the same time, economic development and the progressive extension of citizenship rights equipped them with the means to restore a certain balance in their relation with the patron – or to exit it altogether. But even when the bargaining space seemed nil, it is argued that the clients would skillfully manipulate the terms of the relation with the patron to their favor (cf. Scott 1977, Silverman 1977b, Waterbury 1977). So, the freedom to enter and exit the patron–client relation must be one of the definitional traits and clientelism must concurrently be understood as a free exchange relation. The uneven balance of power between patron and client is, on the contrary, a contingent trait which connotes only some variants of the patron–client relation.

To summarize, patron–client relations are exchange relations whose terms depend on the relative power of the parties, in turn dependent on the contextual circumstances that affect both demand and supply. Some such relations are rather similar to exploitation – the negative end of the spectrum (negative reciprocity) – while others are rather close to gratuitous support – the positive end of the spectrum (generalized reciprocity). In between lies a whole range of relations in all similar to the morally

[18] Silverman (1977b) distinguishes between the objective terms of an exchange relation, which if highly unbalanced could be described as "exploitative" (etic analysis), and the assessment of these terms given by the exchanging parties (emic analysis). Like Scott (1977), she underlines that positive behavioral analysis must start from an apprehension of the actors' assessment of the exchange.

neutral market exchanges (balanced reciprocity).[19] If we interpret clientelism and patronage as strategies we will come to expect that both parties will try to alter the circumstances in which the exchange takes place so as to move the relation to the more favorable end.

Yet even this definition of clientelism raises new puzzles. If what matters to both patron and client is the advantage that can be drawn from the exchange, why then bother to maintain the fiction of a personal relationship? Could this exchange be standardized, as would occur in a market, so as to avoid having to travel the long and cumbersome chains of friends of friends? Would it be conceivable to have an impersonal supply of favors (from the patrons) to meet a demand of favors (from the clients) in a political marketplace? Could we think of patrons advertising their services on newspaper or television and of clients shopping around to find the best cost–benefit balance or the most specialized patron for a given area of favors?

These questions have received three answers. First, an element of personalism may be a desirable, perhaps necessary feature of any public relation, even those between voters and representatives. Already Carl Landé (1977) suggested that a certain amount of personalism in politics may be an unavoidable "addendum," as people may wish to feel represented by real persons rather than by impersonal institutions and organizations. Second, all politicians, patrons included, need to create for themselves a reputation as trustworthy – as getting things done, making the voice of the represented heard, and bringing "the pork" back home. Reputation is inherently personal: hence, the need to establish some sort of real or fictitious bond with the voter (Moss 1995). Third, the clientelist deal is often unspecified and never fully legal. Consequently, compliance is monitored with difficulty. One way of increasing the likelihood of compliance is to

---

[19] Patron–client relations in Europe have historically oscillated between these two extremes: they have probably started from the positive end, and traveled the whole spectrum to the negative end, and it is my impression that in today's Europe they are probably converging toward the neutral center of the spectrum. Already in the postwar period clientelism had become largely a "myth": a "language" which allowed patrons and clients to set the terms of their deals in full knowledge that each side would try to skirt or bend them to its advantage (Silverman 1977b). Korovkin (1988: 113) concurs: "If patronage is myth, then, like myth, it resolves paradoxes by imbuing them with more cultural than social significance. Patronage, in this context, may be seen as an attempt to equalize the impact of socio-economic structure upon itself. Hence patronage should be seen as a dialectical force that constantly brings people 'in' while, at the same time, it promotes exclusivity."

see matters "eye to eye" and to strike a personal deal.[20] So, although a significant degree of impersonalism can characterize patron–client relations, the more categorical and market-like the relation becomes, the more clientelism would tend to blur into other kinds of particularistic politics.

These answers contain some truth, but they do not amount to a compelling argument of why the relation between patron and clients should necessarily be personal. Daniel Verdier's work (1995) shows that neither reputation nor ambiguity in exchange relations necessarily implies personalism and that a depersonalized kind of clientelism is altogether possible. Verdier seeks to explain what determines public subsidies to private industries. The answer is not, as we would expect, industrial structure and technological innovation; it is, rather, the interest of politicians in staying in power by drawing electoral support and campaign funds from industrial lobbies. Far from being the representatives of already constituted interests, politicians constitute these interests by granting subsidies and creating rents. In Verdier's words: "politicians maximize their chances of staying in power through the deliberate use of subsidies to structure the political debate and embed factor owners into stable policy networks" (Verdier 1995: 5).

Subsidies tend to deepen factor mobility. Politicians grant subsidies to the factors of production – labor and capital – according to where they want to draw the mobility line, whether at the sectoral or the territorial level. Four exchange patterns thus emerge. If both sectoral and geographical mobility are to be maintained, subsidies will be given to the entire factor categories, and class politics will result. If geographical mobility is to be increased, then subsidies will accrue to industries, and politics will involve trade associations and sectoral ministries. If sector mobility needs to be encouraged, then subsidies will be given to local governments, and politics will take a territorial connotation. If instead both sectoral and geographic mobility can be kept low, then subsidies can be granted to regional sectors and, in the extreme, to individual firms, and politics will be "clientelistic."[21]

---

[20] Warner (Chapter 6) argues that parties' flanking associations can provide such enforcement.

[21] This is a personal rendition of the discussion in Verdier (1995: 5). This latter label is also mine. Summarizing with Verdier's words: "Variations in political competition determine variations in economic competition. On the one hand, politicians may seek tenure by building narrow, dense networks capable of sustaining abnormally long incumbency – safe seats in the local districts, party dominance in government. In so doing, politicians invite

Verdier's work makes a number of important theoretical points which have emerged in this critical overview of the literature on clientelism and which will inform the empirical chapters of this book. First, whether politics will revolve around classes, functional groups, local communities, or individuals will depend on the level at which interests are aggregated also thanks to public subsidies. Ideologies will be fashioned accordingly to justify the chosen level of aggregation. Instead of representing two opposed modes of mobilization, ideologies and subsidies – programs and divisible benefits – are two faces of the same political game. Second, the politics of rent-seeking are possible if and only if the networks which are created to bind factor owners and politicians are fairly stable. And only if building and joining a policy networks implies fixed costs will the networks be stable.[22] Yet membership in these networks is open to all those who can make a contribution (campaign contribution or vote) and are interested in the related selective benefit. Hence, personalism is not strictly implied by the difficult enforceability of the deal. Third, increased party competition will tend to magnify the importance of the median voter, thus inducing politicians to support factor mobility and embrace class politics ("pie" politics). Such a policy shift will occur through a change in the balance of power, within parties, between back- and front-benchers. While back-benchers will want to keep coddling their safe constituencies through sectoral and geographical subsidies, front-benchers will want to appeal to the median voters by distributing factor-wide subsidies. Thus, whether politics are driven by programs or patronage depends on the level of political contestation. Fourth, if heightened party competition leads to an outbidding war of subsidies to sectoral, geographic, or even narrower constituencies, "pork" alone will soon run out and the "politics of outbidding" will run against unmasterable budget

---

rent seeking on the part of factor owners who, through membership in the policy networks, can win rents that they use to segment factor markets along sector or regional lines. On the other hand, politicians may broaden their appeal to include the median voter into large factorwide networks. In so doing, politicians elicit strategies of market competition among owners of a same factor and lobbying for policies of class redistribution between owners of a different factor" (ibid.: 6).

[22] "Policy networks are defined as systems of informal relations between rational individuals that create a stable infrastructure for the exchange of personal favors" (ibid.: 5). They are a form of investment against the risks involved in the transaction of a rent for campaign resources or of a divisible benefit for a vote. As this transaction is not fully legitimate and cannot be officially enforced, building a stable network will make it safer.

deficits.[23] This, too, will contribute to the demise of clientelism and its eventual transformation into a different type of politics.

To conclude, patron–client relations can be safely assumed to be exchange relations which *may* be more or less personal and more or less balanced depending on the contextual circumstances but which are always voluntarily entered into. The terms of the exchange are known to the parties and command *some* legitimacy. While this is enough to ensure short-term compliance, it does not imply that the parties will not try to bend the terms of future deals to their favor, nor that they may ideally prefer to enter different kinds of political exchanges.

The Comparative and Historical Study of Clientelism

The empirical exploration of patronage and clientelism as strategies is best pursued by studying the contextual circumstances that make the patron–client relation a more or less viable strategy. This book is, therefore, organized around the study of the two sets of circumstances which can be argued to have the greatest influence on the choice of whether to use clientelist and patronage strategies and, if so, how. We denote these two sets as the "supply side" and the "demand side" of clientelism and patronage, respectively.

The terms "demand side" and "supply side" in the debate on patronage were introduced by Martin Shefter in his *Political Parties and the State* (1994: 22–29).[24] Shefter rejects the "neoclassical" theory of political patronage, which sees patronage as a product which political parties, like firms, supply to satisfy the demand of their customers, the voters. According to this view, such demand is independently determined by the voters' preferences, in turn "determined by their social background and cultural heritage" (ibid. 23). In addition to showing that many parties, whose electoral base would lead us to expect the use of patronage to retain voters and

---

[23] The explicit reference to the Italian situation, in which one party regularly won all elections, is in Verdier (ibid.: 17): in this situation, "the logic observed at the level of the local (safe) seat is reenacted at the national level. . . . Party dominance reproduces the backbencher's machine dynamic on the national scale." The implicit reference is to Sartori (1976).

[24] The present volume owes much more that these phrases to Shefter's treatment of patronage as a political strategy, something which will become amply clear in the remainder of this book.

activists, in fact adopt different mobilization tactics (table 2.1, ibid. 23), Shefter argues that the kind of mobilization tactics voters and activists react to is largely determined by the kinds of inducements that were offered to them when they were first mobilized (ibid. 26–27). For Shefter, in other words, patronage is supply driven.

In adopting the demand and supply terminology introduced by Shefter, we decided to look at both sides of the equation and to pay particular attention to their reciprocal interaction. The "supply side" is made of those institutional circumstances that may induce party leaders to adopt clientelism or patronage as a strategy for attracting voters, supporters, and activists to their side. Under this rubric we find: (1) the existence or lack of an independent bureaucracy resistant to partisan pressures, (2) the ideals or other objectives motivating politicians to run for office, and (3) the ideas and expectations about the source of legitimate power that historically developed along with the formation of state structures. These circumstances explain why political leaders may wish to use clientelist and patronage strategies to obtain and maintain control over political representation.

The "demand side," in turn, is composed of those circumstances that make the citizens of a given polity more or less willing to accept the clientelist bid and grant their votes or other services in exchange for divisible benefits. Under this rubric we find: (1) the level of "empowerment" of the citizens, principally affected by their economic status; (2) their cognitive capabilities, especially influenced by the rate of literacy, access to information, availability of meeting places, and so on; and (3) their organizational capacity, that is, their capacity to form secondary associations or join independent organizations which may act as catalysts for collective action (such as people's churches and external political parties). These conditions make the citizens more or less interested in entering clientelist or patronage deals and, if entered, make them more or less capable of defining the terms of the deal in more or less favorable ways.

Why are processes of state-building and political mobilization important for the study of political clientelism? Since clientelism amounts to bending public decision-making to the promotion of individual interests (both those of the patron and those of the clients), clientelism implies the pliability of the structures of public decision-making to particularistic considerations. Attention is, therefore, immediately directed to the process through which such structures were formed, that is, to state-building and the creation of autonomous structures of routinized decision-making, in particular, the administration.

Consistent with the approach to clientelism as strategy, this book argues that politicians and voters are capable of choices which, although inscribed in an institutional and structural context, nevertheless can supersede and redefine it. Institutional and structural conditions do not immediately act as constraints on actors' choices both because they are liable of being modified and because they need to be appraised as constraints before they can act as such. The notion of strategy entails both an apprehension of the context in which choices take place and the purposive attempt to redefine such context. With clientelism, as with other political strategies, actors use the context as a stepping-stone for superseding and redefining it. For our analysis, this means that we avoid as much as possible reading the choices of the individual and collective actors in terms of institutional and structural context. For example, we avoid concluding that, given the institutional and structural circumstances, certain countries (e.g., Greece, Spain, or Italy) were *bound to* become clientelist while others (e.g., England, Sweden, or the Netherlands) were *destined to* become civic. Yet we do not ignore the influence that both institutional and structural circumstances may have had on individual and collective choices and therefore analyze them in detail.

Institutional and structural circumstances cannot be considered as determining factors on other grounds, either. First, because the contextual circumstances of human action need to be appraised, there may be disagreement as to how constraining they really are. Second, clientelist and other forms of particularistic politics run counter to some of the principles – universalism, impersonalism, fairness – publicly espoused in most polities; hence, they inherently contain an ideal tension which can undermine them. While practically expedient, they live a difficult theoretical existence, and are constantly liable to being contested in the name of principles which command a higher legitimacy.

Even the more commonly accepted and celebrated political ideologies (e.g., liberalism) contain contradictions which open up a theoretical space for defending less legitimate, but more expedient, practices such as clientelism. In other words, the relationship between accepted political ideologies and forms of particularistic politics is not that of an ideal to its corruption, but rather a dialectical relationship between what is theoretically desirable and what is practically possible. Clientelism is just one of the historical forms in which interests are represented and promoted, a practical (although in many ways undesirable) solution to the problem of democratic representation.

State-Building

Why did some administrative systems prove less permeable to the appropriation of public resources for private ends than others? What induces politicians to try and distort decision-making rules to win the votes of their clients? When are such practices possible and effective? These questions can be answered by looking comparatively at the political development of Western European countries around two momentous historical junctures: the formation of the administrative system and the onset of mass mobilization. Shefter's thesis (1994), as already noted, is that the relative timing of bureaucratization and democratization – the introduction of universal (male) suffrage – determines whether party leaders will tend to use patronage to mobilize voters, supporters, and activists to their side or resort to programmatic appeals. If, when a party was founded, patronage was not an option (as mostly occurred in "externally mobilized parties"), then party leaders would also in the future use programmatic appeals to attract voters and activists, and these groups will support the party on programmatic and universalistic grounds. If, instead, at the moment of the party's foundation, patronage was an option (as in the case of many "internally mobilized parties"), then the party leaders would also in the future use divisible benefits to attract voters and activists, and these groups will support the party in exchange for patronage. Whether or not patronage was an option at the founding of mass political parties depends, according to Shefter, on whether or not the bureaucracy was already entrenched behind a "charter of bureaucratic autonomy." Hence, to summarize, "externally mobilized parties" – the parties which represent the politically excluded groups and have to build a mass party structure precisely to overcome the barriers to entry into the political-electoral arena – tend to be patronage free, while "internally mobilized parties" – the parties "founded by elites who occupy positions within the prevailing regime" (Shefter 1994: 30) – tend to be patronage oriented precisely because of the different structure of opportunities they were faced with upon their foundation. The use of the spoils of government to partisan goals is too strong a temptation to be resisted.

Shefter gives us the "supply side" account. It explains, *grosso modo*, why political parties in some countries (e.g., Sweden and Germany) avoided the clientelist temptation altogether, while in others (e.g., Greece, Spain, and Italy) they used it extensively. However, his account fares less well in explaining why other countries (e.g., England, France, the Netherlands), in which political parties flirted with patronage, ultimately managed to eradicate or significantly contain it.

In Sweden, the bureaucracy was entrenched early on behind a "charter of bureaucratic autonomy," as in the German case discussed by Shefter (1994: 36–45). Such a charter must not be understood literally as a document in which tasks and privileges of the bureaucracy are spelled out; rather, it must be understood more substantially as a social constellation interested in defending the autonomy of the bureaucracy from political influence. The Swedish bureaucracy, in particular, was staffed mainly by the nobility and the upper bourgeoisie. While having an upper-class bias and, hence, being liable to class patronage, at the onset of mass politicization the bureaucracy was insensitive to partisan pressures and was therefore never drawn into mass clientelism. A look at the demand side only confirms this conclusion.

While creating an independent bureaucracy and staffing it with members of the nobility and the upper-bourgeoisie, the Swedish state also empowered its citizenry both economically and cognitively. The Swedish citizenry was mainly made of independent, literate farmers mostly living at some distance from one another in nuclear families. With industrialization, many relocated to the urban centers of the south and made up a sizable working class. With democratization, individual Swedes were mobilized into mass parties through programmatic appeals, for two reasons. First, they had no other identity than that which linked them to their occupation; neither the extended family nor the village provided a competing source of identity. Second, they had the cognitive tools to articulate their interests as individual instances of broader interests. Not only was there scant supply of clientelism in Sweden, but there was no demand for it, either.

The case of Greece provides a telling contrast with Sweden in Chapter 2, by Apostolis Papakostas. In Greece, universal (male) suffrage was granted before an independent bureaucracy was created and mass political parties entered the public scene early in Greek history. Even though attempts were made to insulate the bureaucracy behind a plethora of written laws and regulations prescribing independence and impersonalism, public officials remained sensitive to partisan pressures, as they had no alternative source of social and economic mobility than through party affiliation. The "charter of bureaucratic autonomy," in other words, was purely formal. Moreover, Greek peasants were largely uneducated and had strong family and village connections, and when they migrated to the cities they recreated there their original family and village networks. Having to articulate and promote their interests, they did so using family and village ties to reach into the state administration: mass parties could do no more than act as a meeting place for supply and demand of patronage.

While the clear-cut cases of Sweden and Greece are in a sense overdetermined, as either supply or demand would probably suffice to explain the outcome, what about the "intermediate" cases of England, France, and the Netherlands, and the uneven geography of clientelism in both Italy and Spain? These more complex cases can be explained only by taking into full account both demand and supply.

In England the supply of patronage never quite met its demand, so patronage never acquired the same characteristics that it did in Italy or Spain. As Chapter 3, by Frank O'Gorman, argues, the kind of patronage which prevailed in England was the expression of community ties between representatives and bureaucrats, at the center, and the common citizenry, in the local constituencies. While nothing prevented the instrumental use of a bureaucracy which, until quite late, was not protected by any written or social charter of bureaucratic autonomy, the fact that the population had both the material and the cognitive tools for promoting their individual interests as part and parcel of their community interests put a brake onto the use of patronage for purely partisan goals. Simply said, people's votes were not for sale. Both public opinion and people in government shared a distaste for "corrupt practices," thus the frequent appeals for, and repeated attempts at, a reform of the public administration. With the onset of mass politicization the supply of patronage had been effectively suppressed, so that mass political parties had to mobilize the citizenry on programmatic appeals instead of on the promise of patronage. As the citizens had their primary allegiance to the local community, they articulated their interests at the constituency level, and as the Members of Parliament represented entire constituencies, it was the constituency's interests which they promoted. For both social and electoral reasons, then, clientelism was averted and a kind of particularism which would elsewhere be condemned as improper – "constituency service" – is present and bears no such stigma in England.

The Dutch case represents a different variant of the same story. During the eighteenth and nineteenth centuries, the scope for patronage in the Netherlands was large. As Chapter 4, by Nico Randeraad and Dirk J. Wolffram, shows, patronage ebbed and flowed in accordance with how tight a control the central authority could establish in the periphery. The

Dutch provinces had a long tradition of self-government, and were thus resistant to bending to a central authority. The Stadholder – the Prince of Orange – amply resorted to the farming of offices to the local nobility in exchange for their acknowledgment of his power. The local nobility, in turn, ruled locally with patronage. However, whenever the centralization drive of the Stadholder lost steam, the supply of patronage decreased correspondingly. The Dutch citizens, having independent sources of livelihood from farming and commerce, were individually rather uninterested in exchanging favors for votes, being more interested in the public goods (roads, canals, etc.) that the state could provide to the local communities. Hence, the demand for patronage was rather low and, if present at all, articulated at the community level. After the Napoleonic rule, when the link between center and periphery was redefined and became administrative rather than political – the provincial "governors" as well as the mayors were appointed by the king, not locally elected – the supply of patronage dried out completely.

An interesting reorientation of interest articulation occurred around the turn of the century which theoretically could have opened up the space for a revival of patronage. With the gradual extension of the franchise, from 1887 to 1917, voters became mobilized into ideological and confessional parties around the highly contentious issue of public funding of private, particularly confessional, schools. The first mass political parties thus represented ideological-religious communities, frequently coinciding with territorial communities. Patronage could have been revived if access to confessional education for local religious minorities had been exchanged for votes. However, given the nature of the political compromise which was reached in 1917, access to confessional education was granted as part of the rights of citizenship. While now the ideological and religious "pillars" became the level at which interests were aggregated and represented, all room for clientelism was concomitantly suppressed.

The fateful interaction between demand and supply of patronage is clearly demonstrated by the Spanish case discussed in Chapter 5, by Georgina Blakeley. In Spain, too, a central power tried to establish its control over the periphery by farming offices to the local nobility, while the local representatives bought electoral support through the distribution of patronage. Because the local populations were economically and cognitively disempowered, they gladly entered this exchange deal. The system was pervasive and well functioning: local *caciques* bought the few votes necessary, particularly in the countryside, to "deliver" elections through the skillful manipulation of the public decision-making machinery which they controlled. The paralyzing omnipresence of the central state in the periphery met with the dependence of the local population on state provisions (permits, exemptions, subsidies, etc.) to yield a foolproof system of patronage.[25] The extension of the suffrage and the onset of mass political mobilization did not change the picture dramatically: even though the supply for patronage changed character – from the limited but vital system which permitted the artificial alternation of parties in government under the *turno pacífico* (1874–1923) to the more fragmented and contested system of the Second Republic (1923–30) – the demand remained as strong as ever, hence the system lived on. Even though, during the Second Republic, citizens were nominally empowered by a state which finally acknowledged their citizenship rights, they remained economically and cognitively disempowered and therefore easily captured in clientelistic networks.

The Spanish case demonstrates the insufficiency of the liberal notion of "civil society." Formally empowered citizens may still need to resort to clientelism in order to obtain the means of livelihood from those who control public decision-making. The independent citizen postulated by liberalism must possess the economic, cognitive, and organizational means to articulate and promote her interests at a higher level of aggregation than that of herself and her family if she does not wish to fall prey to clientelist networks. Moreover, the liberal citizen remains dependent on the state for the defense of her negatively defined liberties and on the historically determined kind of supply of public decision-making that the state provides. During the Second Republic, it was anarchism which propounded a more substantial notion of "civil society," one which postulated citizenship as membership in a community and which could have cut the ties to the state supply of public decision-making. Whether the anarchist project could have actually delivered a different kind of state–society relation than liberalism is impossible to know (even though we have hints from regions, such as Catalonia, in which it loomed particularly large, that it might). What we do know is that the liberal conception of "civil society" is not an antidote against clientelism.

---

[25] Lest the term "patronage" here result in confusion, let me specify that I opt for this term because it applies to a nineteenth-century, limited-franchise political system but that, in terms of its being purely an *instrumentum regni*, it is rather different from contemporary English-style patronage (see *supra* the section on definitions).

The chapters of the first part of this volume, then, refine and correct Shefter's thesis. The relative timing of bureaucratization and democratization cannot per se explain why, in some countries, clientelism became a fixture of political life, while in others it could be expunged or transformed into more defensible forms of (particularistic) interest representation. The analysis of the supply of clientelism needs to be integrated with the analysis of the demand for clientelism if sense can be made of the English and Dutch cases, as well as of the uneven geography of clientelism in Spain.

Mass Political Mobilization

Supply and demand of clientelism do not uniquely depend on the structural and institutional circumstances in which the citizenry gets politically mobilized. Contextual circumstances can be changed through purposive action and, in any event, need to be interpreted before they can act as constraints. For both these reasons, attention must be paid to the autonomous choices of individual and collective actors to make sense of different outcomes even within largely comparable circumstances. The second half of the volume charts the more recent evolution of clientelist exchanges in several European countries to reveal the scope of variation that exists even within largely similar institutional and structural settings. The interpretation of clientelism as strategy implies that we cannot infer the presence of mass clientelism from the previous existence of patronage: while an analysis of the circumstances under which the transition to mass politics occurred will indicate the likelihood of such an outcome, room must be left for the creative choices of the political leaders of each country as well as for the multivariate effect of a number of other factors.

Clientelism becomes a more appealing political strategy the more turbulent the circumstances under which mass political mobilization occurs. This is the story of the Italian Democrazia Cristiana (DC) which, although initially aiming at reforming society according to Christian values like the sister French party Mouvement Républicaine Populaire (MRP), ended up opting for the more secure strategy of mobilizing votes through clientelism in the face of the Communist scare. While the objective circumstances surrounding the strategic choices of these two parties were somewhat different – the line that separated Eastern and Western spheres of influence during the cold war period ran right through the Italian peninsula – the independent assessment of the two party leaderships was crucial.

24

As Chapter 6, by Carolyn Warner, argues, the institutional room for clientelism was equally large (or small) in both France and Italy. The institutional setup of the French state left as much room to clientelist practices as that of the Italian state. The ideological commitment of the respective Christian Democratic parties was also (initially) equally strong. However, because the party leadership assessed the circumstances differently – with the French MRP leaders prioritizing the reformation of society according to Christian values and the Italian DC leaders the fight against communism – their strategies ended up differing. Moreover, internal variation in demand determined the internal variation in strategy choice. In those areas of Italy where the Catholic subculture was particularly strong and individuals could articulate their interests at the community or occupational group level, Christian Democratic leaders could obtain consensus through ideological appeals or, at most, through group-level clientelism and did not need to engage in individual-level clientelist exchanges. In a mirror image, there were areas and social groups in postwar France which pursued their interests as individuals or families along personalistic channels and were, therefore, available for individual-level clientelism. However, most of French society, probably because of its different level of empowerment or, as Warner also suggests, because of the diffusion of norms opposed to distorting public-decision making to selective concerns, was uninterested in individual-level clientelism. They were instead appreciative of constituency-level clientelism, which, however, MRP politicians often did not practice.

The comparison between the strategies chosen by the French and Italian Christian Democratic leaders at the onset of mass political mobilization highlights two important points. The first is that, even under identical institutional circumstances, political leaders remain free to make their own strategic choices – and pay the connected costs. The second is that these choices have, in turn, an impact on the contextual circumstances and, consequently, on the future likelihood that the strategies will be upheld or changed. The Italian case is one where supply largely created (or strengthened) its own demand, while the French case is one where supply destroyed (or weakened) it.

Generalizing from this study, it could be argued that the urgency of the situation faced by the ruling political elites at the time of mass political mobilization determines whether or not, all other things being equal, clientelism will be the chosen strategy. Once the system is in place, though, it would be wrong to assume that it will continue undisturbed. Even if, so to say, the supply side is temporarily given, the demand side will keep changing with social and economic transformations, eventually leading also to a change in the supply. Chapters 7 and 8 analyze which kinds of social and economic transformations on the demand side may trigger a transformation of the institutional and structural circumstances which determine the supply side. Here the historical perspective proves particularly useful, as it is possible to hypothesize that the same factors which were identified in the study of the British case – the political costs and benefits of clientelism, its economic costs and benefits, and the internal logic of clientelism itself – will govern the transformation.

To start with, the political benefits of patronage are all the higher compared with its costs, the less challenged the governing parties are. It can be further hypothesized that, since today's parties – both in government and at the opposition – are well entrenched in the structures of the state (Katz and Mair 1995), even an appearance of competition may hide a fairly stable settlement. However, dramatic political upheavals are possible even in apparently "blocked" systems, as the Italian political developments in the 1990s would seem to show. Not only may external circumstances change, engendering an increase in the economic as well as the political costs of clientelism compared with its benefits, but the very logic of clientelism may cause a "political-fiscal crisis of the state" and trigger a backlash if it leads to large public deficits, widespread corruption, and the disintegration of public institutions.[26] While there is, of course, no guarantee that such dark scenarios will necessarily induce a reaction, it is plausible to assume that, as the danger of a collapse of the system gets bigger, an increasing number of politicians may start to worry about the ultimate and cumulative consequences of their actions and may decide to put a brake on the process.

The comparison between contemporary Spain and Italy contained in Chapter 7, by Jonathan Hopkin and Alfio Mastropaolo, shows how important independent changes in the demand side are, but also how the demand can be skillfully manipulated and transformed by the suppliers of clientelism. The chapter begins by describing the comparable political development of nineteenth-century Spain and Italy, which allowed for the diffusion of the less benign kind of patronage described above. In both countries, patronage served to fashion governmental

[26] This possibility is explicitly acknowledged by Shefter (1994: 13–14).

majorities that had little or no connection to the real needs of the voters. The existence of this precedent, however, does not induce the authors to conclude that clientelism would necessarily develop with mass political mobilization.

In Spain, society modernized and evolved also during the Franco regime, thus becoming less dependent, as a whole, on the system of political patronage. When mass political mobilization finally took place, the demand of clientelism was rather low even in the presence of the supply stemming from the conservative parties. That the demand had become considerably weak is demonstrated by the fact that recourse to clientelism did not grant the conservative parties tenure in government. Governmental alternation, for a while, ensured a relative absence of clientelist practices. Eventually, however, Socialist leaders, in an attempt to get more firmly entrenched in society and to keep power, revived these practices, thus reawakening also the demand for them. Spain in the late 1980s was, once more, surprisingly similar to contemporary Italy.

The Italian story is more linear, unfolding from the strategic choice of the Christian Democratic leaders to employ a clientelist strategy of mass mobilization (as described also in Chapter 5) and spreading also to Socialist and other party leaders. The diffusion of clientelist practices occurred not by "contagion" but rather through the programmatic manipulation of the demand side. The Christian Democratic party created, through legislation, social groups dependent on state subsidies, provisions, and permits, thus inflating the demand of individual- and group-level clientelism. To accomplish this, they systematically undermined the alternative levels of interest articulation – the local communities and the constituencies. This work of decomposition, however, was not uniformly carried out throughout the country – some areas in the North remained long unaffected – and there were even instances of recomposition of interests at the local and regional level (Piattoni 1998). The purposive action of Christian Democratic leaders was accompanied by the autonomous development of society, particularly a decline in ideological commitment. As a consequence, the once ideology-driven Socialist party became interested in using clientelism to win voters to its side, leading to the excesses that became famous in the 1990s.

The importance of the demand side and its malleability by external developments is shown also in Chapter 8 on Iceland, by Gunnar H. Kristinsson. The economic costs of clientelism may increase

27

dramatically in the face of growing external constraints. As clientelism tends to cause chronic overspending, it may lead to the "fiscal crisis of the state." While such crisis can be postponed for a while by cumulating public debt, it finally has to be faced. External economic constraints, however, do not make themselves felt directly on any one society, but rather are filtered and mediated by social groups which, more than others, are sensitive to these costs: in Iceland's case, the university-educated "professionals."

Iceland, although formally belonging to Denmark for many centuries and hence importing from it the formal structures of government (Denmark would be a case similar to Sweden and Germany), had developed a rampant system of patronage during the interwar period. The Great Depression, and the massive state intervention in the economy that it triggered, represented the opportunity for regulating most domestic industries, for fixing administratively the price of many fundamental goods, and for imposing public licenses on most economic activities. Virtually all aspects of economic life ended up being regulated, one way or the other, by the state. This gave ample scope for patronage to public officials and to the politicians that appointed them.

Globalization and adherence to the European Economic Area forced Iceland to privatize many of its industries and to liberalize most economic activities. The inefficiencies bred by the previous system could no longer be tolerated, and a new stratum of university-educated "professionals" spearheaded the drive to reform the public administration. As posts in the public administration started to be granted, again, on the basis of professional competence, they became correspondingly less available for politicians. As these posts had largely served as end-of-career positions for political veterans, the job of the politician became less attractive. Thus, changes originating in the international economic sphere and initially impacting the demand side had repercussions also on the domestic political sphere and on the supply side. While the political old guard still believes that it is their duty, as representatives, to cater to the needs of the constituencies as well as of individual constituents, a new guard of politicians selected through media-dominated primaries is emerging, apparently uninterested in such practices.

Kristinsson concludes that the ease with which a widespread system of patronage has been apparently eradicated in Iceland in the space of few years and without a major political crisis testifies to the existence of unpropitious demand conditions. He advances the hypothesis that the high levels of trust among Icelandic citizens acted as a barrier to the diffusion of clientelist norms, a point frequently made by scholars (cf. Putnam 1993 and, particularly, Roniger 1988, 1990).[27]

Together, the cases in Chapters 6, 7, and 8 argue that clientelism is a dynamic phenomenon for many reasons: because it is actively manipulated by the suppliers, because it is affected by autonomous changes in the demand, and because it is endowed with an inherent logic of evolution that tends to make it increasingly costly. We should not be surprised, then, by its tendency to change: to escalate and implode as well as to retreat and disappear.

Preliminary Conclusions

Starting from the assumption that a certain degree of particularism is unavoidable and that a purely universalistic and impersonal system of interest representation is unattainable, and probably also undesirable, how could clientelism be reformed so as to purge it of some of its worse side-effects? In the light of the European comparative and historical experience, it would seem that two avenues are the most promising for "recycling" clientelism into more acceptable forms of particularistic politics.

The first solution is for clientelism to evolve into "constituency service": while still a form of particularism, "constituency service" has a collective, rather than individual, character which makes it more tractable in view of the harmonization of particularistic interests into "the general interest" of society (the "British solution"). The second solution would amount to recomposing the interests of individuals into those of functional groups – as in corporatism (the "Swedish solution") – or of territorial-ideological subcultures – as in consociationalism (the "Dutch solution"). It is unclear whether in today's Europe there is space for either type of recomposition – indeed, these solutions seem to be under pressure in their original homelands.

There is also, obviously, a third option: that interests continue to be promoted at the level of the individual and her family through personal networks that reach into the bureaucracy through political parties and that

---

[27] The approach proposed in this chapter runs against bestowing autonomous and unmediated explanatory power to norms and values, and rather calls attention to the structure of opportunities actors operate in.

the system degenerates into outright corruption – shall we call it the "Italian solution"?[28] In the concluding chapter we speculate whether this is truly the only realistic scenario or whether there is ground for higher hope.

[28] These labels are only suggestive and, to some extent, also polemical. No polity is uniquely characterized by one system of interest representation only: in all countries there coexist, in different proportions, different systems, which are more or less diffused across social and territorial formations, but which are always accessible and sometimes simultaneously used by every citizen.

2

Why Is There No Clientelism in Scandinavia? A Comparison of the Swedish and Greek Sequences of Development

APOSTOLIS PAPAKOSTAS

Introduction

In a book about the development of the state, Göran Therborn wrote, from a neo-Marxist point of view, that "[i]n the historical development of this social dynamic a number of temporalities affect the organization of the state" (1978: 45). Neo-Marxists are not the only ones who have recognized that temporalities affect the organization of the state. In a standard text about the state, written from a neo-Weberian angle, Gianfranco Poggi wrote that "the particular course taken by the Western state was a highly contingent affair" (1990: 105) and that the development of particular states has to be understood with the emphasis being put upon contingency (ibid. 99–100).

While agreeing on the importance of temporality and contingency, Therborn and Poggi have different temporalities and contingencies in mind. For Therborn, as for other neo-Marxists, the differences between particular states have to be understood with reference to social classes and, specifically, to the different rhythms of two politicized class struggles: one between feudal lords and the capitalist bourgeoisie, and the other between the bourgeoisie and the proletariat (cf. Mann 1993: 45). For Poggi and the neo-Weberians, it is, rather, the temporalities of the state system and the availability of state models that provide the key to understanding the course taken by particular states.

Advocates of each theoretical tradition argue in a rather exclusive fashion as though there were only classes or only states surrounding a particular state. In real situations, however, social classes and other states together constitute parts of the organizational environment of a particular state and interact in ways that are not clearly understood. Of course,

31

the environments in which the states exist are themselves not only the temporalities of classes and other states, but also the temporalities of other social formations, such as voluntary organizations and families, or of social processes, such as urbanization and the spread of literacy. These processes, which are usually not treated in relation to the development of the state, are equally important in understanding it.

I use the same concepts of temporality and contingency to explore the development of clientelism, or the lack thereof, in two European countries: Sweden and Greece. The argument that I develop in this chapter leads me to refine the thesis, put forward by Martin Shefter (1994), that the relative timing of bureaucratization and democratization explains whether or not patronage becomes a tool of political mobilization in some parties' kits. In the course of the chapter, I reintroduce the "demand side" of the clientelistic equation, which Shefter had purposely ignored, not so much to blame it on the "culture" of any particular people as to bring attention to the fact that it, too, was shaped by historically specific temporalities and contingencies.

Bureaucracy or Clientelism?

There is broad agreement that the Swedish public bureaucracies possess two kinds of autonomy: from the central state and from the particularities of civil life. Apart from these two, there is a third kind that has been taken for granted in Sweden, namely, autonomy from political parties. In these respects, the Greek state can be said to be the opposite: the political control of the state bureaucracies by the government is exhaustive. Ministers are usually responsible for and intervene in many matters that would be defined as bureaucratic rather than political in other countries. For instance, it is not uncommon for changes in ministerial posts to lead to changes in the chain of command inside the bureaucracy. State bureaucracies, in turn, are strongly influenced by the particularities of civil life and political parties are intertwined with state authorities to a degree unknown in Scandinavia. It can, for instance, take just a few moments to understand the political sympathies of civil servants in Greece, whilst in Sweden one may still only be able to make qualified guesses about them even after many years.

Non-Swedes probably wonder whether there truly is no clientelism in Scandinavia, knowing that there can exist, for example, fascist practices without fascist parties or socialist politics without socialist parties. To avoid the tendency of Western intellectuals to contrast idealized political *models* with corrupt *practices*, I comment briefly upon this question.

To my knowledge, the Swedish academia has not researched clientelism in modern times. While reviewing the major sociological works on the Swedish state, I did not find the words "clientelism" or "political patronage" mentioned at all (Papakostas 1997). Instead, young sociologists seem to be more concerned about problems stemming from the impersonal implementation of universalistic bureaucratic rules and the transformation of individuals into administrative cases (e.g., Johansson 1992) – questions that researchers in other parts of the world would define as luxuries. My personal impression, however, is that some practices that are defined as clientelistic elsewhere are not defined as such in Sweden, and that therefore one would probably find more "particularism" in Sweden than is generally assumed. The Swedish language does not have an appropriate word for clientelism, and when journalists refer to clientelism in other countries, they usually have to add that this is a practice where politicians exchange favors for political support. Yet, on the whole, the practice of clientelism is relatively unknown in Sweden.

Evidence from scientific research suggests that the Swedish bureaucracy works in a relatively universalistic manner. True, some of those cases that would be defined in terms of clientelism elsewhere are explained in terms of administrative efficiency in Sweden.[1] The character of the discourse in public debates tends to be bureaucratic and rational rather than political, and although power struggles between sectional or class interests are essential in understanding the form and content of state institutions (Ahrne 1989, Korpi 1983, Therborn 1989), the implementation of the rules follows universalistic patterns and is not intermediated through political patronage. According to a standard text on the Swedish public administration, no patronage or spoils system has existed in modern times (Heckscher 1958) and a strong legalistic tradition of loyalty to the government and the public interest has dominated the civil service (Mellbourn 1979, Rothstein 1996: 80).

Students of the labor movements know that asking counterfactual questions such as Sombart's – "Why is there no socialism in the United States?"

---

[1] For instance, recruitment to AMS, the national Labor Market Board – the authority for the implementation of the active labor market policy, a cornerstone of Social Democratic policy and of the "Swedish Model" after World War II – did not follow universalistic rules, but was rather based on ideological commitment to Social Democracy. The motivation

(Sombart [1906] 1976) – could be quite wrong and that it would probably be a better research strategy to explain how the actual outcomes came into being "as the gradual crystallization of a limited array of patterns out of broad spectrum of possibilities" (Zolberg 1986: 401). My major concern here is to answer questions stated factually, such as why state rules came to be applied in a universalistic rather than in a particularistic manner and why political parties became horizontal organizations based on class rather than on vertical networks. I use the expression *rather than* with the intention of avoiding the fallacy of retrospective determinism and of interpreting actual outcomes as the inevitable consequence of antecedent factors. At certain points in time social structures leave several degrees of freedom, opening up a broad array of possibilities, only one of which gets actualized.

When Werner Sombart asked his question about socialism in the United States, he had the predictions of the Marxian doctrine in mind. He believed that socialism was inevitable in modern capitalist industrial societies and wanted to explain the temporal lateness of class-consciousness development in the United States. When asking a similar question about clientelism in Scandinavia, having in mind the virtual ubiquitousness of clientelism in Mediterranean Europe, one cannot rely upon an equally strong theoretical proposition. There is no theory that predicts the inevitability of clientelism, although advocates of modernization theory would argue that clientelism should disappear as societies become more modern.

The fact is that clientelism is not associated with a particular type of society, although some people think that it is more typical of un(der)developed societies or that it depends on some kind of "mystical" preservation of their traditions. It is not unusual, for instance, to find that clientelism in Greece is attributed to the "oriental values" stemming from its Ottoman past, or even to the patrimonial structure of the Byzantine state. Such a narrow cultural explanation falls far short of the mark when clientelism is detected in societies without an "oriental" past or a Byzantine state.[2]

---

given was that of administrative efficiency (Rothstein 1996: 116–30). When historians write about class or family recruitment in earlier periods, they usually explain it by referring to social capital: individuals were "socialized" in the administrative culture of these families (Frohnert 1993: 71).

[2] While reviewing the literature on clientelism, Eisenstadt and Roniger (1980) mention different kinds of clientelist practice in areas as culturally different as Mediterranean Europe, the Middle East, Latin America, southeastern Asia, Japan, the United States, the former Soviet Union, and parts of Africa – by this alone undermining the culturalist argument.

If culture fails to explain clientelism, could economic development do better? Would people living in a prosperous society with a high standard of living ever become engaged in clientelist exchanges? One might anticipate that the answers would be yes to the first question and no to the second, and I certainly believe that there is more behind economic than cultural explanations. Yet clientelist practices are not a common phenomenon in all economically underdeveloped societies, whereas they can also be found in prosperous ones. A detailed Greek historiographic study of work mobility of the urban poor reports, for instance, that about 80 percent of the time, people found jobs thanks to kinship networks and not to political intermediation (Pizanias 1993). Looking at what kinds of practices are associated with clientelism, one can see that they are not purely economic. Intermediating entrance into working life is a common clientelist practice, but not the only one. In reality, nearly all administrative matters can become opportunities for clientelist exchanges. Clientelism is more a social and political phenomenon than an economic or cultural one and the Greek experience – and of course the experience of many other countries (cf. Eisenstadt and Roniger 1980: 46) – suggests that it does not automatically disappear with economic development.

Still, social scientists have taken the development of universalistic state structures as something natural, which automatically comes with economic development. A closer reading of the historical facts and the sequences of development in Europe, however, suffices to call this assumption into question. As a Swedish political scientist has correctly observed (Blomqvist 1992), the development and maintenance of universalistic state structures has to be explained as much as the development of particularistic state structures – and I think that it is rather more difficult to explain the development of the taken-for-granted universalistic state in a few quite atypical societies in the world.

The Contours of a Macro Sociological Explanation

I try to sketch the contours of a macro sociological explanation by using pairs of contrasts between the Swedish and Greek sequences of development to illustrate my argument. The comparison between Sweden and Greece provides the researcher with a situation comparable to multiple natural simultaneous experiments enabling one to analyze different trajectories that lead to the development of predominantly universalistic structures, in one case, and to a mixture of universalistic and particularistic ones, in the other.

To interpret social practices as the outcome of history is as fallacious as saying that culture or economy alone explain everything. The elements in history that were important to a particular development must be clearly identified. To explain present practices with reference to historical legacies that have persisted for centuries – a popular research activity in some variants of historical institutionalism[3] – is problematic, particularly as there is always a plurality of social forms in whichever country's past and a low rate of innovation of new ones. Whatever the accepted practices today, it is always possible to find some roots for them in the past. The problem is not to show that there is a legacy from the past or that there is some kind of continuity between present and past practices, but rather to examine how history makes some of these forms dominant and suppresses others.[4] On the one hand, there were many forms of particularism in the early modern Swedish state – among them patronage – many of which disappeared in the course of time and gave way to more universalistic practices.[5] On the other hand, the ambition to create a universalistic state was present in Greece from the time of national liberation, but in the course of modernization Greece did not manage to free itself of the particularist elements. So, looking at Greece and Sweden from the point of view of the spectrum of possible alternatives, these societies were more similar historically that has been assumed. They have become more different as this spectrum of alternatives was gradually narrowed down to the established alternatives.

To make my argument clear, I use a comparative logic in which historical outcomes are understood with reference to the concept of timing by placing them at the intersections of social processes with different temporalities. In the words of an art historian, it is like seeing historical outcomes as the product of many disparate "wheels of fortune" (Kubler 1962). There are many social processes and plenty of ways to describe and analyze them. My concern is about organizational processes in a broad sense and my approach is materialistic – similar to Michael Mann's "organizational

[3] See Demertzis (1994) and Putnam (1993) for this kind of explanation of modern political culture in Italy and Greece, respectively.
[4] Compare this idea with Barrington Moore's notion of suppressed alternatives (Moore 1978).
[5] On the existence of patronage until the middle of nineteenth century in Sweden, see Englund (1993), Rothstein (1998), and Von Platen (1988).

materialism" (Mann 1993: 36). The underlying theoretical theme is based on the idea of the social landscape developed by Göran Ahrne (1990, 1994) and the theoretical movement of organizational realism. One of the ideas behind these concepts is that organizations are the tissue of social life and that social phenomena should be understood primarily with reference to organizations and the relations between them, and not with reference to an all-encompassing system or to a logic intrinsic to societies. Combining Kubler's metaphor of the disparate wheels of fortune with the idea of the social landscape, historical developments appear to be the outcome of the relative timing and the historical conjunctures of four histories with different temporalities: the histories of states, enterprises, voluntary associations, and families. Thus, one must understand the forms of the state in terms of the state's relations to the other organizational contexts.

In a book about modernization in general, and about state modernization in particular, Marion J. Levy writes that "[n]o activities of the members of any governments can be fully understood in terms of the structures of the governments alone. The structure of political allocation in terms of which the members of the society operate in organizational contexts other than that of government are [*sic*] always to some extent relevant to the governmental context itself" (Levy [1966] 1996: 394). I define such an organizational context as a constellation of organizations (Ahrne and Papakostas 1994) and I try to understand the development of state structures in Sweden and Greece with reference to their respective constellations.

Clientelism is usually studied as an exchange relationship between individuals with unequal power resources. The cultural frame for this relationship has been the major focus of analysis: the literature on clientelism, with its deep roots in social anthropology, has mainly tried to understand clientelism as a phenomenon stemming from the morals or cultural codes of small, "backward" societies (cf. Chapter 1). Without denying that local cultures have some impact, I follow the way of macro analysis and move from the powerful organizations to the local community. I try to portray clientelism as a problem of "boundary setting" and of "intertwining" between different types of organizations, where complicated historical sequences of organization establishment create different boundaries and intertwinings between different types of relatively "modern" organizations. Perceived from this angle, both clientelist and universalistic practices are consequences of different historical ways of drawing up organizational boundaries.

This means combining and going beyond two other traditions in social science: one that perceives clientelism as an organizational attribute of the state – a specific form of particularism – and the other that views it as an organizational attribute of a given political party.[6] Clientelism, in particular, and particularism, in general, are thus seen as problems of intertwining between social organizations operating with different logics.

I also use the metaphor of *vacancy chains* (White 1970) to illustrate how, at different times, some sequences of organizational establishment create open spaces where certain social practices can flourish, while some other sequences do not allow such openings to appear. Two reservations must, however, be stated. In the strict vacancy chains model, effects are felt through the system because moving individuals leave an opening behind them. Organizations do not have to leave an opening behind them when they expand to a new space. The other reservation has to do with the notion of *intertwining*. In new social spaces, social practices and organizational principles can become intertwined in a plurality of forms that is impossible in strict vacancy chain models, where one person occupies the open position. However, although used loosely and evocatively, these concepts prove useful.

For example, the organizational culture of modern Swedish welfare authorities seems to be characterized by a mixture of bureaucratic remoteness and popular proximity. In other words, friendliness in Sweden does not imply preferential treatment, two concepts which are often conflated under the rubric of "particularism." Looking back at the organizational history of the modern Swedish public administration, one finds that it has resulted from the intertwining of social movements and Weberian style bureaucracy (Lindqvist 1990). In the Greek welfare administration, and in the public administration more generally, one does not find such a mixture; it is either remoteness or proximity. Access to familiarity inside the bureaucracy is possible only through personal, often family, networks; otherwise, Greeks face bureaucratic indifference to a degree unknown in Scandinavia. In other words, both friendliness and preferential treatment are assigned on a selective basis. This organizational culture results from the intertwining of kinship, or extended families, and bureaucracy. This is one aspect of Greek authorities' particularism, the other being the intertwin-

---

[6] As the PASOK experience in Greece has shown, clientelist practices do not disappear when the organizational form of the governing party becomes bureaucratic, although they change into what has been referred to as "bureaucratic clientelism" (Sotiropoulos 1966: 60).

ing of political parties and state bureaucracies. At the end of the chapter I use some concepts from relational sociology (Tilly 1998) to analyze the problem of intertwining.

The differences between the Swedish and the Greek cases I have mentioned up to now can be summarized as four analytically distinct, but in reality highly interrelated, boundary relations.

The first of these includes relations between the realm of politics and the realm of the state. One aspect of these relations concerns the degree of *organizational differentiation between the realm of politics and the realm of the state*. In ideal-typical situations these can be completely separated or completely interlocked, but in real situations there can neither be complete separation nor complete interlocking: it is a question of degree rather than of category. Thus, on a scale, I would place Sweden toward the separation end and Greece toward the interlocking end. A second aspect of this same relation concerns the *relations of domination* between the above-mentioned realms. Here again there can be, at one end, cases of total politicization of the state or, at the opposite end, cases of complete bureaucratization of politics. Generally speaking, though, in countries with democratic traditions such as Greece and Sweden, there is a balanced situation between these extremes. Each country then presents particular deviations from this pattern. In Greece the government is formally the highest state authority, while in Sweden the principle of the administrative autonomy of state authorities is institutionalized. Although, in practice, the difference is not as big as it looks at first sight – Swedish ministers do exercise informal control over state authorities – the primacy of politics is an entrenched element in the Greek political culture.

The second set of boundary relations can be denoted as the problem of the *insulation of the state bureaucracy from the "particularities of civil life"* (Bendix [1964] 1996: 139–141). One aspect of such insulation is the one discussed above, which is achieved through the separation of the realms of politics and the state. Other aspects concern the insulation of the state activities from economic, kinship, and local interest. The totally insulated state is, again, an ideal-typical construction. In the real world, states can be characterized as being predominantly universalistic or predominantly particularistic (Levy [1966] 1996: 141). Generally speaking, there are two ways of creating insulation: through institutional devices and through social differentiation. Laws forbidding public employees from having a second occupation or from working at their place of origin are examples of administrative devices. Recruitment on the basis of social distinctions, for instance, recruiting from religious groups different from that of the population as a whole or recruiting from a special social stratum are examples of insulation through social differentiation. The Greek state is characterized by a high degree of institutional devices, but is defectively insulated from civil life. In modern terminology, it is embedded in social relations. In Sweden one finds surprisingly few institutional safeguards intended to create distance between state and society, yet the state is socially insulated.

The third boundary relation concerns the *modes of inclusion of the lower social classes into national politics*. One must distinguish here between the "integrative" and the "incorporative" modes of inclusion (Mouzelis 1986: 73–94). The integrative mode denotes a horizontal and autonomous inclusion, as took place in several of the capitalist core countries, while the incorporative mode denotes a vertical and less autonomous, often plebiscitarian and paternalistic, inclusion, which characterized many countries of the semiperiphery. Clientelism can be seen as one of the historical subtypes of the second mode.

The fourth boundary relation regards the form of the state–citizen relations. *Citizenship* is usually studied from a comparative perspective by using T. H. Marshall's distinction between political, economic, and social rights. It is usually the quantitative aspect of the latter which is studied in a comparative perspective by relating it to the power resources of the major social actors (Esping-Andersen 1990). However, the qualitative aspect of

Table 2.1. *Boundary Relations in Greece and Sweden*

Boundary relations between	Greece	Sweden
1. State and political parties	Toward interlocking and conflation	Toward separation and differentiation
2. State and upper classes (economic interests)	Many institutional devices, social penetration	Few institutional devices, social insulation
3. State and lower classes (kinship and local interests)	Incorporation through controlled associations and vertical networks	Integration through autonomous associations and horizontal representation
4. State and citizens	Bureaucratic indifference, but selectivity of treatment	Popular proximity, but bureaucratic impartiality

state–citizen relations has not been studied as much and the researcher cannot rely on an existing conceptual framework to illustrate differences between countries. Thus, I elaborate this latter relation with the aid of the categories, that I developed above, of remoteness/proximity and preferential/impartial treatment (see Table 2.1).

Having defined the major dimensions along which the Swedish and the Greek cases differ, I now turn my attention to the social landscape in these countries, examine the temporalities that may account for them, and give some tentative answers to the questions raised at the beginning of the chapter.

Disparate Sequences of Political and Social Development

The Expansion of the State and the Extension of the Franchise: First and Fourth Boundary Relations

Generally speaking, Greece belongs to the group of countries that introduced modern institutions in a primary, precapitalist social formation after the end of the Napoleonic Wars and throughout the nineteenth century. These institutions were of two kinds: modern institutions of political representation and a modern state. The electoral reforms were inspired by ideas associated with the French revolution and, therefore, common to many post-Napoleonic countries.[7] Yet, in contrast to what happened in other, similar countries, it is surprising to see how easily modern institutions of political representation got a strong foothold in Greek society. Universal male suffrage was introduced in 1844; a modern constitution guaranteeing liberal freedoms dates from about the same time; parliamentarism was introduced in the 1870s.

Creating a modern state based on the Western European prototype proved more difficult. In contrast to what happened, for example, in Italy, the process of administrative unification lasted for about 100 years. On the whole, the process was rather uneven: building military and police forces and, to a degree, judicial courts was relatively easy, but establishing a school system for primary education and a uniform tax system took time. In this respect, the nonuniformity of the school system is quite striking. Until recently, primary education excluded a relatively large proportion of the

---

[7] With this expression, I mean the countries which were occupied by Napoleonic armies and in which many Napoleonic institutional reforms were implemented.

population, while, proportionally, Greek universities produced more students than economically advanced countries. About 40 percent of those students were students of law. As the labor market could not absorb them, they usually turned to politics. Borrowing blueprints from Western Europe, they gave the state an extremely legal-formalistic character and implanted the widespread idea that social and political problems are juridical problems that can be solved by the law. Many of the roots of the bureaucratic indifference of the Greek administration can be found here.

As is well known, the Western European state is historically based on taxation (Tilly 1990a). The war-driven need for financial resources forced kings to establish structures to register and collect taxes. This laid the ground for the infrastructural power of the state (Mann 1993). Structures built in periods of war were later used to penetrate social life and logistically implement decisions. At the same time, direct relations between the state and its inhabitants were established, but not without protests, revolts, and negotiations that defined the content of citizenship. For reasons I do not discuss here,[8] the Greek state was slow in this vertical penetration of civil life. In this matter, the Greek state was weak, leaving a space between itself and its inhabitants.[9]

In contrast, political institutions spread through the country at a high pace and gained a strong foothold in Greek society. In a referendum in 1863, six out of ten men aged twenty to sixty-five voted, a percentage that was attained only fifty years later in Sweden. Politics thoroughly penetrated Greek society. The English historian William Miller begins the chapter on politics in his treatise on Greece by writing: "It is impossible to write about Greek life, whether in town or country, without saying something on the subject of politics; for they affect every profession, every trade and almost every family to a degree unknown in other lands" (Miller 1905: 21). Historically, political parties based on universal male suffrage came before the bureaucracy in Greece and occupied the space between the state and the social life. As a consequence, peoples' concerns were defined as political matters, making it impossible to depersonalize them and define them as bureaucratic cases. Political parties became intertwined

---

[8] Mainly, the availability of international loans in the nineteenth century, slow economic development, and the low extractive capacity of the state.

[9] Tax collection was initially accomplished through tax-farming. Later, when it was bureaucratized, it did not succeed in becoming effective. An estimated 30 to 35 percent of the GNP still remains untaxed.

with kinship and local interests, thus failing to aggregate them as class or occupational interests, but rather representing them in their disaggregated form. In this way, interests and even citizens' concerns were made manifold – each family had its own interests – which made it almost impossible to treat them with bureaucratic rules based on the average individual. Having established themselves as mediators between social interests and state authorities, political parties occupied a pivotal role in both social and political realms.

The formation of the Swedish state followed a different path of development. Generally speaking, Sweden belongs to that group of countries for which the formation of the state predated the creation of modern democratic institutions. While administrative unification was accomplished in the early modern era, the democratic transformation of the state took place after a period of rapid and thorough industrialization. Problems such as the unification of the judicial system, the incorporation of the church under the state, and the homogenization of the population were solved before the cultural and the industrial revolutions, and the social cleavages they created, could affect their outcome. A system by which to register the population and its resources was established early on by using the organization of the church, which facilitated the collection of taxes and simultaneously created direct relations between the state and its subjects (Nilsson 1990: 56–104). The church was also used to administer the school system, which, by the middle of the nineteenth century, provided nearly all children of school age with access to primary school education. A generation later, it had raised the literacy level of the population to 90 percent, enhancing its overall organizational capacity.[10] If early political representation is the outstanding feature of the Greek state-building process, mass education, uniform taxation, and regulation of social life are the corresponding features of the Swedish process. These different features gave citizenship a distinct tinge in each country. Citizenship rights in Greece were the result of an isomorphic process which gave citizenship a legal-formalistic status. In Sweden, they were the result of tax negotiations, which gave citizenship a substantial content. Thus in Sweden the expansion of the state and the extension of the franchise to the lower classes followed a sequence opposite to that in Greece.

The early modern Swedish state was, in this respect, unique: it regulated, and in many occasions actually changed, social relations to a degree

---

[10] For the relationship between literacy and organizational capacity, see Stinchcombe (1965).

that states established later never managed to achieve. It could intervene in social life and implement its decisions because early expansion had equipped it with the capacity to collect information and control transactions (Nilsson 1990). It also established direct relations between itself and its subjects at a time when there were no other social formations that could occupy the interstices between the state and the people. The political parties and social movements which developed with the extension of the suffrage and the industrialization of the country could aggregate social interests, but could not find a foothold from which to mediate the relation between the state and the citizen.

The realms of the state and of mass political parties, respectively, remained differentiated and separated, thereby, at least in principle, avoiding altogether the problem of political domination of the state. The major task of mass parties and social movements became the definition and aggregation of citizens' interests. As the state did not intervene in the social question, the labor movement – and to a lesser degree other social movements – tried to solve the everyday problems of the working class by creating a whole world of social insurance organizations located very near the everyday experience of the people. Later on, when these social organizations became part of the welfare administration, they transmitted the popular proximity that they had already acquired into the welfare state, making for a bureaucracy that was sensitive to popular feelings and yet implemented welfare policies impartially.

In stark contrast with the even process of state building, political representation remained a rather exclusive matter up to the end of industrialization. In 1890, a year that falls in the middle of the period of rapid industrialization between 1870 and 1910, only one in four adult males had the right to vote and just one in ten actually voted (Carlsson 1953: 14, 23–25). Political parties at that time were exclusively self-organized class parties. Their social base was restricted to the rich quarters of the cities and the landowning peasants. These political parties are known in Swedish as *Riksdagspartier* – parliament parties – one meaning of which is that they functioned inside the parliament, excluding the vast majority of the proletarianized peasants and the industrial workers. Outside the parliament, in the social spaces that were left between the class-exclusive parties, the organization-tolerant nonintervening state, and the nuclear family, a whole world of independent political and social movements found fertile ground in which to develop by using the high organizational capacity of the excluded social strata (Papakostas 1995). These movements defined and aggregated citizens' interests in categorical terms, largely according to class and occupation. They expressed the social demands and needs of specific social groups to the bureaucracy in categorical terms, making it easier to construct bureaucratic rules based on averages within these categories. Citizens' multiple, and in many ways exceptional, demands and needs could thus be transformed into routine cases with few exceptions.

The Location of the Upper and Lower Classes in Public and Social Life: Second and Third Boundary Relations

In both countries, the process of state-building occurred before economic development. Meanwhile, the mechanisms by which capital was accumulated and the ruling classes entrenched their power were quite different in the two countries.

As Constantin Tsoucalas (1978) pointed out, a distinctive characteristic of Greek society after liberation was the absence of a ruling class that could use exploitative mechanisms outside the state to accumulate capital. In the absence of such mechanisms, old nobles turned en masse toward the state, the most important device for the collection and distribution of economic surplus at that time (Tsoucalas 1978). Thus in Greece state and economic activities became intertwined from the beginning, with the latter transmitting their exchange codes and morals to the former. This explains why it later became so important to introduce institutional devices to ensure some degree of separation between public office and private interest.

In Sweden, the aristocracy had originally exclusive rights to higher state positions: being a civil servant almost automatically implied being of aristocratic origins. The intertwining of state and class was pervasive, making the Swedish state a perquisite of a particular class in a way that the Greek state never was. In a study of the social origins of the civil servants in three central state bureaucracies between 1810 and 1870, it is reported that 70 to 84 percent of the civil servants were sons of other civil servants, most of whom were of aristocratic origin (Nilsson 1997: 21). The Swedish state was built on one side of a deep social cleavage, which created social insulation between the incumbents of state positions and the rest of the population. Initially, this did not imply a bureaucratic distinction between private interest and public office. As Göran Therborn (1989) pointed out, such a separation of roles became possible only later, in a developed capitalist economy, when the owners of state positions became state employees (cf. Rothstein 1998).

From the second half of the nineteenth century, when the Swedish bourgeoisie began to develop its own economic base and did not depend on the state for its markets (Tilton 1974: 68), the close intertwining of class and state began to loosen. While the upper classes in Greece turned en masse from economic activities to the state, in Sweden a weaker movement was observed in the opposite direction. Torbjörn Nilsson reports in a new study (1999) that, as the Swedish economy expanded during the second half of the nineteenth century, many civil servants became industrialists and tradesmen. So, whereas in Sweden the early intertwining of state and class left behind traces of the bureaucratic distance, in Greece the apparently looser intertwining of state and precapitalist economic activities proved to be more pervasive, keeping alive the mentality that public goods are exchangeable and the attitude that rules are negotiable.

Apart from being intertwined with the state, the upper classes in Greece developed through politics links to the masses that the Swedish aristocracy and later the bourgeoisie never succeeded in developing. In Greece, electoral reforms changed the power relations between the upper classes and the rest of the citizenry very early on. While the power of the aristocracy in Sweden was based on ascription, tradition, and corporate privilege, the traditional power of the Greek nobility had to be transformed into political power based on the votes of the electorate.

In a society whose population had low organizational capacities at a time when the knowledge of mass organization was in its embryonic state internationally, the only available way to organize people was through the family – a social organization which, in spite of local variations in its structure, has always played an important role in the social life of modern Greece. As Nikiforos Diamandouros (1984: 59) pointed out, in Greece the family has been the major social actor, which operated on multiple levels and fulfilled many economic, social, military, and political functions. When liberation weakened the position of the noblemen, with many of them losing large parts of their fortune during the war, they turned inward toward the family, the main "capital" at their disposal at that time. With politics as an imperative for survival and kinship as the only existing organizational device, extensive family coalitions were built using the quite widespread institutions of adoption, marriage, fraternization, and godfatherhood (Petropulos 1985: 69–73).

Initially these family coalitions were horizontal. The extension of the suffrage imposed their expansion at a time when a weak state did not have the organizational capacity to enlarge its scope and establish direct relations with its citizens. At the interstices between state and local communities, the system of family coalitions found fertile ground in which to develop vertically, creating hierarchies of families with quite unequal power resources, but also relations of mutual dependence. Families at the top of the hierarchy drew their power through their intertwining with the state and access to its goods, and those at the bottom through their capacity to aggregate and deliver the votes of their members. Just like the families at the bottom were dependent upon the families at the top for access to state goods, the families at the top could not secure their position without the political support of those at the bottom.

As well as the families, villages became units for interest aggregation in Greece. Local cultures were never damaged by agricultural reforms, as they were in Sweden; rather, they were strengthened. At the same time, class divisions within the peasantry were weakened by the distribution of the cultivated land to all peasants, thereby creating a relatively homogenous village population with strong local identities. This population was one of illiterates with low organizational capacities and without the means to create independent peasant organizations. Hence, in many parts of Greece, citizenship became relational and derivative, materializing through family networks and political parties and not as the effect of the direct integration of the people into the state.

Family played an important role in Sweden too, but in a different way. For instance, it was not unusual that positions in state authorities would be passed from one generation to the next in the same family.[11] At the same time the delayed electoral reforms in Sweden did not create the need to establish bonds with civil life outside the state. It would have certainly been difficult to do so through kinship relations given the weakness of the social institution of the extended family in Sweden.[12] Thus there was neither the

---

[11] The historian Pär Frohnert (1993) reports that during the Gustavian period (1773–1809), 75 percent of *kronofogdar* – the leading state employees at the county level – were sons of *kronofogdar*. He also reports widespread kinship relations between civil servants. Torbjörn Nilsson (1997) identifies many sons and fathers working together in central state bureaucracies throughout the nineteenth century and many positions that passed from fathers to sons or to other relatives. No social group in Greece ever succeeded in establishing such exclusivity over state positions.

[12] A simple comparison of the household structures in villages in the two countries is quite telling in this respect: While in the village of Syrrako in Greece, 39 percent of the households were extended families (Psychogios 1987: 106), in the parish of Dala in Sweden, only 7 percent of them were extended families, and among the proletarianized peasants, the extended family was almost nonexistent as a social institution (Winberg 1997: 193).

imperative nor the possibility to create links between the leading classes and the entire population through kinship ties.

Furthermore, the possibility to create bonds between the entire population and the elites on the basis of strong local identities was eliminated by the agrarian reforms. While the agrarian reforms in Greece redistributed the arable land but did not change the social structure of the villages, the Swedish agrarian reforms concentrated the land and the reform of *lagaskifte* changed the village structure dramatically by moving the farms out to the estates (Helmfrid 1961). In this way, Swedish local cultures were seriously undermined: geographical distances became social distances (Thörnberg 1912: 77). Later, as migration patterns became a mixture of "coerced" migration and "career" migration,[13] the inhabitants of the cities became rather anonymous in the sociological meaning of the term as described by Georg Simmel ([1902–3], 1950) and Louis Wirth (1938). The Swedish state could thus recruit civil servants from the ranks of the nonnobles without being interwoven in social networks. An already distanced bureaucracy now faced atomized individuals aggregated in categorical terms. It could therefore easily transform peoples' concerns into bureaucratic cases, and as the vast majority of the population were able to read and write and could understand the use of general principles to handle their cases, the need for political mediation was eliminated.

In Greece both the kinship and the social structure of the villages remained intact. As a consequence, urbanization became a mixture of "chain" migration and "circular" migration, which affected the social structure of the cities preventing the atomization of their inhabitants. In this respect, Greek cities can be described as "cities of peasants" and their inhabitants as "urban villagers": a high level of social cohesion in the cities is based on interwoven networks and a high frequency of primary contacts with familiar faces (cf. Gans [1962], 1982, Pahl 1968). As the state bureaucracy was built with people coming from these extensive social networks, it became deeply embedded in social relations based on kinship and local identities. It was therefore difficult to transform the matters of the citizens into impersonal administrative cases. In an attempt to solve these problems, several institutional devices were used, but most of them without effect. Instead, their major, but unintended consequence was to reinforce the bureaucratic indifference with which the legal-formalistic Greek state treated the unconnected citizen, giving political entrepreneurs the oppor-

---

[13] For definitions, see Tilly (1990b).

48

tunity to mediate between the citizen and the indifferent bureaucracy and thus exact a clientelist fee.[14]

Theoretical Implications

Although the question posed in the title is formulated in a counterfactual manner, this chapter sought to answer a question stated in factual terms: Under what conditions will a predominantly universalistic state emerge rather than become embedded in social relations or intertwined with political formations?

One way to approach this issue from a historical-comparative perspective is to give attention to the *suppressed alternatives* and understand the actualization of some historical alternatives by placing them at the intersection of trajectories with different temporalities (Aminzade 1992: 466). As Charles Tilly elegantly noted, "*when* things happen within a sequence affects *how* they happen" (Tilly 1984: 14, emphasis in the original). In this chapter I have devoted some attention to the suppressed alternatives by pointing to the particularistic elements in the early Swedish state and the universalistic ambitions that were present at the beginning of the process of Greek state formation. Using the idea of the *social landscape* (Ahrne 1990, 1994), I have tried to understand the historical outcomes by placing them at the intersection of the trajectories of states, families, enterprises, and voluntary associations.

Some years ago, Martin Shefter, in his *Political Parties and the State* (1994), followed a similar logic of comparison. He tried to understand the emergence of patronage parties in the United States by comparing the different sequences of development of state bureaucracies and political parties in the United States and some European countries. Shefter criticized earlier sociological interpretations of political patronage in the United States where the "demand side" of the phenomenon was overemphasized. The strategy political parties adopt is not totally constrained by the characteristics of the voters, he argued (Shefter 1994: 25, 59). Instead, he turned his attention to the "supply side" of patronage at the time political parties were being formed. If the parties had mobilized a broad electorate before bureaucratic autonomy was established, they had the option of using the resources of the state in clientelist exchanges. Parties founded after a bureaucratic autonomy had been created, or which developed

---

[14] It is instructive to compare the work of Robert Merton (1968: 126–36).

outside the political system, did not have this option available in their formative years and, hence, were bound to become ideological parties.

By turning the conventional arguments upside-down, Shefter's approach sheds light on the relationships among organizational fields in social life, established through the different sequences of development in different countries. The approach is a healthy corrective to the old sociological approaches to the study of patronage in the United States, and also to its social anthropological equivalents in the study of clientelism in Europe. The parts of this chapter dealing with the relationship between the realm of the state and the realm of politics are in line with Shefter's argument. However, this study includes more complicated sequences of development. The analysis here seeks to answer the same questions as Shefter's by examining the development of a wide range of state–society relations besides those that are mediated through the development of political parties and which are analyzed by Shefter. Against this background I now discuss how Shefter's arguments might be developed further.

By placing the supply side of clientelism at the intersection between state and political parties, Shefter gives the impression that state–society relations are shaped *only* by state–party relations and thereby constructs an overpoliticized conception of these relations. Relations between state and political parties matter, but under what conditions do they matter? As the Swedish case illustrates, a state with direct relations to citizens limits the space available for political parties to mediate between state and society. In the Greek case, the delayed expansion of the state left considerable space for political parties to develop strong ties with society and mediate the relationship to the distant state. State–party relations become crucially important when state–society relations are weak and loose. Without available space between state and society, the historical sequence of bureaucratization and mass mobilization affects only the boundary relation between the state and political parties, yet this sequence alone is not sufficient to yield clientelism.

Shefter's argument even seems to imply that institutional barriers between the state and the political parties are sufficient to hinder the development of patronage, but as the Greek development illustrates, this is not the case. Given that interests were defined in local or kinship terms – the "demand side" in Shefter's terminology – institutional safeguards to insulate the bureaucracy had the effect of creating more distance between the citizen and the state, thereby giving more space to political entrepreneurs to mediate between them. In Sweden, on the other hand, very few institutional devices could work effectively because the state was insulated initially through the incorporation of social distinctions and later through the modernization of society. And it was the early expansion of the state that atomized and "modernized" its subjects through institutional reforms and high rates of literacy, thereby minimizing the need for clientelism. This means that the working of institutional safeguards against clientelism in particular, and of political institutions in general, cannot be taken for granted a priori because it is contingent upon broad social processes – even upon the "demand side" of clientelism. Although the history of the states does not seem to correspond perfectly to the history of their societies, the intended and unintended consequences of state organizations cannot be understood without reference to the contingencies of state–society boundary relations.

Shefter makes some very important points by investigating the "supply side" of political patronage. From the sociology of markets, we learn that demand and supply are like hands shaking each other.[15] Not only do we need to study both sides, but we also need to understand how they meet each other. It would appear, for instance, that the persistence of clientelist practices in Greece has to do with the strong institutional and social bonds which constitute the tissue of social life, connect the supply and demand of clientelism, and constantly reinforce each other. In Sweden, on the other hand, it is not the absence of the supply of patronage that explains the absence of clientelism in modern times, but the fact that supply – patronage in the early Swedish state – and demand could never become connected with each other because of the different sequences of development. Thus the practice of patronage remained limited to a restricted class, without expanding to the entire society.

In concluding, I return to these links by using concepts from relational sociology as developed by Charles Tilly (1998). Tilly starts with five elementary social configurations – chain, hierarchy, triad, organization, and categorical pair – and studies how different combinations produce, cement, and change durable inequality (Tilly 1998: 48). For the sake of simplicity I conflate chain, hierarchy, and triad to one configuration: a complex network. I then add another configuration, atomized and anonymous individuals, in the sociological meaning of the term. Thus we have four elementary configurations: atomized individuals, complex networks,

---

[15] I am indebted to Richard Swedberg for turning my attention to this old Weberian argument.

organizations, and categorical pairs. These elementary figurations can combine in two general ways: combinations of the same sort and combinations of a different kind. Most organizations, and, between them, states, are like mosaics that interweave with these configurations connecting organizational life and social life in a multitude of ways. At different times the combinations that are available are rather limited because of sequential phenomena.

The Swedish and Greek states became interwoven with different configurations. The Swedish state was initially built on complex networks located on one side of categorical pairs. The incumbents of state positions were connected by strong links with class, but not with society. Thus a social distinction became an organizational distinction, and the state could establish direct relations to society without running the risk of being exposed to network contagion. An internally particularistic state could, at the same time, be universalistic in its relations to society, cynically reminding us that a universalistic state is not necessarily democratic (Levy [1966], 1996). In the course of time, the categorical pairs, which were basically the aristocratic distinctions the Swedish state was built upon, lost their meaning, but the bureaucratic distance they created remained there and was not undermined by social pressures. Someone could make arguments about historical legacies, pointing to inertial tendencies that characterize social institutions, by stating that, once created, institutions tend to sustain themselves. However, from the analysis here it seems reasonable to argue that the perpetuation of the universalistic traits was contingent upon two other social processes: the creation of organizations promoting categorical interests in society and the modernization of the individuals. Thus the embryo of patronage could not find a glade in the Swedish social landscape in which to develop into mass clientelism.

Clientelism did grow in Greece, although particularism was never institutionalized there as it had been in Sweden prior to 1809. One part of the answer to this paradox can be found in Shefter's argument: The sequence of development in Greece opposite to that in Sweden meant that politics and state became intertwined in Greece, placing politics in a dominant position vis-à-vis the state. This was coincident with the slow and uneven expansion of the state and a limited modernization of social life. In the interstices between state and social life, two sets of analytically distinct – but in reality mutually interchangeable and in many cases overlapping – complex networks developed: social networks connecting families and the distant state through kinship, and political networks that made the same connection, but in a political fashion. In contrast to Sweden, where these networks connected the state and a slowly disappearing leading class, in Greece these networks connected the state not only with the ruling class, but also with the entire social life. While in Sweden the realms of state, politics, and social life became differentiated with relatively clear-cut organizational boundaries, in Greece these realms became partly overlapping and even intertwined with strong social ties. These same ties prevented the atomization of the individuals and the full development of categorical interests. They constituted the social ground for clientelism and made the universalistic tendencies in the Greek state, for long periods, look like islands in a sea of particularistic networks.

3

Patronage and the Reform of the State in England, 1700–1860

FRANK O'GORMAN

Introduction

Eighteenth-century England is the classic case of state "corruption." Even today, some of the words we use to describe this *ancien regime*, such as "unreformed" or "premodern," tend to confirm the stereotype of rampant corruption. Is this reputation deserved? Moreover, what happened to the system – was it a system? – of patronage during the nineteenth-century transition to mass politics? England was one of the first countries to effect the transition from "corruption" to "meritocracy." How did this happen? Although between about 1780 and 1860 a fundamental shift in values respecting certain aspects of state patronage occurred and a limited reform of patronage was implemented, the fundamental principle of patronage was not called into question. Why was this the case? This raises the interesting question of the role subsequently played by patronage when a national bureaucracy was established, after about 1830, and successive reform acts established increasingly democratic political structures. To what extent did patronage still play a role in Victorian politics in the second half of the nineteenth century?

That, then, is the agenda of this chapter. The term "patronage" is employed to describe the pattern of allocation of office, influence, and power which obtained in England during the decades preceding the emergence of meritocratic processes for appointments to office. Patronage, in this sense, may be taken to be a premodern spoils system of a limited character, typical of a number, probably a majority, of European and non-European countries characterized by limited popular participation in politics. In early modern England, like in many other European countries, the patronage system rested upon personal relationships of mutual advantage between unequal partners. The patron offered political and social protection, advancement, and even security in return for the client's support, service, and public endorsement – his or her deference being often expressed in highly symbolic terms through gestures, courtesies, and specific forms of language. These powerfully personal relationships were capable of hereditary transmission, and were often symbolized in public ideologies, languages, and even in the adoption of specific liveries.

In England, patronage acquired its bad reputation at the hands of early nineteenth-century radicals such as William Cobbett and George Wade. Cobbett and his fellow radicals denounced "old corruption" as a system of government which enabled ministers and the crown to purchase political support, notably in parliament, at the expense of free and open political debate and administrative efficiency. At the same time, according to this critique, rich patrons could advance their own interests and those of their families by purchasing office, influencing promotions to office, and raising expectations of future receipt of office. Such a system was further denounced by Cobbett because it penetrated all government departments, the armed services, the professions such as the law and the church, and, not least, local government. Furthermore, this expensive and unnecessary fabric of corruption was financed out of the taxes of the mass of the people who paid, as it were, for their own exclusion from power and office, and subsidized the expensive life-styles of the elite (Harling 1996: 1–2, 9–11).

Astonishingly, these partisan, contemporary denunciations have been taken by generations of writers as accurate, empirical descriptions of the political realities of the time. Even today, distinguished academics use them to supply a teleological and even an ethical framework to their narratives of administrative reform. These include respected and eminent authorities such as W. L. Guttsman, who, in an influential work, writes, "Worldly success went hand in hand with the exercise of political power and it was the very venality of the system which made it so. Members (of Parliament) bought or bribed the electorate, and ministers, in turn, if necessary bought members' votes" (Guttsman 1968: 17).

Such distortions cannot survive even casual analysis, especially when unusual and atypical circumstances are presented as accepted conventions, and aberrations from the norm are presented as the norm itself! It is all too easy to shift from using words such as "patron," "client," and "influence" to using much more dangerous terms such as "corruption" and "venality," forgetting that the norms, purposes, and functions of the political system to which those words are referred are quite unlike those with which we are familiar today.

More recently, Martin Shefter has approached these issues from a less ideological standpoint. In *Political Parties and the State* (1994), Shefter does not condemn systems of patronage but enquires into the conditions in which they existed. According to Shefter, England was a decentralized polity whose vital functions – the maintenance of public order, the administration of justice, and the distribution of poor relief – were lodged in the hands of local men and institutions. Parliament itself was under the control of hereditary local families. Yet for Shefter, like so many others, it is not enough to claim that the eighteenth century was the classic era of patronage in politics. It must follow that appointments to major administrative positions were made for flagrant party political reasons. "The governing classes of England . . . were not tied to a bureaucratic regime. In the absence of any such constituency for bureaucratic autonomy, party politics, or at least the politics of parliamentary parties, was patronage-ridden" (Shefter 1994: 46).

Shefter proceeds to investigate the relationship between the emergence of mass political parties and the establishment of democratic political forms, on the one hand, and the steady elimination of political patronage, on the other. This he does with authority and with considerable ingenuity. Professor Shefter is a political scientist: how far his interpretation of the relationship among the processes of administrative reform, party development, and democratic evolution in the nineteenth century squares with an historical approach forms one of the central threads of this chapter.

The Patronage Structure of Eighteenth-Century England

The structure of patronage in eighteenth- and early nineteenth-century England has almost always been depicted in negative terms by radical writers reveling in righteous moral indignation against an incontrovertibly corrupt political system, by Whig historians determined to claim for themselves (and their version of English history) the credit for its reform, and by left-wing historians naturally hostile toward any manifestations of aristocratic oligarchy. But what was it really like? And to what extent has recent scholarship revised traditional caricatures?

The first point to note is that historians no longer adopt a moral standpoint when treating the issue of patronage in eighteenth-century England.

Following the work of John Brewer, historians now generally utilize a very different vocabulary, adopting the notion of a "fiscal-military state" (Brewer 1989; see also Brewer 1994: 52–71). Brewer argues that, largely because it had kept out of European wars in the 250 years before the Glorious Revolution of 1688–89, Britain enjoyed a political system relatively free from the worst forms of venality. It was England's involvement in six major wars in Europe between 1689 and 1815 which led to the creation of a centralized, bureaucratic state which, if no paragon of virtue, was more efficient than many of its continental counterparts. It was also rather bigger. In the 1720s the state had in its service around 12,000 permanent employees, most of them in the revenue departments (Holmes 1982: 244–55). This compares with about 3,000 in Prussia (Brewer 1994: 59). By the second half of the eighteenth century the English figure had risen to 16,000 (Brewer 1989: 65, Hanham 1969: 318). During the French Revolutionary and Napoleonic Wars the figure expanded to 24,000 in 1815 and to 27,000 by 1821 (Gash 1979: 51). To pay for this new bureaucracy, taxation as a percentage of national income had to rise from 3 percent in 1665 to 16 percent in 1815 (Brewer 1989: 89–91).

It follows – and this is the second important element of Brewer's interpretation of eighteenth-century patronage – that the British patronage system was not markedly different from those of many of Britain's continental neighbors. Such a conclusion coincides with that of revisionist scholars such as Jonathan Clark and Jeremy Black (Black 1984, Clark 1985). In the work of these writers, the English *ancien regime*, like those of the continent, was solidly based on the three pillars of monarchy, church, and aristocracy. Like them, England was a strongly hierarchical society in which offices were sought informally and were distributed on the basis of personal connection and family loyalty, rather than on the basis of merit and efficiency. In other words, recent scholarship has exploded the myth of English fiscal and administrative exceptionalism.

A third tendency in recent writing has been to minimize the extent of patronage in eighteenth-century England. For example, it is often assumed that the English government enjoyed significant influence over the House of Commons through the votes of its civil servants or placemen. Yet placemen were unreliable supporters, and, in any case, their number was diminishing. In the early eighteenth century there had been over 250 of them in a House of Commons of 558, but their number thereafter steadily declined. In 1780 there were about 200, and by the early nineteenth century only 80 to 90 of them in a House swollen in size, by the admission of Irish Members, to 658. As for contractors – MPs who held government contracts – there were only 18 of them at the height of the American War, despite the universal assumption among opposition writers that the government was sustained by such individuals (Harling 1996, Namier and Brooke 1964: 81, 134–36).

Similar exaggerations characterize also the subject of reversions, that is, the legal right of inheritance to certain public offices, usually sinecures. As is often the case with such matters, the truth was much less exciting than the myth. In fact, there were only 100 such offices in 1809 in Britain and the whole of the empire. Radicals also popularized the view that governments bought support through the use of pensions. It is, in fact, impossible to estimate the exact number of those in receipt of state pensions, but perhaps only around £200,000 per year was spent on pensions at the end of the eighteenth century, much of it for entirely nonpolitical purposes (Brewer 1994: 61–62). By whatever measure, then, the extent of patronage, while certainly considerable, was much less extensive than is conventionally assumed.

Paradoxically, the values, practices, and traditions of the patronage system itself actually prevented the growth of some of the worst abuses. The very fact that an office was legally regarded as a piece of freehold property prevented a spoils system from developing. Any attempt to exercise political coercion over state officials would have met with national uproar. It is true that dismissals for political and party purposes were by no means unknown. After the purge of the Tories in 1722–23, however, they became much rarer. The only subsequent such purge occurred in 1762–63, when several dozen members of the Whig opposition were deprived of their offices. By this date, however, such an exertion of the will of the executive was looked upon with considerable disapproval, especially by the parliamentary opposition, who denounced it as unconstitutional (O'Gorman 1975: 64–65). Such a purge was not repeated.

There were very good reasons for this. By the end of the eighteenth century habits of constitutionalism had become deeply entrenched. Politicians who had been boasting for decades of Britain's constitutional purity were now hoist with their own petards.

In other words, patronage was less an instrument of rule than the process by which public office, and the power and influence that went with it, was distributed. If political purges were rare in eighteenth-century England, it remained true that officials in most government departments were recruited and promoted via informal processes of petition, recommendation, seniority, or even purchase. There was always a massive demand for patronage. So long as those with office did not scandalously exploit their position or neglect the national, or indeed the local, interest, such practices were generally tolerated in an age which knew nothing of allocation of place and power through systematic training and public examination.

There was criticism aplenty of this system but such criticism came largely from those excluded from office for political reasons: the Tories, opposition Whigs in the first half of the century, and certain opposition Whig groups in the second. The century is studded with convulsive waves of popular hostility, particularly when it was suspected that the King and his favorites were exploiting their official positions for their own benefit. Traditional hostility to a standing army bred a suspicion of the growing bureaucracy of the "fiscal-military state," while popular perceptions of individual independence and privacy fostered a powerful hatred of excise officers, who had the legal power to enter people's homes. This was powerfully illustrated in 1733–34, when Sir Robert Walpole's government tried in vain to extend the excise tax to tobacco and wine. The public was outraged and a vigorous petitioning campaign forced the government to drop its proposal.

The patronage state thus contained within itself powerful self-correcting mechanisms which placed boundaries around the extent of corruption. At the same time, there are grounds for believing that this patronage structure delivered a number of powerful benefits, facilitating the survival of successive governments and lending consistency and, arguably, administrative continuity at all levels of the body politic. It may even have delivered political confidence and continuity and thus, conceivably, by enhancing the power of the governing elite in both national and local affairs, promoted political stability and thus economic progress.

The Reform of the Eighteenth-Century Patronage System

The reform of the eighteenth-century patronage system has its origin in the later years of the American War of Independence. In 1780, the government of Lord North, reeling from defeat and demoralization in the war and shocked by the emergence of widespread public protests against the inefficiencies and misadministration which accompanied its humiliations, appointed six Commissioners to Examine the Public Accounts. Between 1780 and 1787 they issued fifteen reports. This was followed by a

Commission for Enquiring into Fees in the Public Offices and then by House of Commons Select Committees on Finance in 1782, 1786, 1791, and 1797. Administrative reform was now on the political agenda. Government departments were increasingly subject to regular scrutiny, and abuses were publicly highlighted. In the next few decades, governments of all complexions pursued policies of economical reform, that is, the abolition of useless sinecure offices and pensions and the removal of antiquated structures of government. The impulse for reform had come from Edmund Burke's 1782 attack on sinecures and useless departments. Yet more was done during William Pitt's long administration (1783–1801). Useless posts, especially in the revenue departments, were abolished, 765 in 1789 alone and another 196 in 1798. Normally, however, posts were quietly allowed to wither and die (Harling 1996: 31–55). Pitt's unobtrusive yet effective work in these years was not without real effect. Slowly, the idea that public office was a piece of property was replaced with the idea of public service and public accountability. In these years the term "civil service" was coming into circulation and officials were beginning to enjoy greater security of tenure.

The period of the French Revolutionary and Napoleonic Wars intensified public criticism of the existing patronage system because they led to "an enormous growth in taxes, public debt, central government agencies, and bureaucratic sclerosis" (Harling 1996: 2). Reform was now more urgent than ever, especially once Tom Paine's *Rights of Man* (1791, 1792) had popularized biting criticisms of the restrictive monopoly of offices among the aristocracy. The parliamentary opposition, led by Charles James Fox, constantly criticized government corruption in this period. Pitt had been responding to the reports of successive commissioners, albeit in a cautious, piecemeal fashion that was "at variance with the boldness and urgency of their pronouncements" (Harling 1996: 61). Consequently, he was neither as ruthless nor as radical as he might have been. In any case, Pitt and his colleagues had neither the time nor the will to carry out the comprehensive reforms which the Reports demanded in the middle of the most dangerous war for national survival that the country had ever faced. Political action to curb patronage was hazardous. Indeed, in an attempt to maintain the momentum of economical reform, Pitt appointed a Finance Committee in 1797. It reported in radical terms, criticizing the government for permitting fees to increase during the war and condemning in general terms the entire system of administration. It proceeded to issue no fewer than thirty-six reports covering most aspects of financial administration, which provided regular and detailed public criticism of the government's handling of money. No wonder Pitt was cautious. It was not a simple fear of reform that inhibited him. In fact, Pitt wanted to keep the issue of administrative reform out of the parliamentary arena, preferring to maintain his freedom of action to act as he wished and to move at his own pace. However understandable, such timidity was incapable of silencing the critics of patronage. Consequently, the extent of reform in the 1790s was disappointing. Sinecures and reversions were gradually abolished while salaries began to replace the fees and profits of office. Regulations were laid down to compel officials to transact the business of their offices in person.[1] But the record of reform achieved by the time of Pitt's departure from office in 1801 was disappointingly slight.

A combination of political circumstances led to a renewal of the campaign for economical reform in the early years of the new century. Pitt had always been reluctant to control those of his friends who had their fingers in the public purse. Several of his political allies made huge fortunes out of the public service, and Pitt, dependent upon their support, did not have the will to discipline them. However, in 1805 Viscount Melville, one of Pitt's closest political colleagues, was accused of misappropriation of public funds. This issue became part of a broader revival of radical agitation for the reform of parliament and a growing reaction against the apparently endless war against France. Pitt died in 1806, in time to avoid dangerously mounting criticism of the system of government administration over which he had presided for so long. His successors in office, and the opposition Whig party, continued to adopt the principles of Economical Reform. There followed a gradual reform of sinecures, reversions, and pensions. In 1807 a new Committee on Public Expenditure was established. Its report condemned sinecures in much the same terms as those adopted by extraparliamentary radical critics. In 1809 it became illegal to make a profit out of public office. In the same year a bill prohibited the purchase and sale of public offices, thus further weakening the assumption that public office was a piece of property. In 1812, a bill for the abolition of sinecures was introduced. Although it did not pass, it served to highlight an abuse which in many circles was thought to be indefensible.

The "fiscal-military state," in other words, once it had won the war against Napoleon, had to be cut back, as it was too expensive to be

---

[1] We have no method of calculating what proportion of officeholders had attended to their duties in person.

maintained. Immediately after the conclusion of peace, in 1815, there was popular outcry over its costs. Previous agitations against "old corruption" paled into insignificance at the mass revulsion against what was now perceived to be an exclusive and indefensible system of government. Press and pamphlet roused the people. The publications of George Wade (1820, 1826(?), 1832) patiently spelled out in great statistical detail the extent of influence and appointments. Wade's lists of officeholders, and those who had appointed them, marked the culmination of the radical critique of "old corruption" and have been enormously influential among historians (e.g., Rubinstein 1983). On this, as on earlier occasions, however, the demand for the reform of the patronage system was not lost on the politicians, who proceeded to respond to it as they had on earlier occasions. By so doing, they could at least ensure that they could retain some room for maneuver. Had they dragged their feet and allowed public anger to mount, they might have become its prisoners.

So, the stately process of administrative reform from above continued. Lord Liverpool's government (1812–27) committed itself to retrenchment and reform of administrative offices as early as 1816, when salaries of officials in public offices were made a parliamentary rather than a departmental responsibility, a crucial step toward the emergence of a unified civil service. In the following year, Liverpool swept away dozens of sinecures, leaving very few in the civil offices. Even more significant, in 1821 he abandoned the First Lord of the Treasury's customs patronage to the heads of departments, a critical step toward ensuring that merit would be rewarded. Indeed, in 1822, one of the Joint Secretaries to the Treasury lamented the fact that if the influence of the crown were reduced any further "it will be quite impossible for any set of men to conduct the government of this country" (Foord 1947). In reality, the reforms took time to work through.

In fits and bounds, the "fiscal-military state" was cut back. As we have already noticed, the size of the civil service peaked at 27,000 in 1821, but by 1841 it had declined to 17,000 (Hanham 1969: 318). By the end of his long ministry, Liverpool had taken significant steps toward the creation of a civil service based on expertise rather than on patronage. Indeed, by 1830, it was common for departments to use a probationary period to weed out unsatisfactory new appointees. Most departments now had age limits for new entrants and were even developing some form of simple qualifying examination. The Whig governments of the 1830s followed similarly stringent policies of retrenchment. After decades of criticizing in opposition the morality of Liverpool's administration they had little alternative. After 1837 "the policy was increasingly followed of deciding internal promotions in the revenue departments by merit rather than by seniority" (Gash 1979: 52). Such a system was the consequence of the tension between the values of an increasingly professional civil service and the reluctance of politicians to surrender the political power which patronage continued to give them.

This growing professionalism was reflected in at least three further developments which were generated internally and had the effect of tilting the balance of power within the civil service.[2] First, Whitehall and, in particular, the Treasury succeeded in imposing control over the entire administrative network, even over that of the Irish administration which by 1830 had been effectively absorbed into the administrative control of the English Treasury. At the same time, the Treasury assumed responsibility for the control of all the other spending offices. In 1822, for example, the Treasury was able to force reductions in the spending of all the other departments of state. Second, all departments had to become more professional and more efficient in their administrative activities because the Treasury was now responsible for inspection, oversight, and working practices specification. Third, the scale of business was expanding. The amount of parliamentary legislation and enquiries, for example, at least doubled between 1780 and 1830. More remarkable, the number of letters dealt with by the colonial office rose five-fold between 1806 and 1824, that by the Treasury no less than twenty-fold, admittedly during a longer period, from 1767 to 1815.

The final, formal victories against patronage came in the middle of the nineteenth century. The establishment of central boards to administer activities as various as the Poor Law, Tithe Reform, and Education in the 1830s enabled the commissioners to innovate and attempt rational reforms. At this point, the history of patronage reform intersects with the influence of Jeremy Bentham and his disciples. The characteristically Benthamite solutions to administrative problems included central government supervision, a salaried inspectorate, and professional training. These were to be of the greatest importance in the middle of the nineteenth century. The followers of Jeremy Bentham persuaded the Poor Law

---

[2] I am indebted to Professor Peter Jupp for a pre-publication examination of his latest book, *British Politics on the Eve of Reform: The Duke of Wellington's Administration, 1828–30*, in particular, chapter 4.

Commissioners to appoint only on merit and after interview. Even more spectacular, under the influence of James and John Stuart Mill, the India Office was comprehensively reformed on utilitarian lines.

These developments culminated in the Northcote–Trevelyan report of 1853, produced as a consequence of a series of departmental inquiries initiated in 1848. The Conservative Sir Charles Trevelyan, who was head of the Civil Service between 1840 and 1859, and the Liberal Sir Stafford Northcote launched an inquiry into the Civil Service. Their report, published in 1854, set forward the principles that appointments to the civil service should be made only through a process of open, competitive examination and not by personal appointment, that promotions should be through merit only and not through seniority, and that the Civil Service should be considered as embracing all departments. These principles were so revolutionary and aroused such an extraordinary amount of internal opposition that they could not be implemented at once. Only a watered-down scheme could be enacted in the first instance. Instead of open competition for Civil Service posts, an Order in Council of 1855 appointed Civil Service Commissioners to ensure that appointments to the civil service had the requisite qualifications; the departments were still allowed to nominate their own candidates. This compromise lasted until 1870 when a genuine system of open competition was enacted. Even then, the Foreign Office remained outside the scope of the new system and it was not until 1877 that it was applied to the Colonial Office. It took another forty years and three more royal commissions before the Home Civil Service actually began to resemble a single, coherent career service based on merit.[3]

Explanations of the Reform of the Patronage System

What underlying lessons may be learned from this case study? To what extent does a succession of finely calculated bureaucratic reforms make the political uses of patronage unacceptable and illegitimate? What explanations for these changes in the patronage system have been forthcoming? This section considers a number of such interpretations.

A first type of explanation for the decline of patronage in England lies with the historians of administration (see, inter alia, Chester 1981, Cohen

---

[3] On the later stages of the reform of patronage, see Burn (1964), Gash (1986), Hanham (1969), and Roseveare (1973).

1941, and Finer 1952). While it is unquestionably an advantage to consider the process of administrative reform from the inside, as it were, the focus of administrative history has normally been regrettably narrow. In these accounts the search for cheap government and efficient administration become rational goals in themselves, with little or no reference to wider public and political pressures. Explanations of reform tend to go little further than the unpopularity of high taxation or concern over the size of government debt. Even the best of these accounts, that of Binney (1958), which devotes considerable importance to the activities of Lord North and William Pitt, tends to ignore the broader political and public context. In general, such accounts give excessive prominence to theories of administration, especially those of Bentham, and involve the reader in labyrinthine details of administrative structures and their reorganization.

A second category of explanations of the reform of the patronage system may be found in the works of a number of political historians. Professor A. S. Foord (1947: 506–7) had a deeper understanding of the politics of the period but, like many scholars writing in the 1940s, was preoccupied with the narrow issue of the "waning of the influence of the crown" (see also Guttridge 1963, Keir 1934, and Ritcheson 1954). This was understandable at a time when the allegedly authoritarian activities of George III fascinated historians and the reforming endeavors of the King's parliamentary opponents thus appeared to be significant. Such a position could perhaps be justified in the closing years of the American War and at the time of the early Economical Reform legislation of 1782, but thereafter it is difficult to regard the Whig opposition of Charles James Fox as seriously committed to reform. Although their criticisms of government scandals and administrative abuses were directed at extraparliamentary opinion, they rarely brought forward detailed proposals for the reform of patronage and it is not easy to demonstrate that as a party they had any serious interest in the issue. Indeed, it is the clear verdict of historians that it was the government of William Pitt, not the opposition of Charles James Fox, which began the reform of patronage (Harling 1996: 27–28). According to this view, William Pitt appears as a politician much given to commonsense analysis of essentially practical problems of administration, guided by experience rather than by theory, and dedicated to good (and cheap) government and efficient administration as acknowledged goals in themselves.

A third and still very influential kind of explanation of the reform of the patronage system has come from historians with a background in social and even radical history. They have popularized a view of "old corruption" and its demise which in many respects owes much to Marxist analyses of the political system which, in their turn, derive from the propaganda of radicals such as Cobbett. Historians such as E. P. Thompson and Roy Porter, in influential texts, have roundly condemned a system of government based on "old corruption" (Porter 1982, Thompson 1963). This condemnation is part of their general repudiation of aristocratic oligarchy, Anglican establishment, and class hegemony. Not surprisingly, they tend to view the reforms of the patronage system undertaken between 1780 and 1830 as little better than image refurbishment. As Harling (1966) notes, what historians of popular radicalism seem to deny is that the financial and administrative reforms executed before 1830 contributed anything to the weakening of the "old corruption." Indeed, the old leftist, progressive narratives of nineteenth-century reform need to be replaced by less slanted interpretations which stress the durability of the old regime in England. It is, in fact, that very durability that lends some credence to left-wing accusations that reformers and radicals, and particularly the Chartists of the late 1830s and 1840s, were entirely justified in their criticism of the 1832 Reform Act which effectively excluded the lower orders from the franchise.

A fourth explanation of the reform of the patronage system remains one of the most influential. In his *Constitutional Bureaucracy* (1969), Henry Parris argued that patronage could not survive the arrival of fully fledged party politics. Before the arrival of a mature party system, according to Parris, the political and bureaucratic arenas had been manned by the same personnel. With the arrival of mass politics and a mature party system, the amount of work involved in these arenas became so heavy that a separation of the two became inevitable. Parris argues that it was in both the short- and long-term political interests of ministers to choose civil servants on their merits and thus to exercise efficiency in administration (Parris 1969: 73).[4] Insofar as this was recognized to be the case, and in some respects it was, then Parris certainly has a point. But surely the original initiative for the reform of patronage did not come from party sources but from deep within the nonparty governing oligarchy of William Pitt. Indeed, party leaders often opposed Economical Reform. In any case, the arrival of two-party politics may at the earliest be dated from the second decade of the nineteenth century, at least thirty years later than the origins

[4] In what follows I am following the argument of Harling (1996: 25–30).

of Economical Reform in the 1780s. Furthermore, as much of the evidence in Parris's book in fact demonstrates, the arrival of party politics tended to reinforce the temptation for politicians to use patronage for party purposes, whether it was to please well-connected friends in the party or to reward useful local party contacts and their dependents (Parris 1969: 51). Furthermore, even Parris concedes that one of the consequences of this kind of partisan usage was to "retard the development of a non-partisan civil service." He goes on: "If ministers could not count on permanent civil servants to be neutral between parties, the next best thing would be to ensure that their own party was well represented among the officials" (Parris 1969: 66).

Yet in one further respect Parris's arguments have some force. At the electoral level, at least, patronage was becoming less effective at a time when the size of the electorate was growing. In fact, it had been increasing fairly steadily since about 1780. After the Reform Act of 1832, which increased the size of the electorate from around 440,000 to around 660,000, patronage was now inadequate as a means of rewarding loyal electoral supporters. After 1832, there simply was not enough patronage to go around to feed the hungry political dependents of Whig and Tory party leaders at local as well as at national levels. In any case, even before 1832 the number of the electors was already so great as to render patronage in many constituencies of little consequence. Perhaps in the closed boroughs, several dozens of which the Reform Act of 1832 abolished, patronage might have been an effective instrument of electoral control, but even in these places it was far from being an adequate and reliable method of controlling a parliamentary constituency (O'Gorman 1989, chapter 4).

Of greater sophistication than many of the foregoing explanations is that offered by Martin Shefter. In his *Political Parties and the State* (1994) he argues that the reason why England was able to reform her patronage system was because a "bourgeois constituency" set about reforming the administration *before* the development of a two-party system. According to Shefter, therefore, when modern, mass parties developed in nineteenth-century England, patronage was no longer available to their leaders on any scale. As a consequence, they were compelled to employ ideological and programmatic appeals in order to attract electoral support and, indeed, to retain the support of their activists. In his analysis, Shefter proceeds to make a crucial distinction between "internally mobilized parties" – which are founded by politicians who occupy leadership positions in the prevailing regime and who undertake to mobilize and organize a popular following behind themselves – and "externally mobilized parties" – which are established by leaders who do not occupy positions of power in the prevailing regime and who seek to bludgeon their way into the political system by mobilizing and organizing a mass constituency. For Shefter, "internally mobilized parties" have the choice between using patronage and adopting programmatic appeals to the public, while "externally mobilized parties" can employ only the latter strategy.

Shefter's provocative analysis merits positive assessment. Its recognition of the vital significance of high politics reminds us of the extent to which "the strategic behavior of leaders is shaped by and in turns shapes political institutions" (Shefter 1994: 3). Shefter is surely justified in pointing to the ability of the ruling elite to maintain its control of the political system by making a series of judicious reforms of the administrative system. Nevertheless, he is worryingly ambiguous about where the demand for reform of the patronage system came from. He asserts that it came from a coalition of a "rationalizing bourgeoisie" with "older political and social elites," a coalition which "may thereafter serve as a nation's constituency for bureaucratic autonomy" (Shefter 1994: 45), but such a description scarcely identifies with accuracy any elements in the complex social structure of England at the end of the eighteenth century. Who are the groups which form this "rationalizing bourgeoisie" and where are they to be found? Which "social and political elites" are involved in this coalition? Are they to be identified by their social characteristics and/or their political dispositions?

Shefter's attempts to answer such questions are disappointingly vague. He almost entirely ignores the eighteenth-century origins of the reform of the patronage system and chooses to concentrate solely upon nineteenth-century developments. He identifies two subgroups within his "rationalizing bourgeoisie," one which was "oriented towards the concerns of the older, more established segments of Britain's middle classes" and which "sought to rationalize the nation's traditional institutions" (Shefter 1994: 46). Such men advocated a liberally educated professional elite to govern the country. Shefter identifies this group with an Oxbridge-educated elite of "the aristocracy, the gentry and established members of the liberal professions" (ibid. 47) but he omits to give it names and dates. The second subgroup was "oriented more towards the concerns of the emerging entrepreneurial class" (ibid. 47), among whom Shefter identifies Edwin Chadwick and John Stuart Mill. Such men favored a system of technical training for civil servants over a more traditional liberal training. However plausible such correlations of opinions with (obligingly unanimous) social groups may be, they tend to ignore the personal endeavors of Sir Charles Trevelyan and Sir Stafford Northcote. They entirely neglect the dimension of political narrative.

According to Shefter, the Northcote–Trevelyan proposals of 1854 were defeated because they failed to win the support of the aristocracy and this second, entrepreneurial group. The situation was considerably more complicated. The greatest opposition to the 1854 proposals came not so much from "the aristocracy" as from a much wider constituency of opposition. The process of wearing down that opposition between 1854 and 1870, the relevance of events such as the Crimean War, and the spectacular defects in administration which it revealed cannot be ignored. According to Shefter, only when a plan was fashioned which was backed by the aristocracy and by both sections of the bourgeoisie could civil service reform be adopted without controversy (ibid. 48). Yet there was still considerable unease with and opposition to the measures of 1870.

These shortcomings notwithstanding, Shefter's analysis does throw light on the acceptability of the measures. Because the 1870 program divided the civil service into three grades – administrative, executive, and clerical, each with its corresponding educational requirements – namely, liberal, modern English, and technical, respectively – it provided outlets for all kinds of talents. As for the aristocracy, the Reform Act of 1867 and its extension of the franchise to householders and rent-payers persuaded it to relent on civil service reform. The 1870 reform, indeed, by insisting upon a liberal education for the administrative level, kept open promising avenues of access to the highest echelons of the civil service for its younger sons.

Shefter's analysis of the process of reform offers a useful, if limited, degree of analytical clarification. How useful, however, is his much-vaunted distinction between "internally mobilized parties" and "externally mobilized parties"? He is, in fact, on firm ground in asserting that the "internally mobilized" regime – in this case the Whig regime of eighteenth-century England – relied heavily on patronage for its survival. As Shefter points out, it appealed for popular support only when it was compelled to do so by competition from "externally mobilized" groups without necessarily embarking on a program of mass mobilization and organization. Moreover, he is surely justified in arguing that the continuation of patronage strategies depended upon: "(1) the demands and expectations of the party's rank and file supporters; (2) the material and organizational resources available to the party; and (3) the orientation of the party's leadership and its cadres and the interests of the elites who are allied with the party or who are capable of sanctioning it" (Shefter 1994: 32). Yet the Whig regime in the second half of the eighteenth century was not a party regime. It was intended to be a coalition of groups. Furthermore, Shefter erects a contrast between a somewhat elitist patronage structure, on the one hand, and the possibility of a mass base, on the other. I am not convinced that such a contrast is justified. In fact, the Whig patronage system of the eighteenth century ultimately extended into many localities and into many minor appointments of a local nature, tending, in its own way, to build its own mass base, as Shefter actually concedes (Shefter 1994: 61). I believe that Shefter underestimates the degree to which Whig notables depended upon the support and loyalty of the middling orders and their dependents.[5]

More damaging, however, is Shefter's treatment of "externally mobilized parties" in later Hanoverian England. The idea that the Rockingham Whigs and, later, the Foxite Whigs and their descendants needed to "gain entry" into the political system, a system that their ancestors had done much to create, seems fanciful. True, their exclusion from power in the central administration no doubt persuaded them from an early date to organize the political forces at their disposal, and this they did in the 1780s (O'Gorman 1967). However, they did so precisely by mobilizing their local patronage as a means of strengthening their electoral support. Again, patronage and opinion are not necessarily conflicting and contradictory concepts. Furthermore, when the Whigs came to enjoy a lengthy spell in government after 1830, there is no sign that they wished to dispense with patronage in order to keep the party in power and to maintain a linkage with their subordinates and followers. Shefter, thus, ignores the extent to which parties used patronage as a mechanism to build up and consolidate mass support both before and after the Reform Act of 1832. It is simply not the case that patronage was not available to the mass parties of the second half of the nineteenth century. Shefter may be justified in arguing that in some ways overt patronage could discredit the political process and that it might be in the interests of politicians to abandon it. This they did, of course, but only when it had already become redundant and when their objectives could be attained by other means, as we see in the next section.

---

[5] On the ability of the Hanoverian elite to employ and to associate with members of the lower and middling orders, see Langford (1991).

These reservations may not go to the heart of Shefter's analysis but they do signify that the approaches of the historian, on the one hand, and the political scientist, on the other, yield very different empirical and analytical results. After all, Professor Shefter's principal concern is to investigate the nature of political parties, as the title of his volume reminds us, not the reform of the patronage system in England. Nevertheless, the generalizing approach of the political scientist and the empirical research of the historian frequently yield qualitatively different conclusions. Rather than treating the Whig regime of the 1780s as an example of an "internally mobilized party" it may be more enlightening to underline what can be verified, namely, that the reform of the patronage system in England had its origin not in any conflict between the ruling oligarchy and the "bourgeoisie," bracing though such confrontations may be to relate, but between Pitt and his ministers, on the one hand, and their critics within the political establishment, on the other. Public debate perhaps became a factor sustaining the momentum of reform in the 1790s when the process was already well under way. Even then, it was not always the confrontation between a radical public opinion and a recalcitrant government which prompted the debate. Although public opinion remained touchy about administrative abuses, most radicals of the 1790s remained uninterested in administrative reform. More commonly it was a combination of Independent Members of Parliament and Whig opposition politicians who criticized and coaxed ministers into furthering the cause of administrative reform. After 1815 public opinion became a more active component in the process of the reform of patronage, and the momentum to reform gained weight correspondingly, yet the effective dynamic of reform continued to be generated from within the governing establishment rather than from outside.

Survivals of the Patronage System in the Victorian State

The process of the reform of the patronage system was so gradual that it is difficult to declare that at any given point it was finally accomplished. Many aspects of the old practices continued well into the second half of the nineteenth century. Indeed, the language of radical and liberal criticisms of "old corruption" were still to be heard long after 1850. For example, the language of Gladstonian liberalism constantly challenged aristocratic exclusiveness and elite monopoly of power and office. Nevertheless, the great days of popular agitation against "old corruption" were over. They were replaced by campaigns for political, for party, and later for class objectives. As Philip Harling has persuasively argued, the reform of patronage had done much to maintain the confidence of the new electors enfranchised by successive reform acts, and of those beneath them in the social and political scale, in the responsiveness of the English political elite (Harling 1996: 256–59). As he puts it: "The reduction of the cost of the British central government and the patronage at its disposal, the reform of its more glaring administrative abuses, the more equitable distribution of the tax burden it imposed, and the increasingly conspicuous probity of its ministers, were all bound to allay popular suspicions of the motives of elite politicians" (Harling 1996: 262).

Yet many of the old elements remained. Landed proprietors remained supreme in politics. Until the 1850s, most cabinets contained a clear numerical majority of members of the House of Lords over the House of Commons. Genuine members of the bourgeoisie were notably rare. Out of the 103 cabinet ministers who served between 1830 and 1868 only three can be described as bourgeois. Members of the House of Commons continued to number less than one quarter as late as 1865 (Guttsman 1968: 36–41). As we noted earlier, patronage could be utilized by governments of both political parties. Disraeli, for example, regarded the distribution of patronage as one of the principal foundations of his political power during his government of 1874 to 1880. He authorized his patronage secretary to inform him of all proposals to abolish offices, and he was always ready to use political influence to bestow offices which had no recognized ladder of appointment or promotion (Parris 1969: 51–52).

Why were so many elements of the old practices continued? One reason must have been the speedy expansion of government functions. We remarked earlier that the number of civil servants had declined to less than 17,000 in 1841. The trend then turned sharply upward. By 1870 a massive expansion in the functions of government, which by then covered a wide range of public activities, including the poor law, health, transport, emigration, education, and prisons, raised the number of civil servants to 70,000. By 1901 the number had reached 116,000 (see Evans 1983: 285, Hanham 1969: 318, McCord 1991: 424). It was in fact in these newer areas of administration, among the lower echelons of the civil service, that the Northcote–Trevelyan reforms exerted their most significant influence. However, it would have been astonishing if politicians had been completely blind to the competitive advantage they might enjoy over their opponents if they permitted party interests to influence official appointments, especially at the higher levels. Furthermore, what is often lost sight of is the even more remarkable expansion in the functions of local government, especially in urban areas, many of which had known little coordinated administration in the past. The introduction of party politics into the municipal corporations after their establishment in 1835 almost certainly proved a great temptation to party men in town councils to indulge in favoritism when appointing to office.

One further reason for the persistence of old forms of patronage was the uneven rate at which reforms were being enacted. There was nothing smooth or continuous about them; they tended to come in sudden bursts, such as in the 1830s and the 1850s. Indeed, the work of Gladstone's ministry of 1868–74 was so comprehensive and so thoroughgoing that it took time for contemporaries to adjust to it. The government passed bills to reform the church, the ancient universities, the civil service, the legal system, and the army. It would not have been surprising if politicians and civil servants had clung tenaciously for a time to familiar routines of administration and appointment which were deeply embedded in social patterns relating to birth, education, landownership, and life-style. Politics could not be separated from status. The world of politics at the top was a closed and intimate world. Personal knowledge, preference and prejudice, political sponsorship, and the operation of factors such as family loyalty and party political advantage continued to influence appointments to and promotions in administration. This kind of social pattern was much less pronounced in the towns of Victorian England, but even here personal knowledge, sectarian dispositions, and economic competition no doubt had predictable consequences.

The Northcote–Trevelyan reforms had opened up appointments, albeit belatedly, to the most able. But who were the most able? At a time of very limited educational opportunity it was not at all surprising that the civil service elite continued to be drawn from the landed and aristocratic classes. Competition was very limited and many of those nominated were able eventually to secure a place. Appointments at the highest levels of the civil service continued to be made from within a narrow range of public school-educated personnel. "The most prestigious and rewarding positions in both the home and foreign Civil Service remained perquisites of men drawn from the dominant minorities; they alone possessed the resources, the connections and the education to win them" (McCord 1991: 424).

As we have seen, some of the more conservative and traditional sectors of the central government administration managed for some decades to avoid the new system entirely. Moreover, it was hardly to be imagined that conventionally minded political leaders in London would wish to take risks with any of Britain's peripheries. Local needs had to be consulted and traditional regional feelings had to be massaged. To achieve these objectives informal means were preferred. Consequently, the reforms were not applied to many sectors of the administration of Scotland and Ireland.

Finally, the patronage system of England in the second half of the nineteenth century, even after the effects of the Northcote–Trevelyan reforms had been felt, continued to exist as a structure of power supplementary to the official political system, although enjoying something less than full and complete independence. It was, in short, very much in the interests of politicians in office to leave the legacies of patronage in place. Consequently, the personal actions of individuals, whether making a gift, visiting a friend, or even directly petitioning for an appointment, may have interacted with the formal political structure. This, of course, goes against the grain of principles of civil service autonomy and even, arguably, against the principles of democratic accountability. But may there not at least be one advantage in it? May it not have helped to smooth the transition from one system of allocating power and influence to another? Might not the untidy overlap of one system with another have facilitated the passage from a form of appointment and promotion based on personality to one based on merit?

Conclusion

To what extent does the English experience in reforming patronage suggest broader ideas and approaches? It was, of course, a slow and complex business, taking almost a century to effect even at the formal level. It is impossible to reduce such a process to a single factor such as the rise of mass politics, the activities of a parliamentary opposition party, or the alleged intersection of (suspiciously homogeneous) social groups and subgroups, although all of these forces no doubt played their part at various times. The reform of the patronage system in England was principally, if intermittently, the process of internal government reform prompted and influenced, from time to time, by the above-mentioned factors. It largely preceded the emergence of mass politics and mass political parties. It had its origin in the political response to public outcries against the perceived corruption which accompanied the prosecution of the American War of Independence in the late 1770s. It was for the next quarter of a century taken up within the portals of the political and bureaucratic structures of the state, encouraged by occasional but, after 1800, increasingly frequent, bursts of radical indignation against the structures of elite power. These were exploited by the extraparliamentary radicals and by the parliamentary opposition, usually the Whig party, although it is difficult to take their posturing seriously. The reform of the state was not on the whole the product of party competition because between 1780 and 1830 and again between 1846 and 1866 there was little alternation of the parties in government.

The reform of the state administration by successive governments was undertaken less to conciliate a particular social group than to placate a wider public opinion and, by doing so, maintaining the confidence of the public in the social and political elite. Indeed, even before the end of the eighteenth century, public opinion had become a powerful and irreversible feature of political life in England. Traditions of dynastic and party conflict had bred a readiness on the part of the public to discuss and to criticize, as was vividly revealed by the rapid growth in statistics of newspaper circulation, up from 9 million newspaper stamps a year in 1760 to 12.6 million in 1775 to over 16 million in 1801 to 22 million in 1816, and to a staggering 39 million in 1839 (Christie 1970). The passion for information, especially political information, was almost insatiable. The growth in newspapers and periodicals was matched by that of cheap printed caricatures and cartoons, all readily available in the rapidly multiplying coffee and debating clubs which were to be found in all towns and even in some larger villages. It was no accident that Pitt and later Liverpool and Peel were constantly aware of the need to play to this opinion. Politicians of all descriptions were aware that while public opinion might be influenced it could not, in the last analysis, be controlled. This is not to suggest that the English ruling class simply conducted an effective press campaign, seeking to satisfy an anxious public opinion with superficial evidence of reform. There can be no doubt that the political leaders took administrative reform seriously. They looked to improved governmental structures and to greater fairness and efficiency, not simply to the blind retention of the status quo.

The timing and the context of the reform of patronage are central issues. According to Professor Shefter: "Patronage in the civil service was finally restricted in Britain, and a system of competitive examinations was instituted, when a reform plan was fashioned that could be supported by the landed and entrepreneurial classes as well as by professional elites"

(Shefter 1994: 48) While there is some truth in this generalization, it is weakened by its distinctions between "landed," "entrepreneurial," and "professional" classes and the inference that patronage reform occurred once these classes had established some common interests. Such distinctions have their dangers. Even during the eighteenth century, the landed classes had been highly entrepreneurial and professional, whether in politics, estate management, or even to some degree in their private lives. Furthermore, the landed orders had always collaborated and interacted with the middling orders during the period covered by this essay.

Indeed, I would argue that the manner in which patronage was reformed provides important clues for understanding the persistence of landed power in English politics down to the end of the nineteenth century and even into the twentieth century. There are, of course, economic and social explanations for this persistence but the process by which patronage was reformed in the late eighteenth and nineteenth centuries helps to explain why the mass of the voters and even the mass of the people were prepared to tolerate a highly elitist political system and to acquiesce in the continuation of an immensely hierarchical political and social order. These continuities are of primary importance in seeking to understand England's ability to survive the great social changes of the nineteenth century without significant internal upheaval. In Ireland the situation was to be tragically different. It is surely significant that the emergence of mass political parties in the 1870s coincided with the effective liquidation of patronage in some key areas of the civil service. Furthermore, it can be argued that England disposed of its patronage system when it was no longer indispensable to its system of government. In this sense, the *political* costs of patronage, not least the immense public suspicion which it created, had become troublesome, while the *economic* costs were not significant. By the middle of the nineteenth century the governing establishment was satisfied that political stability could be maintained by a range of alternative strategies, including extensions of the electoral franchise, the mobilization of mass political parties, the modernization of local government, and, not least, the meritocratic system of appointment to and promotion in the public administration.

4

Clientelism in the Building of State and Civil Society in Spain

GEORGINA BLAKELEY

Introduction

Spanish political history provides the opportunity to study the transition from patronage to clientelism by examining how state–society relations have altered during this transition and how politics as a linkage between state and society has also altered (Weingrod 1968). The particular way in which both the state and civil society have developed, and the interactions between the two, denote both the circumstances in which clientelism increases or declines as well as the type of clientelism present. State action is crucial to explaining how clientelist structures may be reinforced or weakened in two key ways: first, the type and extent of resources, in terms of public decision-making, that the state provides; second, the state's ability to enforce the rule of law and demonstrate its autonomy from class interests to counteract the inequalities inherent in civil society.[1] These are the structural and institutional circumstances which Shefter draws attention to in his "supply side" account of patronage (Shefter 1994). The "demand side" of this account is provided by looking at civil society. Civil society is an important explanatory variable in terms of its ability to ensure state accountability and to provide a check and counterbalance to state activity. This depends on the extent to which citizens become economically and cognitively empowered to organize and form associations in civil society independently of both the state and political parties.

However, it is crucial to highlight the limitations of the liberal notion of civil society. First, the "free" and "equal" citizen postulated by

---

[1] As Waltzer points out, "left to itself, civil society generates radically unequal power relationships, which only state power can challenge" (1992: 104).

liberalism tends, in reality, to be neither free nor equal. This gap between potentiality and reality is where clientelism as a functional strategy may enter the picture. Second, the inequalities which result from this gap between the potentiality and reality of liberal civil society can be tempered only by state intervention. Unable to rely solely on the horizontal links binding individuals together in civil society, the liberal citizen must look to the state for protection. This necessary vertical linkage between citizen and state may provide further opportunities for clientelism by preserving intact the "supply side" of clientelism.

To illustrate the development of both state and civil society in Spain, I look first at the limited democracy of the *turno pacífico* from 1874 until 1923 in which the figure of the *cacique*, as the linchpin of that political system, was a clear manifestation of the clientelist nature of the Restoration political system. The existence of patronage reflected the fact that Spain remained a predominantly rural and agrarian society as well as the fact that the central state was so weak and inefficient that it was incapable of integrating the majority of citizens into its orbit save by means of its extractive and repressive arms. *Caciquismo* was a strategy to link people to the central state in the absence of any other effective linkage mechanism such as political parties.

The second period to be examined is that of the Second Republic between 1931 and 1936. This period, I argue, is the odd one out in relation to the two periods of democratic politics which flank it. During the Second Republic there is not just one concept of civil society but two: the liberal elites' project of extending the democratic state and strengthening civil society from above, as well as an alternative anarchist project of building a collectivist civil society from below and against, rather than for, the liberal state. Whereas the liberal project faced the limitations outlined above, the anarchist project did not. Anarchism entails a far more substantial notion of civil society which relies exclusively on strengthening horizontal links between citizens in civil society rather than the vertical links between citizens and the state. As such, anarchism had the potential to negate clientelism by empowering citizens to be free and equal, not just potentially but in reality, too, as well as by denying the viability of the state and thereby obviating the need for mechanisms, clientelist or otherwise, to link the citizenry to it.

During the Francoist dictatorship from 1936 to 1975, a whole series of socioeconomic changes, which were often unintentional by-products of the regime's policies, set the foundations for the post-Franco transformation from the traditional patronage of the past to the kind of clientelism typical of fully mobilized polities of the twentieth century. Increased state intervention in the economy and the need to provide some form of social provision, however meager, strengthened the "supply side" of patronage. However, the "demand side" of patronage was gradually weakened: first, the increased role of the state served to strengthen civil society by providing it with a focal point. Organizations came to engage with the state rather than ignore it, as they had done in the past. Second, the process of socioeconomic modernization during the 1960s, which was largely despite state policies rather than because of them, nevertheless empowered people both economically and cognitively, thereby weakening the demand for patronage.

Finally, I examine the liberal democratic regime established after the death of Franco in 1975. This period is marked by several contradictory tendencies. On the one hand, opportunities for clientelism have grown due to the increased strength of the state in terms of the resources it has at its disposal as well as the increased strength of political parties which are now capable of linking state and society and of acting as conduits through which the state's resources are distributed. On the other, clientelism is checked by the state's ability to uphold the rule of law and by the increased ability of civil society to hold the state accountable (see Chapter 7).

In conclusion, this chapter argues that it is unhelpful to posit a false dichotomy between "clientelist" and "civic" systems (cf. Putnam 1993). First, Fox argues that within the same nation-state there may be different enclaves, placed along a continuum, going from areas of authoritarian clientelism, where clientelist practices are reinforced by the threat of coercion, to areas of pluralism, where access to state resources is not conditioned by political subordination, with "gray areas of semi-clientelism" in between. In the latter, compliance is induced "more by the threat of the withdrawal of carrots than by the use of sticks" (Fox 1994: 157). It is these "gray areas of semi-clientelism" which are problematic and difficult to distinguish from the "normal" bargaining process of politics.

Second, I argue that some kind of clientelism is a natural feature of liberal democratic polities because it results from the gap between the normative ideals of how a liberal democracy ought to function and the reality of how it actually operates in practice. In other words, the areas of clientelism found in otherwise "civic" systems result from the limitations of liberal democracy arising from the fact that liberal democracy is not liberalism extended and made more democratic, but rather democracy narrowed and restricted to liberalism (Wood 1995: 229): hence, the gap between the potentiality of equality and freedom, which such systems hold aloft, and the reality of a formal political equality separated, and based upon, economic and social inequalities. Clientelism, therefore, is a symptom of the fact that liberal democracies basically fail to live up to the normative standards set by democratic theory.

The *Turno Pacífico*

The dominance of patronage under the Restoration political system from 1874 until 1923 was a symptom of a liberal democratic system, artificially constructed and imposed from above, which lacked any real foundations within society. The Restoration political system was based on the *turno pacífico*, an arrangement whereby the two dynastic parties – the Conservatives and the Liberals, led by Cánovas and Sagasta, respectively – agreed to the peaceful alternation in power. On paper this arrangement resembled the British system from 1832 to 1867 of which Cánovas, the architect of the *turno pacífico*, was a fervent admirer. In practice, however, the rotation of the two parties did not rest on normal electoral procedures. Rather, the King, with the agreement of the incoming government, would dissolve the Parliament and call elections. Elections therefore were a pure formality which in no way reflected public opinion. As González Calbet summarizes: "This system was a result of political demobilization, but at the same time it favored it. There was a government responsible before the parliament and those parties which organized within it, but they didn't attempt to establish a link nor to appeal to the support of the people *because they didn't need to*" (González Calbet 1986: 110, emphasis in original). As Shefter also remarks, the governmental party found it more convenient to collude with the opposition party rather than to try to engage in competitive mobilization, which may have mobilized strata of the population *against* the incumbents (Shefter 1994: 8).

This strategy was possible because, in 1878, the voters numbered only around 847,000, approximately 5 percent of the population. Moreover, in subsequent years, this figure fell to 2 percent of the population. Only with the introduction of universal male suffrage by Sagasta in 1890 did the number of voters increase substantially, to 4.8 million. But even then, in reality, many voters were deprived of their right to vote, mostly in rural areas, by Article 29, which stated that where the number of candidates presented for election did not exceed the number of seats available, no election was necessary. This benefited the dynastic parties almost exclusively (Artola 1991: 54–55). Thus, the "real" vote of the urban areas was constantly distorted by the "false" vote of the rural areas. This explains the otherwise anomalous fact that the rural areas constantly showed participation rates of around 80 percent compared with the high abstention rates in urban areas (Carr 1980: 12).[2]

In urban areas, the *turno pacífico* began to disintegrate at the turn of the century as the electorate was open to mobilization by parties outside the system. As Shubert writes: "Alejandro Lerroux's Radical Party was able to control local government in Barcelona in the early years of the twentieth century with only 10% of the vote. This was because *caciques* did not try to compete in the realm of real politics" (Shubert 1990: 186). However, although by the turn of the century it was no longer possible to control the urban vote, the *turno pacífico* continued to function because the urban vote could still be watered down by the rural vote, which the dynastic parties continued to control.

The agreement between the two parties to alternate in power depended for its success on the ability of the government to manage elections systematically. Agreements to "make" elections would be forged initially between the national leaders of the two dynastic parties, Cánovas and Sagasta, who had to take into account and reconcile the interests of a number of conflicting groups. In particular, it was necessary to accommodate the leaders of the various factions within the governing party, the leader of the opposition, and even certain representatives of the nondynastic parties such as the Republicans, who were often allotted seats to encourage them to take part within the system rather than to act against it. But the story did not end at the national level. To ensure the acceptance of these national agreements at the local level the figure of the *cacique* was crucial.

The *caciques* were local party bosses whose power depended on their manipulation of the administrative machinery for their own personal benefit and that of their clientele. The *cacique* was not necessarily a wealthy person, nor did the *cacique's* power rest exclusively upon the distribution of material resources, for these were in short supply at all levels of the state apparatus. Rather, the *cacique's* power rested upon the discriminate

---

[2] Such high participation rates in rural areas were clearly engineered. In contrast, the high abstention rates in the urban areas reflected the urban electorate's perception that their "real" vote would be distorted by the "false" vote of the rural areas.

distribution of "state decisions" as the following quote illustrates: "Authorization, certificates, court and police sentences, exemptions, and the like, were as important to the *cacique*, if not more so, than jobs and other resources allocated to clients and non-clients" (Romero-Maura 1977: 56). In many senses, the *cacique* operated much like a constituency MP would have done in Britain. As Carr says: "They served their constituents well. La Cierva, without whose permission, it was said, not a leaf fell in Murcia, got his district everything from secondary roads to a university" (1982: 368).

Tusell Gómez also agrees with this interpretation of the *cacique*, whom he likens to the "boss" in United States politics. He says: "The term *'cacique'* should be reserved for those professional politicians whose form of action did not differ too much from that of the 'boss' in United States politics; congenial . . . , their power derived from the patronage that they practiced with regard to the electorate and from their role of promoter for concrete material advantages from the central government for their constituents" (1976: 14). Moreover, many *caciques* worked for both parties. Regardless of his own party affiliation, the *cacique* guaranteed the return of deputies from either party in return for the disposal of government patronage within his district. As Romero-Maura argues, "the strength of its local *caciques* guaranteed to each party that it would retain a strong minority and considerable influence whenever it was the other party's turn to 'make' the election from the Government" (1977: 57).

To operate, the *caciques* required a highly centralized state from which a wide range of favors could be extracted, coupled with financially starved municipalities unable to provide services of their own. The ability to use the central administration as a provider of spoils was the result of the highly centralized administrative system established by the Liberals. In such a context, local government was totally lacking in power. The fact that nearly all decisions, whether small or large, were taken in the capital Madrid meant that the *cacique* served as a crucial intermediary between a remote state in Madrid and the citizenry. As Carr points out, the *cacique* "always protected his village clientele from the laws, taxes, and conscription levies of the outside world of the state" (1982: 369). In this sense it is difficult to overestimate the importance of the state administration in Spanish political and social life, especially given the lack of economic development in Spain, which meant that few opportunities for advancement existed outside of the state. The centralized and omnipresent administrative system was simultaneously a source of political power as well as a channel for social mobility. Even the postman or village schoolteacher in the depths of rural Spain owed his appointment to the *cacique* or the local party boss. Trice states that estimates show that at each rotation of the *turno pacífico* 5,000 to 10,000 political and administrative positions changed hands (1974: 11).

Patronage during the *turno pacífico* resulted from a particular configuration of state–society relations where both the "supply side" and the "demand side" of patronage were strong. It was a functional response to the early establishment of advanced liberal government in what was still an economically and socially backward country. *Caciquismo* solved the problem of how to establish some kind of link between a narrow elitist political system, on the one hand, and a demobilized society, on the other, between a remote, highly centralized state and an atomized and mainly rural society. The *caciques* were the local agents of a political oligarchy which was isolated in the national capital, and as such they arranged electoral support and handled local affairs. In most places there was nothing else in the way of political organization apart from the figure of the *cacique*. Political parties had no roots in society and they lacked meaningful ideological identity. The political class won power by manipulating elections and controlling the state apparatus rather than by fulfilling the functions of interest aggregation and representation. In the absence of effective political parties, the figure of the *cacique* became the only way of linking the people with the state.

Patronage also reflected the weakness of civil society in Spain characterized by low levels of associational life and a "particularistic" political culture. Only in those areas where an incipient industrialization had taken off – the Basque Country and Catalonia – could one find the stirrings of associational life spurred on by the development of an industrial bourgeoisie and an urban working class. In these areas one could point to the growth of an independent entrepreneurial class whose power and wealth came to be based on controlling the economic means of production within civil society rather than the political goods of the state. In the rest of Spain, though, the political and economic remained closely entwined with the result that the state administration remained the key channel for social advancement and patronage remained a viable strategy to achieve such advancement.

Thus, "[c]*aciquismo* turned out to be a functional mechanism to establish communication between a parliamentary regime and a demobilized society" (Varela 1982: 64). For the state, *caciquismo* was a necessary means of overcoming its inefficiency and weakness at the local level: in short, the state needed the *caciques* to operate at the local level given the state's own limited capacity to intervene in and to regulate society. To rely on a distinction made by Michael Mann (1988), the Spanish state may have been strong in terms of "despotic power" but it was weak in terms of "infrastructural power": it met few constraints in keeping law and order, but its ability to penetrate society and to organize social relations by means other than coercion was severely limited. For the clients patronage was a means to provide some measure of security against a state which generally touched the lives of its citizens purely in a negative way, either in its "extractive" or "repressive" capacity. Indeed, for most citizens, the most visible manifestation of the state in their daily lives was the Civil Guard, responsible for maintaining law and order in the countryside. In this sense *caciquismo* and the Civil Guard were two sides of the same coin.[3] As Shubert points out: "The expansion of the *Guardia Civil* was the foremost example of the growth of the liberal state in Spain. At the same time, however, it can also be seen as marking a crucial limitation of that state: an essentially suspicious, if not openly hostile, attitude toward the bulk of the population" (1990: 181). Most people therefore saw the state "not as a potential instrument for their own aspirations, but rather as an alien agency, from which, at best, transactional benefits may be obtained" (Clapham 1982: 23).

The Second Republic

Although a period of dictatorship under General Primo de Rivera (1923–30) separated the Second Republic from the Restoration political system, vestiges of the latter were still present when the Republican elites embarked upon their project of modernization and democratization. Those vestiges, particularly patronage, would be an obstacle that the Second Republic would find difficult to overcome.

Although an extremely complex period in Spanish history, the Second Republic can be interpreted as an attempt to construct a liberal democratic state from above via a series of modernizing/democratizing reforms (Shubert 1990: 189–90). Rather than looking at the separate reforms individually – agrarian reform, reform of the church and the military, labor legislation reform, and reform of the state structure – it is possible to see them all as a means of asserting state authority and autonomy vis-à-vis the

---

[3] I am grateful to my colleague Andrew Taylor for pointing this out to me.

established interests of the military, the Church, and the landed oligarchy, and as a concomitant result, strengthening civil society.

A snapshot of some reform areas will suffice. Anticlerical legislation aimed to strengthen the role of the state and threaten the hegemony of the Church by demanding the withdrawal of the religious orders from primary and secondary education in an attempt to extend public, secular education to everyone. Agrarian reform attempted to strengthen the state's autonomy vis-à-vis the land-owning oligarchy and claimed the right of the state to expropriate private property for reasons of social utility, thereby stressing the primacy of the public good over private interests. Military reform which attempted to reduce the size of the officer corps, and hence the amount of the state budget which it received, also helped to bolster the political authority of the state, as did the various attempts to make the military subordinate to civilian control.[4] Even the Statutes of Autonomy granted to Catalonia and the Basque Country can be interpreted in the light of bolstering the state's authority and legitimacy, as they were an attempt to adapt the existing state structure in order to better reflect the reality, and therefore the diversity, of the Spanish nation-state.

The expansion of the state's authority also served to strengthen civil society primarily by attempting to provide, for the first time, an effective state apparatus capable of guaranteeing the rule of law on an equal footing to all without regard to "particularistic" criteria. In this way, the state guaranteed the people's right to associate free from retribution by employers or landowners. Simply by enforcing the law in rural areas the state challenged the political and social supremacy of the landed oligarchy in local life and strengthened civil society by providing the space within which peasant organizations could form without the fear of reprisal from landowners.

The arrival at the Ministry of Labor of the Socialist trade union leader, Largo Caballero, meant that "the power of the state would now be put behind the basic aspirations of the rural proletariat" (Preston 1993: 165). Two legislative changes, in particular, had a huge effect in the south. One was the decree of municipal boundaries issued on April 28, 1931, which forbade the hiring of outside labor while local workers were unemployed. This was an obvious blow to one of the main repressive weapons of the landowners: no longer could they break strikes or keep down wages by bringing in outside labor. The second measure was the establishment of

---

[4] The War Ministry, for example, was brought under civilian control.

"mixed juries" made up of representatives of employers, unions, and the state, which undoubtedly strengthened the organizational capacity of both the rural and the urban working classes. That they were effective can be seen in the following quote: "In Oviedo, 84.7% of the cases brought to the arbitration committees in 1932 were decided in favor of the workers and only 15.2% in favor of the employers" (Ramírez Jímenez 1969: 320). The downside, however, could be seen in those areas where traditional structures of patronage were still entrenched. In such areas, "the percentage of decisions favorable to workers goes down considerably even to the extent that in some towns of Toledo and Ciudad Real, they are exceeded by those in favor of the employers" (Ramírez Jímenez 1969: 320).

Herein lay the difficulty. Although under the Second Republic the extension of the democratic state helped to bolster civil society primarily by guaranteeing people's right to form associations without fear of retribution, in many areas of Spain, civil society remained weakened by entrenched systems of patronage. *Caciques* remained firmly in place in many rural areas throughout the whole of the Republic. Many of the Socialists' legislative changes remained on paper as they lacked the machinery and the power to enforce them against the obstructionist tactics of the *caciques*. As Preston comments: "Socialist deputies from the south regularly complained in the Cortes about the way in which the civil governors of their provinces displayed little energy in preventing the local *caciques* (political bosses) from simply ignoring legislation and even less in ensuring that the Civil Guard did not continue to side with landowners in defiance of the new laws" (1993: 168). Thus, the imposition of a liberal democratic polity at the national level, while of great import, was not enough to reinforce state structures and penetrate civil society at all levels and in all areas of Spain.

The modernizing/democratizing project of the Second Republic was not experienced equally by all. For many citizens the state remained synonymous with coercion. Incidents such as the massacre at Casas Viejas in January 1933 in which government forces shot twenty-five anarchists after they had spontaneously declared the village's independence, struck a familiar chord with many. While such incidents did not necessarily typify the nature or the extent of state coercion during the Second Republic, they were indicative of the state's continued weakness and reliance on coercion.

For many the Second Republic was far from an empowering experience, as in their daily lives they remained powerless to mobilize the basic resources necessary for survival. Spain remained a poor and predominantly rural country where the basic struggle to survive weakened the possibilities for the development of either civil society or the state. Clientelist practices therefore coexisted at the local level with more democratic practices at the national level. Azaña himself complained that the Republic had failed to reach huge swathes of Spanish life even after five years or so of its existence, as Ramírez Jímenez points out: "It is precisely in his speeches where we find the lament that, quite a lot of time after its establishment, the Republic had not reached the towns" (Ramírez Jímenez 1981: 35).

The Liberals' attempt to construct a liberal democratic state structure from above was blocked from two very different sources. First, much of the agrarian and social legislation which the state elaborated during the first two years of the Republic when Largo Caballero was Minister of Labor was blocked by the intransigence of the big landowners, backed by the violence of the Civil Guard. The landowners saw in such legislative changes a far bigger threat to their hegemony than the usual spontaneous rebellions of the peasants. The latter was easily dealt with by calling on the repressive capabilities of the Civil Guard, whereas the former was far more difficult to challenge as it constituted an attempt to alter permanently the balance of power between landowners and peasantry. Second, the liberal democratic project stumbled against the strength of anarchism in Spain. As Preston writes, "the intransigence of the owners was matched by the opposition of the CNT [the anarcho-syndicalist trade union, the Confederación Nacional de Trabajadores] to both the *jurados mixtos* and the law on municipal boundaries" (1993: 169).

Anarchism, which denied the legitimacy of the state and the parliamentary process, was perhaps the biggest obstacle to the development of a liberal democratic polity. Nor are we talking about a minority radical current: the anarcho-syndicalist movement represented the largest percentage of the Spanish working classes; thus its absence from the traditional political arena meant the continuing weakness of the parliamentary process and political parties.[5] In a sense it was a vicious circle, as one author comments on the effects of anarchism in Andalusia: "one did not vote because the system was corrupt, but it was corrupt because one did not

---

[5] Whereas by the 1920s the CNT, the Anarcho-Syndicalist trade union, had over 800,000 affiliates, the UGT, the Socialist trade union, despite being created in 1888, numbered only 100,000 (Arango 1978: 41).

vote" (Tusell Gómez 1976: 18). The corruption of the electoral process alienated a large part of labor from the regular sphere of political action and pushed it toward extraparliamentary action.

The strength of anarchism in Spain seriously affected the ability of other parties to develop. Whereas the socialists were willing to work within the parliamentary system and even to work with those bourgeois groups which favored reform, they were not the foremost representatives of the working classes in Spain. Until the 1930s their representation in the countryside, where the majority of the active population was employed, was minimal. The socialists first gained seats in Andalusia and Extremadura in the municipal elections of 1931. Equally as important was the fact that the socialists failed to gain more than a nominal foothold in the most industrialized part of the country: Catalonia. This prevented the integration of a large part of the urban working class into liberal democratic politics through democratic elections.

To combat their continued weakness, parties often resorted to clientelist strategies in an attempt to effectively link state and society and overcome the persistent weakness of each. During the two years when the socialist Largo Caballero headed the Ministry of Labor at the beginning of the Second Republic, the Socialist Party and its affiliated union, the Unión General de Trabajadores (UGT), used the state apparatus mostly in the form of the "mixed juries" and other legislative measures to try to establish clientelist networks, particularly in Andalusia, in order to gain a foothold in such an Anarchist stronghold. As Gillespie writes: "In spite of an impressive spread of UGT influence in the south during the 1930s, Socialist support here had been poorly rooted and dependent upon the State patronage of Andalusian workers that had existed under PSOE ministers" (1989: 202).

The use of patronage by the right-wing parties was similarly indicative of their inability to gain support by other means such as interest aggregation and representation. Right-wing parties tended to eschew party politics in favor of influence via the Church, the military, and the bureaucracy by means of "a highly personalized system of political organization, using local notables, brokers, *caciques* and clientelism" (Barnes 1986: 64). Generally speaking, the oligarchy was accustomed to exercising power directly and privately without the intermediation of parties or other associations. They tended to prefer more traditional means of influence, such as "the traditional visit to those in charge, the letter of recommendation" (Linz 1967: 242).

Patronage remained a viable strategy. For the Socialist party on the left, and the Confederación Española de Derechas Autónomas (CEDA) on the right, patronage was a means of establishing themselves as mass parties capable of performing a linkage function between state and society. Anarchism, however, by not recognizing the need for such a function, had no need for patronage, either. In areas such as Catalonia a combination of a vibrant associational fabric with the triumph of anarcho-syndicalism meant the virtual eradication of patronage. But, in Andalusia, despite the strength of anarchism, a much weaker civil society meant that it was far more difficult to uproot clientelist practices.

As such, the anarchist project of building civil society from below and against, rather than for, the liberal state conflicted with the liberal elites' project of extending the democratic state and strengthening civil society from above. Although it is true that there are differing interpretations as to what exactly the anarchist project entailed, what it certainly did not imply was a civil society in the liberal sense of simultaneously encouraging horizontal links between citizens as well as vertical links between citizens and the state. In the rural south and in urban Catalonia, anarchism put forward a more substantial notion of civil society which relied exclusively on engendering a sense of community between individuals by strengthening the horizontal bonds between them, thereby obviating the additional need for vertical linkages between individual and state.

However one interprets either the project of the liberal elites during the Second Republic, on the one hand, or the anarchist vision, on the other, they were certainly not compatible. The victory of Francoism in the Civil War signaled the end of both conflicting visions of civil society. Francoism would be a negation of everything the Republic had represented and would instigate a complete restructuring of the relationship between state and civil society. The anarchist vision of civil society would remain buried forever; the liberal vision would remain dormant for well over thirty years.

Francoism

During the first period of Franco's dictatorship from the end of the Civil War in 1939 to the first Economic Stabilization Plan in 1959, both the "supply side" and the "demand side" of patronage were strengthened as the regime embarked upon a policy of autarky. In practical terms, the isolation of Spain following the victory of the Allies in World War II meant that the adoption of a policy of economic self-sufficiency was as much a necessity as it was a deliberate choice. In ideological terms, autarky was the economic corollary of fascism.

Autarky signified massive state intervention and regulation of all aspects of economic life: domestic industry was heavily regulated, the price of key goods was fixed administratively, and public licenses were needed for most economic activities. In 1941 the National Institute of Industry (INI), based on Mussolini's IRI, was created in order to develop those industries in which the private sector was unable or unwilling to invest.[6] In agriculture, the INI's equivalent was the National Wheat Board, created in 1937 to guarantee a market and price for the country's main grain crop. In such a context of widespread state regulation of the economy, the state became the focal point for clientelist demands and provided ample scope for patronage to public officials.

The political structure of the state also favored patronage. Franco was in effect the supreme patron and all clients were linked vertically to him. All important state officials were appointed by Franco, either directly or indirectly, and were responsible to him. Franco appointed the President of the Government, who, in close consultation with Franco, chose the other members of the Council of Ministers. The Minister of the Interior, again following consultation with Franco, appointed the civil governor of each of Spain's fifty-one provinces and the mayors of each major city. In turn, the civil governor appointed the mayors of towns and cities with populations under 10,000 (Gunther 1980: 35).

The extensive network of the Falangist party with its central and provincial bureaucracies and its plethora of affiliated organizations also served as a mechanism of patronage whereby jobs, official contracts, and licenses were all subject to arbitrary distribution. Grugel and Rees (1997: 38) remark that the membership of the Falangist party mushroomed to just under one million members by 1942 largely as a result of the opportunities it provided for patronage within the numerous governmental agencies and local government bodies of the expanding state structure. Recruitment to the state administration tended to follow clientelistic criteria whereby jobs were often allocated on the basis of personal contacts and recommendations.

During this initial period of autarky, the "demand side" of clientelism was also strengthened. The precarious position in which many people

---

[6] INI concentrated principally on fuels, fertilizers, and electricity, but rapidly extended its activities to include transportation, iron and steel, cars, and many other industries.

found themselves, both economically and politically, and the lack of any opportunities for collective action in the face of widespread repression reinforced the tendency to use personal influence as protection against the state's often arbitrary demands. For the working class, in particular, the increase in state norms and controls in the sphere of the economy and labor relations signified an increase in social discipline and exploitation designed to place the burden of industrialization exclusively on their shoulders, without disturbing the social power of landed wealth (Richards 1995).

The flourishing black market which was a direct result of the economic policy of autarky highlighted the importance of having good contacts simply to be able to survive. The supply of food, like work, was controlled by the state. Richards points out that: "[t]he provision of 'supplementary rations' which could mean the difference between life and death, was controlled by a local board made up of the mayor (usually a local industrialist or landowner), the parish priest and the local head of the party" (Richards 1995: 180–81). Moreover, local Falangist chiefs, along with the parish priests, were responsible for issuing certificates of political reliability and good conduct, which were often necessary for anything from obtaining work, accommodation, or even food to being allowed to travel.

Franco's labor relations framework, based on corporatist Vertical Syndicates which represented employers and employees alike, was also designed to break the collective defense of working-class interests and to force these to be defended on an individual basis. In the absence of collective action, contacts with public officials were perforce concerned with highly disaggregated and particularistic matters. Balfour contends, "Workers were encouraged to respond individually to their work problems by turning either to the array of legal advisers of their local union or to private lawyers specializing in labor legislation. No other way of rectifying grievances was offered by a system in which collective organization was banned" (Balfour 1989: 199).

The organization of society was thus corporatist and highly centralized. The former horizontal solidarities of civil society such as political parties and trade unions were rejected as "unnatural" to the Spanish way of life. Instead, citizens were vertically linked to the state via the family, the municipality, and the syndicates. Even organizations such as the chambers of commerce and the professional colleges were subordinated to national, frequently Falangist, control. Such associations were headed by government appointees whose "selection responded to political criteria and clientelistic ties with the new political class" (Linz 1981: 388). Gunther (1980) highlights the importance of personalism and clientelist criteria in the policy-making process during the Franco regime. Private-sector interests tended to make exclusive use of particularistic, clientelist links to state administration officials rather than official channels of interest representation. He writes, "Clientelism exists to some extent in all political systems, but rarely to the high degree found under the Franquist regime. It is most unusual to find that (in the opinion of hundreds of State administration officials) particularistic and/or clientelistic channels of interest articulation were used far more frequently than the bureaucratic and corporatist channels provided by the state; . . . it is unusual to find that the most persuasive explanation of elite recruitment patterns was exclusively clientelistic" (1980: 259)

An unexpected consequence of increased state intervention, however, was the increased dependence of citizens on the state, which became responsible for everything and expected to solve everything. The Vertical Syndicates played their part in making citizens look to the state via the vast range of services which they provided, such as housing, schools, sports clubs, holiday resorts, and leisure facilities. More important, from 1941 to 1957, the head of the Ministry of Labor, the Falangist José Antonio Girón, presided over the expansion of the social security system, which provided both unemployment insurance and old-age pensions, and the creation of a national health service.

This increase in welfare state activities, although still a long way from reaching the scale achieved in other European countries, was crucial in terms of providing an impetus for the corresponding growth in civil society. An increase in associational activity goes hand in hand with the expansion of state services, which suggests that the growth of civil society is dependent upon the state's ability to provide it with a focal point (McDonough et al. 1984). Thus, instead of ignoring the state and concentrating exclusively on self-organization within society as the Anarchists had done previously, organizations within civil society were forced to engage with the state and to seek solutions from it. This reorientation of civil society toward the political-institutional sphere was strengthened by the process of economic modernization from the late 1950s onward.

By the mid-1950s, it was clear that autarky was untenable. Rather than the creation of a self-sufficient industrial economy, government policies had resulted in economic stagnation, bottlenecks, and corruption. In ideological terms the raison d'être of the autarkic system had also disappeared with the fall of Fascism across Europe. Thus, in 1959 the first Economic Stabilization Plan was instituted, with the aim of creating a market economy and reintegrating Spain into the international capitalist system. State intervention did not disappear, however, but was in fact enhanced through the adoption of a series of development plans inspired by French indicative planning. This was the starting point for Spain's so-called economic miracle.[7] Most important, this extended period of economic growth throughout the 1960s stimulated a series of socioeconomic transformations – rapid urbanization, changes in the class structure, and increased associational activity in civil society – which would change state–society relations irrevocably.

One of the main consequences of Spain's economic growth during the 1960s was the massive migration from the countryside to the cities.[8] Urbanization also transformed the balance of classes. While the working and middle classes grew considerably, the size of the traditional landowning class declined. The agricultural labor force fell from 42 percent of the population in 1960 to 20 percent in 1975 (De Riquer i Permanyer 1995: 262); the industrial working class rose from 32 to 37 percent and the amount of people employed in the service sector rose from 26 to 40 percent in the same period (Shubert 1990: 208).

This process of rapid industrialization and urbanization highlighted the inadequacy of almost every aspect of public service provision – education, health, sanitation, leisure facilities – despite some growth of state investment in these areas. As public demand grew for a solution to these inadequacies, it became clear that there was an increasing disjuncture between a rapidly modernizing economy and society and an antiquated political regime, which was incapable of responding to public demand for fear of disturbing the balance of forces on which it rested.[9] This anomaly sparked off a growth of oppositional activity in civil society, among which the labor

---

[7] Certainly, growth rates seemed nothing short of miraculous as the following set of figures shows: from 1960 to 1974 the economy grew at an average of 6.6 percent overall, and 9.4 percent in the industrial sector, a rate exceeded only by that of Japan (Shubert 1990: 207).

[8] Official figures, which are probably on the conservative side, estimate that some 5.7 million Spaniards moved from one province to another between 1962 and 1976 (Shubert 1990: 218).

[9] Despite considerable growth in public expenditure, the Spanish state remained relatively poor due to the Francoist elite's continuing reluctance to expand the state's tax base by increasing direct taxation, rather than by using the indirect taxes which it had always depended upon.

movement and the neighborhood movement were the strongest. *Pace* the current trend among academics to diminish the role and scale of the opposition movements, oppositional activity within civil society forced both the pace and extent of the negotiated political transition following the death of Franco in 1975 (see Chapter 7). In short, socioeconomic structural changes which had empowered citizens economically and cognitively set the stage for the subsequent political change, which demanded that Francoism had perforce to die with Franco.

Liberal Democracy since 1975

The liberal democratic regime which was established following forty years of authoritarian rule rests upon a set of state–society relations which differ dramatically from those discussed above. The most notable change is that each element is stronger than before. Certainly, the Spanish state is stronger and more closely approximates other states in Europe than at any time in its history. The state bureaucracy and the portion of national income devoted to the government sector have grown, as have the functions assumed by the state. Total public expenditure as a percentage of gross domestic product increased from a meager 20 percent in 1965 to 44 percent by 1994 (Gunther 1996: 41). Such an increase is not just a result of the expansion of the central state but is also due to the establishment of seventeen autonomous communities, each with its own parliament and budgetary powers.

Associational life, while still weak compared with other European countries, has also grown in Spain. Although the increase in the number of associations from 1965 to 1990 has been continuous, the years of the transition were notably the most intense period. From 1977 to 1980, a period of only four years, more associations were established than in the twelve preceding years, thereby representing an increase of 221 percent in relation to 1976 (Prieto-Lacaci 1992: 201). The number of associations has continued to increase during the decades of the 1980s and 1990s, albeit not as intensely as during those initial years of democracy. The number of associations has increased by 106 percent from 1981 to 1990 (Prieto-Lacaci 1992: 202). Despite these spectacular increases, however, it still appears as if Spain is among the group of countries with the lowest rates of associational activity in the European Union. A survey carried out in 1989 showed that the portion of the population who joined associations in Spain was 31 percent, a rate which placed Spain above only the countries of Portugal and Greece, with figures of 24 and 25 percent, respectively (Prieto-Lacaci 1992: 205). Nonetheless, although associational activity in Spain still remains below the European average, given the length of the preceding authoritarian period, such growth as currently exists should not be underestimated.[10]

During the present liberal democratic period, two conflicting dynamics are at work. On the one hand, the "demand side" of clientelism is weakened by a stronger civil society, bolstered by the greater autonomy of organizations within civil society and the ability of the state to guarantee the rule of law. On the other hand, the strengthening of the state has increased the supply of patronage available to any government, due to the huge increase in the amount of resources at its disposal as well as its increased economic role. In comparison to the traditional patronage of the past where the *caciques* generally distributed nonmaterial rewards from the state, today the rewards to be distributed from the state are material and increasingly numerous, especially given the strengthened regional tier of government in Spain.

Just as there has been a change in the nature of the rewards to be distributed, so has there been a change in the nature of the patrons. In place of the landlord or *cacique* as "individual" patron, one finds political parties as "collective" patrons who in their role as intermediaries between state and society increasingly link the distributive and electoral realms via clientelist strategies (Lyrintzis 1984: 104). In particular, the majority of parties in Spain have used clientelist strategies to corner certain constituencies which, as in the past, are mainly rural enclaves. The Partido Popular (PP), for example, has targeted Galicia in this way, whereas the Partido Socialista Obrero Español (PSOE) has targeted Andalusia. In both cases there appears to be a direct exchange of electoral support for either employment or benefits. In Andalusia this takes the form of the agricultural unemployment payment scheme (PER), while in Galicia employment opportunities are channeled through private businesses belonging to people with close ties to the PP party (Cazorla, Jerez, and Montabes 1997: 14).

The PER in Andalusia is perhaps the most notorious case of such discriminate targeting. In 1983, the high rates of unemployment among

---

[10] It should be noted, however, that mere numerical growth of associations does not necessarily mean an increase in the effectiveness of civil society.

agricultural day laborers in Andalusia and Extremadura pushed the PSOE government into introducing a special type of unemployment payment scheme which entitled day laborers who could provide evidence that they had worked the land for sixty days in any given year to qualify for nine months' unemployment benefits. This unemployment scheme was also complemented by a government-sponsored community works scheme which allowed workers to claim days worked under this scheme toward the PER. As Cazorla comments: "The clientelist aspect arose from award-ing help to a particular person in preference to others with the necessary qualifications, or indiscriminately, even to those who were not entitled to claim. Moreover, the collection of the payment is *personalized*. The person selecting and the person being selected to work meet face to face, which in the rural context inevitably generates a feeling of gratitude which can be shown – and taken of advantage of – in many ways including that of giving political support" (1995: 49). As Hooper comments, "the mayors – most of them Socialist – have taken over from the landowners as the arbiters of local fortune. Small wonder, then that the PSOE's vote has gone up in the countryside even though it has gone down in the towns" (1995: 249).

Without an examination of civil society in this context we are left with only a partial picture, for the greater strength of civil society – its greater associational autonomy – means that many voters may take the socioeco-nomic rewards offered by the parties but are generally not compelled or coerced into offering their political subordination in return. The parties use clientelist strategies, often with no guarantee of any concrete results. Likewise, it is difficult to decide, in the case of the PER at least, who has the upper hand in this relationship – the parties or their constituents. As Hooper points out: "Most mayors go along with the fraud for fear of what will happen to them otherwise. 'Uncooperative' mayors can expect to be voted out at the next local election. One went into hiding after refusing to oblige" (1995: 249).

This, therefore, raises the question as to whether we should be using the concept of clientelism to describe this phenomenon at all. This skep-ticism about the continued usefulness of clientelism as a concept is also shared by other analysts. Hopkin, for example, who argues that the "col-lective," rather than the "particularistic," nature of the distribution of resources both to party supporters and to constituencies as well as the "col-lective" nature of rewards, in the sense that voters reward the party rather than particular individual candidates, questions the appropriateness of the term "neo-clientelism." He writes: "This form of resource distribution appears to take the logic of 'mass party clientelism' to its limits, to the extent it becomes difficult to describe it as clientelism. It appears to involve collective rather than selective incentives" (1997a: 19).

Clearly, the parties attempt to connect the distributive and electoral spheres via clientelist mechanisms, but if they can do no more than trust or hope that voters go along with the bargain then this may be just a normal part of the political bargaining process rather than clientelism. As Cazorla et al. write, "electoral clientelism – conditioned by electoral rentability – often integrates legitimate governmental actions" (1997: 10). The geographical targeting of swing regions – in Spain these are Catalonia and Andalusia, which together account for just under a third of parliamentary seats – does not necessarily mean that access to benefits is systematically conditioned by and dependent upon forms of subordination, nor that targeted spending will reduce the freedom of voters to vote as they choose. As Fox writes, "more and more citizens may well accept pork-barrel funding but still also vote their conscience as civic activism broadens and deepens" (1994: 180). Here the state's increasing ability to guarantee free and fair elections in Spain, as well as its ability to enforce the rule of law, is also crucial.

Although parties attempt to buy political support in Spain, they are unable to enforce political compliance in exchange for resources. This is due, on the one hand, to the strength of civil society and the ability of associations within civil society to avail themselves of the state's resources without compromising either their aims or autonomy. On the other hand, this is due to the increased strength of the state, in terms of not the increased resources at its disposal but its ability to ensure the rule of law.

Evidence garnered from interviews conducted by the author with associational leaders and activists in Barcelona during 1997 supports this hypothesis. Associations there are well aware that parties utilize clientelist strategies in their ability to gain electoral support. One neighborhood leader defined the policy of the local administration toward the neighborhood associations as being one of keeping the associations "contained and contented." The ruling party of Catalonia, the Convergéncia i Unío, in particular has been accused of using clientelist strategies in order to strengthen its position within civil society. On the one hand, what is known as the "Comas phenomenon" involved the targeting of public funds to those associations known to be sympathetic to the CiU.[11] As many associations rely exclusively on public funds for finance, such clientelist attempts may constrain the associations' autonomy. On the other hand, the CiU has attempted to set up parallel organizations of its own to counteract the strength of those that already exist. For example, it established a confederation of neighborhood associations (FAVIC) to counteract the strength of the one that already existed (CONFAVC) which was seen to be controlled by the Socialist and Communist parties. While the CiU has poured money into this alternative confederation, as one neighborhood leader pointed out wryly, all the neighborhood leaders still belong to either the Socialist or Communist parties. On the whole, then, such practices do not appear to compromise the associations' autonomy. Neither do they seem to deliver any significant increase in the amount of votes received by the parties who indulge in such clientelist strategies. It is widely acknowledged, for example, that the "Comas phenomenon" failed and did not deliver the expected returns in terms of an increase in electoral support. It would not be unreasonable to assume that over time clientelism of this type will gradually decline.

The fact that parties still have a tendency to resort to clientelism, however, is a reflection of their weak roots in civil society, just as patronage was a reflection of their weakness during the period of the Second Republic. This type of electoral clientelism is a result of the nature of parties in Spain, organizations which have been created from the top down which are far closer to, and therefore far more reliant on, the state than civil society (see Chapter 7). Unable to rely on their links with civil society, parties rely far more on the state and its resources in order to consolidate their power. This is a phenomenon detailed by Katz and Mair (1995), who identify a new type of party labeled the "cartel party" which is more reliant on the state than on civil society. While this is undoubtedly a tendency in most European countries, it is arguably more noticeable in the case of Spain because, as Amodia has pointed out, Spanish parties have gone from being notable parties in the nineteenth century to being electoral parties in the twentieth century without ever having been mass parties (1990: 46).[12]

---

[11] Antonio Comas, the former Minister of Welfare, was accused of going "cheque book in hand" to buy votes and support from different associations by several of the neighborhood leaders interviewed.

[12] To what extent the particular nature of Spanish parties, unencumbered by the baggage of the mass parties, affect their propensity to use clientelist strategies is a point which needs researching.

Conclusion

The present nature and extent of clientelism in Spain therefore bears little resemblance to the patronage of the past. The increasing strength of civil society has checked the ability of parties to avail themselves of the ever-increasing quantity of state resources for clientelist purposes. Although parties still use clientelist criteria when distributing state resources, particularly in terms of targeting public spending to key constituencies, it appears that such clientelist strategies are on the decline, not the least because parties are not guaranteed any fixed returns in terms of electoral support. Additionally, whether such practices amount to clientelism at all or are simply a feature of the transactional nature of politics generally is by no means clear.

This points to a certain amount of linguistic "hypocrisy" by analysts. There seems to be a tendency to label such practices as "clientelism" in countries such as Spain which historically have been described as clientelist systems, whereas in other countries not usually associated with such phenomena, almost identical practices are given the more benign labels of "brokerage politics" or "constituency service," that is, politics as usual. Some form and degree of clientelism, whatever the strength and nature of civil society and the state, appears to be an inevitable feature of liberal democratic politics whether clientelism or other more benign terms such as "brokerage politics" or "constituency service" are used. This is due to the limitations of the liberal democratic project with its gap between its normative promise and its reality. A vibrant civil society in the liberal-individualist sense needs to engender a sense of community between "mythical" individuals who are conceived of as "free" and "equal." The fact that many individuals are neither free nor equal undermines the potential of civil society to be either civil or social. Moreover, unable to trust solely on the horizontal ties binding individuals together in civil society, the liberal individual also needs to be tied vertically to the state upon whom she is dependent for the defense of her negatively defined liberties. In these interstices between the ideals of liberal democracy and the reality of liberal democratic polities lies clientelism. It is a manifestation of the fact that liberal democracy offers only the potentiality of equality, freedom, and universalism, but holds out no guarantee of their realization. It is that disjuncture between potentiality and reality that clientelism steps into. As Güneş-Ayata points out, "clientelism involves inequality, but so does the society at large" (1994: 24).

Clientelism and other kinds of particularistic exchanges akin to it are symptoms of the transactional nature of politics in liberal democracies within which, to quote a well-worn phrase, politics is about who gets what, when, and how. Clientelism, in particular, can be seen as a functional strategy or as a logical response by disempowered citizens to the disjuncture which obtains from having won the prize of formal political equality, often following protracted and bloody struggles, only to find that it leaves intact the inequalities of market life.

Thus, as political scientists, when explaining clientelism we need simultaneously to explain why the notion that democracy empowers people tends to be contradicted by the reality that many individuals may be powerless. Clientelism is a result of inequality, "predicated on the differential control by social actors over the access and flow of resources in stratified societies" (Roniger 1994: 3). As such clientelism is likely to remain an inevitable feature of liberal democratic polities. It may not be everywhere, but it is certainly here to stay.

5

Constraints on Clientelism: The Dutch Path to Modern Politics, 1848–1917

NICO RANDERAAD AND
DIRK JAN WOLFFRAM

Introduction

The study of clientelism in the Netherlands is exclusively linked with the Republic of the Seven United Provinces. Although the social and political structure of the Republic radically differed from the absolutist monarchies in Europe and therefore did not know of royal patronage, its internal stability and wealth rested upon the continuous support of the urban oligarchies whose power was inextricably linked with their control of patronage networks at the local level. Complaints about the all-pervasive nepotism and corruption greatly contributed to the crisis of the Republic in the last decades of the eighteenth century. Nevertheless, the obscure system of negotiation and compromise was not inherently inefficient. To some extent, it even sustained the undisputed administrative continuity of the Republic. The highly particularistic tax system, for example, lacked the uniformity that would become the norm later in the nineteenth century, but it was adaptable to local circumstances and, in comparison with absolutist states, resulted in a relatively equitable tax burden (De Vries and Van der Woude 1995: 141). Local elites took care of primary education and poor relief, which took the sting out of social protest.

The Batavian–French period (1795–1813/15) marked an important transition in the formal and informal state structure. The unitary state which took shape in these years concentrated more power at the central level of government and was less dependent on painstaking compromises among urban oligarchies. There was no turning back after the fall of Napoleon. In 1815 the new rulers of the Kingdom of the Netherlands carefully announced an update of the political institutions of the old Republic. The restoration was limited to a return to representation by estates and to a distinction between towns and countryside aiming at reducing the Napoleonic centralization and uniformity. However, on the whole, the "administrative monarchy" that developed in the wake of the Constitution of 1815 adopted the Batavian–French project of institutional modernization.

With the transition of the Republic to the monarchy and the concomitant waning of the political power of the urban merchants, the notion of patronage seems to have vanished from the research agenda of Dutch historians and political scientists. This is only partially justified. From the center, King William I (1815–40) was clearly trying to turn the state into an extension of his court by nominating sympathizing ministers and provincial governors and by granting privileges to the aristocracy. Royal patronage became a distinct possibility, although it was held in check by a rudimentary form of parliamentarism (Worst 1992: 74). The bureaucracy was small and largely recruited from a small number of Protestant families in the provinces of North and South Holland (Van IJsselmuiden 1988: 98–99). A complex electoral system with indirect representation preserved the power of traditional elites at the local level, where they continued to control access to public services. At the same time, their influence on national politics was restricted.

The opportunities for patronage did not change dramatically with the outcome of the events of 1848. Admittedly, the short panic in the royal palace which followed the news about the outbreak of a revolution in Paris resulted in a substantially reformed constitution, which included direct elections and ministerial accountability, but the franchise remained limited to less than 5 percent of the population. "Modern" politics did not make its entry until the end of the nineteenth century. It was triggered by a first extension of the franchise in 1887 followed by a second extension in 1896 but, more important, by the appearance of centrally organized political parties in the same period. At the same time, the central and local levels of government became more and more involved in the management of the disruptive influences of urbanization and industrialization, causing a growth of the bureaucracy at both levels and an increase in the availability of resources for clientelistic exchanges. Last but not least, the process of pillarization – the segmentation of society along sociopolitical and religious lines – started to work its way up from the localities to the center, thereby lending modernization an ambivalent character.

As recent studies have demonstrated, these developments may favor the transition from patronage as a strategy of kings and notables to mass clientelism. Clientelism not only has to be discussed as a remnant of traditional social and political relations, but may also be analyzed as a concomitant of political modernization (Briquet and Sawicki 1998, Roniger and Güneş-Ayata 1994). It is our purpose to investigate whether the traditional arenas of patronage in the Netherlands evolved into anything like clientelism with the modernization of politics around the turn of the century.

The onset of pillarization is tightly connected to this transition and may go a long way in explaining why clientelism never took root in the Netherlands. The first critical studies of pillarization, which appeared in the 1950s (e.g., *Socialisme & Democratie* 1957), emphasized the general social and political deadlock, the tight grip of political elites on their supporters, and the high costs of pillarization – aspects that are familiar to the discourse about modern clientelism. Echoes of this view are sometimes found in the literature today. In his account of Europe's twentieth century, Mark Mazower has no difficulty in comparing the clientelistic methods of Christian Democrats in Italy and Belgium with those in the Netherlands (1998: 340). We argue, however, that although there have certainly been "clientelistic moments," by 1917 – with the introduction of proportional representation and the linking of compulsory attendance at the polls with the enfranchisement of all adult men (in 1922 extended to women) – it was clear that political elites had chosen a different electoral strategy.

Patronage during the Dutch Republic

Patronage in the nineteenth century was but a faint reflection of the clientelistic system of the Republic. In the seventeenth century, patronage was ubiquitous in local and central government. To avoid social unrest, local elites were often busy bargaining with representatives of the people about popular demands. Brokers of various types mediated between burghers and officials, administered bribes, and managed access to citizenship, trade permits, posts as administrative or tax collectors, and the like. Central authority, represented by the Estates General and the Stadholder (the Prince of Orange), depended on this clientelist system for purposes of tax collection and political support. At the same time, the endemic antagonism between the House of Orange and town magistrates limited the power of both. After the death of Stadholder (and King) William III in 1702, the power of the central government began to crumble, which resulted in the increasing importance of local interests.

To some extent the decline of the Republic in the eighteenth century weakened the clientelistic relations which had tied local and central government together. The filling of public offices remained an internal affair of the elites, but it missed the "national" dimension of the seventeenth century. However, one could claim that the difference lies not so much in the general economic and political character of the seventeenth versus the eighteenth century as in the administrative difference between the periods of rule of a Stadholder and the Stadholder-less periods (1651–72, 1702–47). The presence of the Stadholder (1579–1651, 1672–1702, and 1747–95), whose power required continuous support from the various provinces, almost naturally led to an expansion of clientelistic exchanges (Israel 1998: 701).

In the course of the eighteenth century, the reciprocity which had characterized the relationship between regent families and their clienteles at the local level decreased. Competing elite factions closed their ranks, making use of corruption and nepotism. Of course, in the political climate of the late Republic attacks on corruption were as widespread as the actual cases of this vice. Furthermore, as Simon Schama justly remarks, "as in other European states, large and small, venal office did not necessarily make for incompetent government" (Schama 1992: 48). A series of local studies has shown that, despite the enclosure of office within the ranks of a small elite, numerous cases of glaring nepotism, and the objectionable practices of tax farmers, local government remained fairly efficient at least until the 1780s (De Jong 1985, Kooijmans 1985, Prak 1985). In the last quarter of the eighteenth century, international crisis and semi-civil war disrupted local and national government to such an extent that the checks and balances of yore proved painfully inadequate. In 1795, a French invasion decided the fate of the Dutch Republic.

Dutch Patronage in the Nineteenth Century

Under French influence, centralization of government was inevitable, not least because it dovetailed with the administrative vision of Dutch revolutionaries. After a few constitutional experiments wavering between federalism and unitarism, the internal appeasement after the turn of the century paved the way for a series of legislative innovations which can be regarded as the main legacy for the institutional layout of the country in the nineteenth century.

In the first years of the nineteenth century, the administration of private and public law, the tax system, and primary education – to name but a few areas in which the transition toward a unitary state manifested itself – were thoroughly and durably reformed. Losing their ancient autonomy, towns were thrown into a turmoil. Some *homines novi* had entered the scene, but they had to allow for the gradual return of the Republican elites. At the local level the old regent families lasted in office well into the nineteenth century. Under the Constitution of 1815 and further local government decrees, the members of municipal councils were nominated by a board of electors, which in its turn was chosen by a small number of enfranchised notables. The office of elector was a lifelong function. The limited franchise and the indirect elections ensured local elites a lasting and unchallenged leadership in the local political arena. Hence, it is hardly surprising that the local political elite constituted a closed and homogenous group, even more so than in the eighteenth century, when in the larger towns they were usually divided in competing factions.

The local ruling class was mainly involved in commerce, agriculture, and leisure. The scope of local government was small, and was bound to remain small, as long as its raison d'être was to keep expenditure as low as possible. This meant that the local notables disposed of few public goods to trade for electoral support. Hence, on the local level, the incentives to build up clientelistic relations were severely limited. However, a limited form of patronage persisted: the elites continued to distribute the small number of public offices among themselves and showed hardly any inclination to use public means for private interests. The mayor was by far the most important and powerful local official. As he was appointed by the King and controlled by the provincial governor, he could always justify his aloofness from local vicissitudes. His career did not depend so much on clientelistic exchanges as on his ability to be impartial and serve what was perceived as the "general interest," that is, to counter social unrest, control municipal finances, and take care of public primary education. Finally, the high degree of urbanization, the omnipresence of the market economy, and the relative absence of large landownership rendered society less susceptible to the kind of clientelistic relationships that existed, for example, in Corsica and Southern Italy (Briquet 1997, Woolf 1991: 477).

Although William I and William II made extensive use of their power to appoint and discharge officials, all in all they interpreted their kingship in such a way that they offered few incentives for the development of full-fledged clientelism. The Constitution of 1815 granted the head of state many prerogatives. No doubt the kings saw patronage as a means to hold on to key political figures and the interest groups behind them (Van Sas 1981: 113–16). Exerting tight control over the key areas of government, the monarchs showed no interest in any real delegation of power. Cabinet ministers were first of all the King's servants; as such they were in no position to go further than occasional appointments. Apart from that, a certain degree of ministerial responsibility restrained ministers from an overtly cynical attitude toward public opinion and the nation's interests. Belgium was added to the new kingdom at the Vienna Congress, and was probably the only region where a clever policy aiming at consensus among the local elites, possibly through clientelistic exchanges, could have made a difference. Instead, King William I systematically alienated the Catholic and liberal elites in the southern provinces. The Belgian revolt of 1830 and the separation from the Netherlands demonstrated the utter failure of any policy which could have led to conciliation.

The Constitution of 1848, important as it was for the development of the liberal state, had few immediate consequences for political culture at the local level. Elections were direct, but the franchise remained extremely limited and the turnout at the polls was often dramatically low (less than 50%). Under these circumstances it was hardly surprising that the incumbent council members retained their seats and that local government conserved its closed character. The activities of local government remained limited to the traditional fields of government intervention: public order, education, and to some extent public health (the fight against contagious diseases and the surveillance of prostitution). Churches and private institutions had a large share in poor relief, although they left certain areas to the municipalities, for example, certain types of unemployment benefits. Local government, therefore, disposed of very few benefits that could be exchanged for electoral support. Not surprisingly, the recent revival of local history has not yielded many cases of flagrant clientelism. The unpredictable turnout at local elections reduced the chances of clientelistic policies. It was almost impossible to manipulate elections, because voters simply chose to stay at home rather than to cast their vote without a clear view of the electoral result (Leenders 1991: 361–67, Wolffram 1993: 93). In the larger municipalities elitist electoral committees dominated municipal elections, but could be taken by surprise by low attendance at the polls (Van Tijn 1965: 333).

Patronage was still part and parcel of this highly personalistic political system, but the local authorities never lost sight of reasonableness. Formerly excluded groups, such as Catholics and Jews, were allowed to enter public office. As long as they were believed to serve the general interest and did not put forward claims that were exclusively based on their religious background and that favored their group alone, they were accepted and respected, though never in large numbers. The alleged openness of the post-1848 liberal institutions, therefore, was strictly a matter of favors, hardly of equal rights (Fuks-Mansfeld 1995: 225).

The Constitution of 1848 prescribed direct elections and a constituency voting system (single- and double-member districts) for national elections to the Second Chamber. The franchise, based on wealth, was even more restricted than for elections to the municipal councils. Candidates needed an absolute majority of the votes to be elected. This electoral system persisted until 1887, but even thereafter the Netherlands remained a long way removed from the introduction of universal suffrage. Traditional elites, together with an emerging class of liberal notables, continued to play a decisive role in the electoral game. There was no need for them to develop, either directly or through brokers, political relations with broader sections of the population.

Local electoral associations, usually not more than one or two in every larger town, pushed forward candidates in order to prevent the fragmentation of votes. Through these associations, which showed little tendency toward federal organization, local power relations remained important also at the national level. Yet there is little evidence that the consecutive national governments were willing to sacrifice in a systematic way the public good for local or partisan interests. The extension of the Dutch railway system around 1860 is a good example of the limited importance of local interests. Although a number of members of Parliament pleaded for a railway through their constituency, national interests and not local preferences eventually dictated the railroad construction, which meant connecting the main cities and the main harbors with each other and with Germany (Dijksterhuis 1984: 84–89). Significantly, in the elections that followed, members of Parliament were not massively punished even if they had not succeeded in obtaining a railway connection for their constituency.

It was generally accepted that the influence of individual members of Parliament in large infrastructural projects was limited. Since members of Parliament were not required to live in their constituency, national party considerations tended to gain strength compared with local loyalties. As opposed to Britain, there was hardly any tension between party adherence and local interests. Moreover, the small but independent state bureaucracy was a powerful restraint on the spread of particularism. Mayors and commissioners of the king – the Dutch "prefects," the representatives of the state at the provincial level – continued to be appointed by the Crown, at the suggestion of the Minister of the Interior. Their main task was to build consensus, but their careers were not directly at stake if they failed to please notable power. The average duration of office of a commissioner in a particular province was ten years and some commissioners even celebrated their twenty-fifth anniversary in one province – an exceptionally long duration compared with the French and Italian prefects (Randeraad 1998a: 97).

The system of local and constituency-level patronage, based on close personal contacts between candidates and voters within a small political elite, gradually weakened. In the last decades of the nineteenth century, national elections became more and more the playground of party politics. The "old" elites were willing to give up their monopoly in politics, albeit gradually, because they saw that their social and economic status was not really at risk. At the local level patronage persisted longer, particularly when the electorate was economically bound to a candidate. This was the case in smaller agrarian communities, where tenant-farmers were often tied hand and feet to their landlord. These tenure systems were particularly common in the eastern and southern parts of the country. But even in those regions economic dependence did not lead to networks of clientelistic relations, which also affected the working of the political system.

The extension of the franchise, which accelerated as a result of a few minor changes in the electoral system in 1887, reduced the possibilities for local political leaders to control elections through conventional patronage. New forms of mobilization were required. The need for a more modern approach to electoral engineering had been recognized in the 1870s and 1880s but, significantly enough, not by the ruling liberals and the (swiftly vanishing) conservatives.

The Emergence of Political Parties: The External Mobilization of Political Interests

The development of party politics in the Netherlands has been markedly shaped by the "Anti-Revolutionaries," an antimodern movement of orthodox Calvinist Protestants who strongly opposed the liberal principles of the French revolution. The Anti-Revolutionary movement was a reaction to the Dutch Reformed Church, which King William I had created in order to unify the members of all Protestant denominations nationally. Orthodox Calvinists were dissatisfied with the moderate character of this new Church (Wintle 1987: 26). Their movement gained political impetus when it directed itself against the enlightened, state-controlled, generally Christian character of public education. In fact, the foundation of the first modern political party in the Netherlands, the Anti-Revolutionary Party (ARP), in 1879 was a direct reaction to a further modernization of elementary education by a liberal government in 1878.

The ARP was the political expression of an outspoken religious vision of society. The party aimed at recreating the (mythical) seventeenth-century hegemony of Calvinism. Its popular appeal stemmed from the practical applicability of the orthodox ethic to the struggle for Christian primary education. The Anti-Revolutionaries, led by the "titanic" Abraham Kuyper, wanted to replace public education with private, truly Christian education – the so-called School with the Bible. It was difficult for them to raise enough money to found and maintain private schools, particularly because a series of education Acts prescribed sound buildings and qualified teachers without distinction between public and private schools. On top of that, before 1889, orthodox schools, like all private schools, were excluded from state and municipal subsidies.

The struggle for denominational education offered an opportunity for clientelistic exchanges. Orthodox Protestant parents wanted a good, Christian, and cheap education for their children. The Anti-Revolutionary leaders tried to exploit this desire by combining forces in electoral associations and governing bodies of Protestant schools, and by mobilizing "the people behind the voters." For both the political elites and the grass-roots supporters this commitment was a long-term investment. Until 1887 the franchise virtually excluded the Calvinist *kleine luyden* – the lower middle class of artisans, tradesmen, small farmers, and skilled workers – from national elections. Because, until 1887, voting for municipal councils required a lower franchise and because the franchise was proportional to the number of inhabitants, the Anti-Revolutionaries were strong only in the smaller municipalities.

The *schoolstrijd* – the controversy over education – was inextricably bound up with the question of electoral reform. It should be noted that the issue of denominational primary education was not equally salient in all parts of the country. In those towns and villages in which one denominational group had a large majority, religious education in the public school traditionally conformed to the will of that majority. Hence, at first, the *schoolstrijd* did not seriously affect politics in the homogenous Roman Catholic municipalities of the south. There, state schools were automatically Catholic, since the overwhelming majority of teachers and pupils belonged to that religious group (Catholics constituted about 35 percent of the population, of which a large part lived in the South). However, when state subsidies became available for denominational private schools, separate schools with an official Roman Catholic identity did emerge. Local elites, mostly Catholics themselves, took the initiative in establishing these schools in order to relieve the burden of local government (Van Vugt 1980: 49, Verhoeven 1994). In these constituencies, electorally secure elites did not need to resort to the exploitation of personal networks in order to pursue their goals, which they might have if the Catholics had been a minority.

The widening of the franchise in 1887 (and again in 1896) and the Education Act of 1889 were the first steps toward the political emancipation of an hitherto excluded part of the nation and toward an equal treatment of private and state schools. Both questions – political emancipation and the school issue – were finally settled in 1917 with the enactment of universal male suffrage and the provision of an equal grant to all pupils in whatever kind of school. Until then orthodox Protestant and, for that matter, Catholic leaders occasionally sought opportunities to use the school issue for electoral gain, in particular at the local level. Rarely, however, could denominational schools be directly traded for votes: Protestant or Catholic majorities in municipal councils usually pursued a careful policy of discouragement toward public education and, instead, support for denominational schools. In 1893, for example, the emancipating Roman Catholics of 's-Hertogenbosch – capital of the Southern province of North Brabant – challenged the Protestant and liberal Catholic elite, which had ruled the city during most of the nineteenth century, by urging the removal of the public normal school and, subsequently, supporting the foundation of a Catholic normal school, to be funded by the municipality. Such successes were difficult to repeat, but their echo, amplified by the clergy and Catholic media, resulted in continuous support from new voters (Duijvendak 1990: 147).

Denominational education, important as it was in the genesis of pillarization, was a single issue, which eventually proved to have limited potential to become the pivot of clientelism. The Protestants and Catholics managed to form a first denominational government together in 1888, under Baron Aeneas Mackay, but the absence of the Anti-Revolutionary leader Kuyper in the government revealed grave differences of opinion. Furthermore, the temporary solution to the problem of state funding of primary education in 1889 cut across the former denominational alignment. After the fall of Mackay's government it would not be until 1901 that a new confessional cabinet was formed. The real influence of Catholics and Anti-Revolutionaries remained fairly limited: the political parties they had formed were predominantly "externally mobilized." These parties, like the Socialist parties, developed at the fringes of the political arena and did not enjoy access to state patronage in their formative years. Consequently, in Martin Shefter's theory (Shefter 1994: 5), their leaders had to rely mainly upon the support of the clergy and of confessional associations of all kinds, a strong partisan organization, and, above all, a compelling ideology.

The power of ideology continued to be a binding factor, often clearly more important than material issues. Both Catholics and Anti-Revolutionaries displayed a strong aversion to liberalism and socialism. Particularly within the Catholic clergy, the fear of socialism loomed large. Among factory workers the percentage of Catholics was relatively high, simply because many factories were located in the Catholic regions of the country, the South and the East. As the Catholic party wanted to cater to both employers and workers, it carefully avoided an unequivocal stance on the "social issue." Papal and Episcopal influence nourished a belief in corporatism and subsidiarity as the basis for the solution of class antagonism. Catholics, therefore, strongly favored cooperation between labor and capital instead of a continually intervening state. In this sense, they discouraged the creation of opportunities for their leaders to use the resources of the state in order to acquire a following.

To some extent this line of thinking matched Kuyper's view of the relationship between state and society. He, too, believed that the role of the state had to be kept to a minimum. "The state may never become an octopus which stifles the whole of life," he argued in his Princeton lectures of 1898 (cited in Wintle 1987: 66). Instead, he emphasized the individual responsibility and sacrosanct principle of life of all God's creations. He called for "sovereignty in the individual social sphere," which resulted in a series of related standpoints concerning the aloofness of the state: parents needed to assume responsibility for schools; employers and workers had to reach agreement without interference from outside; and so forth. One of the consequences of his thinking was his striving for a considerable extension of the franchise, which in the middle of the 1890s brought him in sharp conflict with other leading Anti-Revolutionaries – another demonstration of the constant threat of internal division within the new parties.

In sum, the confessional parties were typically "externally mobilized" parties, not only in the sense that their origins lay outside the political system, but also in the sense that they strongly relied on ideologies which opposed state interference. Shefter's argument, therefore, acquires an additional dimension: ideology was not merely an alternative to patronage; its actual content, emphasizing the limits of state power, led away from a strategy of clientelism. During the years of confessional government before World War I, in 1901–5 and in 1908–13, the coalition of Anti-Revolutionaries and Catholics limited its support to minority issues in the religious sphere, such as small subsidies for denominational education, the appointment of a few Anti-Revolutionary mayors, and the extension of the official recognition of the Free (Calvinist) University. On the whole, however, the government was held back by the fear of increasing public deficit, a fear which proved to be much deeper than the desire to meet the demands of the voters and thereby leave a confessional imprint on society. In their early days, therefore, the confessional parties were not in a position to develop clientelistic methods of gaining electoral support: they were too small and had no access to state patronage. When from 1901 onward they started to grow and joined in coalition governments on a regular basis, they denied themselves the means to bind their supporters through clientelistic exchanges.

Continuity of Bureaucratic Autonomy: The Public Administration as Mediator between State and Society

Shefter's explanation of the occurrence of modern patronage – clientelism, in the terminology of this book – hinges on the relative timing of democratization – the extension of (male) universal suffrage – and bureaucratization – the creation, usually through a civil service statute and other laws, of an independent public administration. However, the general civil service charter that Shefter seems to have in mind is, in continental Europe, a phenomenon of the late twentieth century. In France a *statut des fonctionnaires* fixing rules on recruitment, payment, and discipline of public officials came about after World War II (if one is prepared to omit the Vichy statute of 1941; Siwek-Pouydesseau 1989). In Italy, Parliament passed a bitterly contested civil service bill in 1908 (Melis 1980: 67–113, 1996: 230–37). In the Netherlands, the first general civil service law was enacted in 1929 (Randeraad 1994: 229). But also on the British Isles, the early promulgation of a "charter" such as the Northcote–Trevelyan reform is no guarantee against patronage (cf. Chapter 3). In short, while the absence of a civil service code as such cannot explain the transition to large-scale clientelism, its existence is no automatic guarantee that clientelism will not in fact develop. What is needed, above and beyond a purely formal charter, is the existence of a "constituency for bureaucratic autonomy" (Shefter 1994: 30–31).

However, Shefter is doubtlessly right in assuming that bureaucratic autonomy discourages patronage strategies. The bureaucratic "safety mechanisms" against the use of state resources for clientelistic purposes do not have to be strictly legal, but may also stem from the civic tradition in a given state. It must be admitted that "civic tradition" is a somewhat ambivalent notion in today's political science and historiography. Robert Putnam's attempt to trace contemporary attitudes toward the public good in Italy back to the High Middle Ages (Putnam 1993) has been met with a lot of criticism. From a historian's point of view the main problem with his analysis is the rigid, unchangeable continuity of civic virtues as well as their counterpart – corruption, irresponsibility, and misadministration – throughout the ages. Nevertheless, we believe that a more cautious use of the term can still be very fruitful. The civic tradition in the Netherlands was deeply rooted in the necessity for the small state to maintain internal peace, not least because the threats of religious and social strife were so manifest.

To analyze the administrative culture of the Dutch bureaucracy of the "long" nineteenth century between the Batavian–French revolution and World War I, we need a few facts. First of all, there is no real takeoff in bureaucratic growth before 1900 (Randeraad 1994: 215–17, Van Braam 1957). The increase in bureaucratic personnel between 1900 and 1914 – still moderate in comparison with the period after World War II – is more or less in accordance with the extension of state activities and the concomitant rise of central and local government expenditure (Van der Voort 1994). This slow growth manifested itself in a rather closed recruitment circuit and a widely shared administrative ethic. Purges or tendencies toward a spoils system were unknown, even after the Batavian–French period and the Restoration. Surely, newcomers were not banned, but the percentage of Catholics in the civil service, for example, remained extremely low. On the other hand, it was fairly common to find members of the same family in various sectors of the bureaucracy. Those officials whose work was not merely clerical were strongly imbued with a dedication to the public good – or, rather, what they perceived as such. Avoidance of religious conflicts, a keen eye for commercial interests, and a general concern with the welfare of the people were their guiding principles.

With the constitutional reform of 1848, which established the principle of ministerial accountability and made a sharper distinction between local and national responsibilities, higher officials in central government became the minister's political and administrative watchdogs. The officials themselves were supposed to stick to professional neutrality. This proved to be an attainable goal. Although the "rule of law" has never been a great issue in the Netherlands, the state bureaucracy has "interiorized" the public good as a natural concomitant of administrative behavior. As Vincent Wright has concluded (1991: 9), the recruitment of public officials has been, in principle, nonpartisan yet, in practice, politicized because of liberal dominance and, later, pillarized proportionalism. Yet the working of the administration has not been partisan or politicized or pillarized. Patronage clearly affected only the distribution of jobs in the public administration and was directed at a large enough societal level – that of the pillar – as to rule out that the distribution of access to public goods would favor selected individuals.

At the local level the dominant official was the mayor. The Constitution of 1848 and the subsequent communal law of 1851 established that any (male) Dutch citizen could be appointed mayor provided that his profession or family status was compatible with the office. He was not required to be elected in the communal council before the appointment, or to be resident in the commune itself. The government's discretion in mayoral appointments has always been enormous, until the present day. The Ministers of the Interior, who in practice made the appointments, have frequently put forward candidates from outside the municipalities in which the mayors were to be posted. In the ten years between 1887 and 1897, for example, 665 new mayors were appointed, of whom 264 had been residents of the town or village in question, and 401 came from elsewhere (Randeraad 1998b: 256–59). Toward the end of the century the dominance of a limited number of elite families – around 1850 an undisputed phenomenon in many municipalities (Wolffram 1993: 12–15) – faded away.

With the disappearance of family rule one of the main sources of local patronage dried up.

The mayor was expected to have administrative capacities and an independent mind, which generally came down to little more than a taste for expediency in administrative matters and sufficient private means. His work was closely followed by the commissioner of the King – the representative of central government in the provinces – and the provincial executive committee (*Gedeputeerde Staten*), which consisted of a few elected members of the provincial council presided over by the commissioner. The commissioners were particularly keen on keeping a close watch of municipal regulations and local finance. In practice this was an important impediment to the distribution of selective benefits among interest groups (Randeraad 1998a, b, 2000).

Until well into the twentieth century a liberal elite dominated the corps of mayors and commissioners. They continued the Republican tradition of *schikken en plooien*, "to arrange and to ply." The administrative tactics of the Republican regents – appeasement and consent – were also important aspects of liberalism in power. The accommodating spirit has left a formidable imprint on public administration in the periphery, particularly where social and religious conflicts would otherwise have threatened public order and, in the long run, the internal cohesion of the country (Randeraad and Wolffram 1998). It is generally accepted in the Dutch literature that the persistence of accommodation as an administrative tool can explain the fact that the religious and political cleavages were held in check and could not critically endanger public order (Daalder 1981, Lijphart 1968). Administrators could embody this tradition only if they held on to the pursuit of the general interest and kept political interference away. Simultaneously, the governments of the day refrained from too much meddling with the bureaucracy, because that could easily turn against themselves. The concomitant spoils system, therefore, has never had a chance. This administrative and political habitus greatly helped to nip clientelism in the bud.

Pillarization and the Politics of Accommodation

In the years between the last powerful liberal cabinet (1897–1901) and World War I, decision-making at the central level seemed to grind to a standstill. Important laws on primary education, the franchise, and social security, albeit all clearly incomplete, had been introduced. For the time being the government did not dare to resort to more radical legislation. Liberal and confessional parties were unwilling or unable to resolve the struggle for the equality of rights of Christian education through equal subsidies and did not succeed in bringing the struggle for universal suffrage to an end. Furthermore, massive strikes and the first socialist successes at elections made clear that social legislation had to be adapted. Party politics went through a profound crisis. The liberals were sharply divided into radicals and moderates. The ARP suffered from a division in "democrats" and "conservatives"; the socialists and the Roman Catholic party were still weak (the latter did not formally establish itself until 1926). Governments were powerless, resting on small and reluctant majorities in parliament. There was a general lack of political leadership. When the war broke out in 1914, the parties accepted a general depoliticization. Although the Netherlands remained neutral, even the socialists declared that the exceptional situation demanded the deferment of ideological disputes. Political leaders committed themselves to overcoming the deadlock over education and elections. To this end they formed committees, which surprisingly rapidly reached compromises. In other words, they succeeded in finding a radically new approach to the settlement of disputes in Dutch politics.

The key to this new approach was a redefinition of the "general interest" in terms of political stability and the unity of the state. The old conception of the general interest, which consisted of a not-too-emphatic pursuit of progress, cutbacks in government expenditure whenever possible, and the advancement of the Netherlands as a trading nation, made way for a modern conception of the general interest in which the preservation of the nation-state was dominant. At the core of this new interpretation lay the recognition that the Netherlands was a nation of minorities: Roman Catholics, orthodox Protestants, moderate Protestants, socialists, liberals, and a few others. It was recognized that, in order to retain political stability, all their interests had to be met with the means available to the state. The best way to reflect these various interests was to accept universal suffrage and proportional representation. The constituency voting system with limited franchise, the basis of nineteenth-century patronage, was abandoned. The resources of the state were also distributed proportionally. The tone was set with the new law on education. From 1920 onward private denominational schools received complete funding from the state. Of course, this was a very expensive operation, especially because the number of fully subsidized schools almost doubled between 1920 and 1930. The questions of social legislation and public housing were solved in roughly the same way.

The key to these changes lay in a different attitude toward public finance. During World War I the Dutch finally got rid of their fear of a national deficit. The national government simply had to resort to loans in order to finance the huge costs of neutrality, such as the permanent mobilization of the army, unemployment benefits, and agricultural subsidies. Municipalities were already used to financing their long-term investments in infrastructure with loans, but at the national level the near-bankruptcy in the aftermath of the Belgian secession in 1830 had led to extreme financial caution. After 1917 the national budget rapidly rose, building a near-permanent budget deficit.

The paradox was that the demands of Anti-Revolutionaries and Roman Catholics for denominational schools, and subsequently for social equality, were eventually met by methods which they had resolutely rejected. The ideals of "sovereignty in the individual social sphere," or the Catholic equivalent of "subsidiarity" – the organization of social relations at the lowest level possible, for example, the family, the company, the school – were realized by greatly increasing the role of the state. Another paradox was that the liberals, supporters of universal suffrage, suffered severe losses at the first general elections in 1918. The Catholic party and the Protestant parties saw their long-term investment of the end of the nineteenth century to mobilizing the "people behind the voters" finally lead to success. They held an absolute majority in parliament from 1918 to 1963.

In 1918, as was predictable, the externally mobilized parties acquired power without resorting to clientelistic strategies. The constitutional explanation must be sought, as we have noted, in the introduction of universal suffrage and proportional representation, which loosened the personalistic relations between representatives and voters in the constituencies. However, even once they became hegemonic, they did not develop clientelist tactics. The confessional parties, which now dominated the political arena, redefined the Dutch "general interest" as the necessity to meet sectoral and minority interests in order to maintain political stability. This demanded further constitutional change. By now it was acceptable to sacrifice the neutrality of the state, which the liberals had cherished so deeply, in educational and in welfare matters. State and municipalities were allowed to pay for Christian schools and welfare organizations.

Financial resources were distributed evenly among the Dutch "pillars." This meant that the state accepted to finance schools (primary, secondary, and higher-level) of the different denominations on the same basis as the state schools. It also meant that the resources that were available for social work were evenly divided. A remarkable proportional distribution took place in the 1920s, when the Christian coalition, which had gained an absolute majority after 1918, distributed radio-broadcast time evenly among socialist, Roman Catholic, orthodox Protestant, liberal, and modern Protestant groups. Although pillarization thus received a clear political component, it remained mainly a social and cultural phenomenon. And there lay the strength of it. A pillar, whether it was Roman Catholic, Protestant, or socialist, offered cultural identification and the security of being among peers. The leaders of the pillars – mainly clergy and politicians – worked hard to keep the pillars strictly separated. The level of interconfessional marriages, for example, remained extremely low. One of the main features of pillarization was that the pillar itself became a means of putting forward private interests. Each pillar wanted to develop a complete political and social world. The largest political parties tried to establish links with trade unions and other large organizations in civil society. The relatively strong position of the confessional parties in the agrarian parts of the country forced these parties to pay special attention to agricultural interests.

The mass electorate was thus tied to the political parties of the pillars to which it belonged, not by means of clientelism, but indirectly by creating a safe haven, a refuge against what existed outside one's own pillar: the dangers of socialism, Catholicism, Protestantism, capitalism, and/or modernism. In the period between 1930 and 1960, as long as the world seemed in turmoil and the future was uncertain, pillarization boomed. With the development of the welfare state, which provided a pillar-neutral protection, and modern means of communication, which opened up the country to the world, the pillars started to crumble. The confessional parties lost their majority in 1967, while the socialists also suffered severe electoral losses.

Local government went through a similar transformation. After 1917 local politics became clearly subordinate to national politics, partly as a result of proportional representation. But already from the turn of the century, when the results of the widening franchise became clear, the old elites had begun to withdraw and the system of elitist patronage had started to crumble.

The Dutch version of proportional representation left no space for clientelism. The people could vote only for a political party, not for individuals. The political parties decided who would represent them in Parliament. Of course, private interests continued to be represented through political parties. For example, trade unions were represented by the socialists, the Catholics, and the ARP. Agricultural interests were looked after by representatives of all parties. But there was no direct connection between these representatives of private interests and voters. The trade of votes in exchange for public decisions of economic significance could not take the form it took in some Mediterranean countries. Within the parties, within the parliament, and within the government private interests had to be weighed and related to the general interest (Daalder 1981, Lijphart 1968).

The changes of 1917 and subsequent decades left the Dutch "constituency for bureaucratic autonomy" virtually untouched, and even strengthened it. Paradoxically, the principle of proportional representation and distribution did not lead to a high turnover of personnel. After 1917, the percentage of Catholic civil servants grew only gradually. Of greater importance was that the old civil service went along with the new interpretation of the "general interest," albeit sometimes rather reluctantly. It was generally accepted, in particular among the officials themselves, that the civil service should be dedicated to a fair distribution of public means and act as a true mediator. Any abuse of the system for personal gain would eventually disrupt the social and political equilibrium, and thus threaten the stability of the nation-state. Again, the Dutch case calls for a modification of Shefter's argument. The existence of a constituency for bureaucratic autonomy helps to explain the absence of clientelism in modern Dutch politics, but there was more to it. It was the capacity of the bureaucracy to adjust to the changing interpretation of the general interest that paved the way for "pillarized" solutions to the main political issues, and thus shut the door on clientelism.

Conclusion

The Dutch case shows that clientelism is not inevitable. There is no general pattern of transition from patronage to clientelism via democratic modernization. In the study of clientelism more attention has to be paid to the mechanisms through which general, categorical, or private interests are created and promoted.

The political system of the Dutch Republic in the seventeenth and eighteenth centuries, based on the economic power of the urban merchants, was a potentially fertile terrain for clientelism. The administrative reforms of the Batavian–French revolution did not fundamentally change the channels of traditional patronage (at least at the local level). Government on the whole remained relatively small until well into the twentieth century. When the scope for public action was dramatically expanded after World War II, an administrative "culture" that shunned from individual-level particularism had already been created and grown roots. In between lay the organization of society into religious and ideological pillars, each proclaiming (with different words) the independence of society from the state and establishing self-help traditions. Individual interests came to be conceptualized as part and parcel of larger societal interests: while proportionalism took care that all societal interests had fair representation and protection, no space was left for individualistic particularism.

Strong formal or informal bonds between political leaders and parts of the electorate do not necessarily imply clientelism. We have focused on the conflict-ridden period between 1870 and 1920. During these years the Dutch political system acquired the form it would essentially keep until the 1960s. Clientelism was no part of it. In the Netherlands the most important constraints on the growth of clientelism were the emergence of an independent bureaucracy, the small electorate until the first decade of the twentieth century, the emergence of the main political issues before the development of mass politics, and the common recognition that accommodation of the private interests of the religious and ideological minorities had to be the core of Dutch general interest.

Equally important was an old tradition of extreme restriction of public spending, which lasted until 1917, when the war conditions finally drove neutral Netherlands to deficit spending. This financial volte-face cleared the way for the expensive but egalitarian system of pillarization, of "*liberté subsidiée*." To be sure, remnants of patronage have occasionally surfaced until the present day. On the eve of the provincial elections of March 1999, an elderly elector from South Limburg confided to the national newspaper *De Volkskrant* that she would vote for the Christian Democrat party because one of its candidates had helped her obtain a piece of real estate. But it is almost perverse to put such isolated events on a par with systems of mass clientelism. In our view there are no grounds for Mark Mazower's reasoning that the Netherlands did not differ from Italy, Belgium, or

Austria with respect to the dependency of Christian Democracy on clientelism. The ruling Christian Democrats in these countries, he argues, were opposed to Thatcherite cutbacks of state spending because "clientelism fed off public-sector growth" and "roll-back thus implied weakening the party itself" (Mazower 1998: 340). Several elements set the Dutch case apart from the others. First, in the Netherlands the support of the welfare state was surely not the exclusive domain of Christian Democrats. Second, the bond between party and voters has never developed into a cynical quid pro quo relationship. Individual politicians did not have the power to control electoral support through state patronage. The comprehensive constitutional changes of 1917 had made way for a political system based upon an impartial distribution of public goods and benefits, which left no room and no need for clientelism.

6

Mass Parties and Clientelism in France and Italy

CAROLYN M. WARNER

We battle, but on our program. The Movement [Républicain Populaire, MRP] is not going to define itself by opportunistic positions, but by courageous positions. (MRP 1951)[1]

But of all of them, the most thorough in every area of evil is surely Mr. Sebastiano Vincelli, who, notwithstanding his young age, has never known other weapons than those of pretense, blackmail, corruption, double play, calumny, [and] continual lying.... It is a fact that he is the main [person] responsible for the disaster of the [Democrazia Cristiana, DC] party in our province. (DC 1958)[2]

Introduction

The consequence of the Mouvement Républicain Populaire's (MRP) abjuring of clientelism was electoral failure; the consequence of the Democrazia Cristiana's (DC) clientelism was also electoral failure.[3] Evidently, clientelism can be a double-edged sword. The question for this chapter is why parties choose to wield it, and how. In analyzing the clientelist practices of two Western European Christian Democratic parties,[4]

---

[1] MRP deputy Leo Hamon, at Executive Committee meeting, April 5, 1951. Archives Nationales (hereafter AN), Archives MRP (hereafter A-MRP), 350 AP/49.

[2] Archivio Centrale dello Stato (hereafter ACS), Ministero dell'Interno Gabinetto (hereafter MinIntGab), 1944–66, fondo Partiti Politici-Democrazia Cristiana, Reggio Calabria, f. 165-P-66, b. 9, anonymous letter, April 19, 1958, "Per l'on. Amintore Fanfani," p. 3.

[3] The MRP dissolved itself in 1969; the DC in 1994.

[4] Christian Democracy is an ideology which evaluates social, economic, and political issues using Christian principles. It values democracy for its individual freedoms and as the fairest means to solve economic, political, and social inequalities but, contrary to classical liberalism, sees the individual as an essential member of a family, a spiritual, even supranational, community. It stresses social solidarity, compassion for the poor, and state intervention to

Italy's DC and France's MRP, for the decade just after the end of World War II, it becomes apparent that the relative timing of bureaucratization and democratization alone – Martin Shefter's thesis (1994) – does not suffice to explain why Italy's DC opted to use clientelism while France's MRP chose not to. To account for their diverging strategies, we need to look at the situation in which these parties' leaders made their choices and at their primary goals.

To the degree that clientelism depends on the institutional context, some possibility of it existed in *both* France *and* Italy. Both the MRP and the DC aimed to appeal to a broad constituency, hoping to acquire a mass base. The MRP's declared ambition was to reform French society, to "awaken" the French to their "civic responsibilities." It was an ambition which militated against using clientelist practices. The DC's declared goals were to become the dominant party of (a non-Communist) government, and to convince the Catholic Church that it could coexist with democracy. The party was less discriminating about the means used to reach those ends.

This chapter takes issue with Martin Shefter's path dependent claim (1994: 30–31) that externally mobilized parties, once in office, will continue to eschew clientelist practices.[5] Several types of clientelist practices were available to political parties in postwar Italy and France, but parties varied in their views of clientelism and, hence, varied in their use of it.

The MRP and the DC came into being during the advent of "mass politics," when suffrage had been granted to the entire adult electorate. Party

---

ameliorate the ravages of industrialization, seeing class divisions as artificial. Christian Democratic parties need not be exclusively Catholic: some parties were developed by Protestants (e.g., the Dutch Christian Historical Union, or CHU); others are bi-confessional (Protestant and Catholic, such as Germany's Christian Democratic/Social Union or CDU-CSU and the Christian Democratic Appeal, or CDA, of the Netherlands). See Warner (2000: 10–11).

[5] Shefter's argument is that new parties, which had no prior access to governmental machinery, must rely on other means to recruit followers and develop an organization. Generally, ideological, programmatic appeals are the solutions (1994: 32–33). He notes that voters, once attracted to a party in this way, will not demand discrete material benefits. He then invokes Lipset and Rokkan (1967) to state that voters in various sociologial groups, once brought into the electorate, are not available for other parties. Finally, if external parties had gotten a large mass following prior to coming to power, they would not need to attract additional voters. Yet, as the MRP discovered, new governing parties often find that their electorates dwindle in the absence of material benefits, that social groups must be repeatedly lured to "their" party, and that most parties need more voters than their "base" electorate in order to retain office (Fiorina 1981; Przeworski and Sprague 1986).

politicians faced the problem of how to get logistical support, attract voters, and, once the ideological hopes had been stripped away by the compromises inherent in democratic governance, sustain the party. The extent of the electoral market had become vast, making the campaigning for and servicing of the electorate difficult. The new parties also faced competitors with established roots: well-organized Socialist and Communist parties, and liberal parties which were long practiced in patronage. While ideological and programmatic appeals could win the first battle for power after the restoration of democracy at the end of World War II, clientelism could help solidify the party's electoral bases and build its internal structure. This, indeed, was the strategy pursued by Italy's DC, while it was shunned by France's MRP. This chapter analyzes this divergent choice and the consequences that it had both on the two Christian democratic parties and on Italy's and France's overall political development.

Clientelism: Its Costs and Benefits

Clientelism can be a useful electoral and party-building strategy as it attaches the voter and the activist to the party through divisible, usually material, benefits. Clientelism is potentially beneficial particularly to a newly formed party that just got into office and whose programmatic record and reliability are unknown. The voter, due to the uncertainty attendant to new political systems, may be strongly inclined to discount the future. Therefore, a party offering material incentives to a voter eliminates some uncertainty and perhaps mitigates hardship. The voter is given tangibles, not vague promises.

Though part of the interim governments as the war ended, both the DC and the MRP were "new," at least in the sense that they had not governed prior to the war. As a result, they could not solely rely on the promise of patronage because they were dependent, for being able to keep this promise, on the vote. Rational voters could not base their vote on a promise that might not materialize. If the DC and MRP succeeded in winning enough seats in the first national election, they could then credibly use patronage to win additional seats. Martin Shefter (1994) would predict that the first elections would mostly be ideological in nature and that only later would patronage be employed. Indeed, up to the first postwar election, the DC and MRP were similar in their strategic choices: their campaign emphasis was ideological and stressed universalist programs. It was only later that the parties diverged.

Patronage can be used to develop clienteles at various levels of aggregation: individuals, collective actors such as organized societal groups (e.g., churches, trade unions, farmers' or employers organizations), and/or an electoral district, which I term "constituency." In each case, the party supplies selective incentives in order to get the individual's or group's support. The mix of individual, collective actor, and constituency patronage depends on the organizational characteristics of the electorate and the party's strategies – respectively, the demand and the supply sides of clientelism. Where societal groups have already created networks of members, the party finds it easier to negotiate with the group leadership, rather than with each individual voter. If interest groups are not critical in an election, and dispensing patronage at the individual level is too organizationally costly (or just not feasible), a party might instead try to target the entire district.[6] Individual-level clientelism is more effective where the client's economic alternatives are severely curtailed.

Yet clientelism is also organizationally costly for parties (Warner 1997) and voters; therefore, its use demands an explanation. If patron–client relations are seen as a contract in which the client exchanges a vote for the selective benefit which a patron delivers, there are costs, including risks, attendant to the exchange. The most glaring for each contractor is getting information on whether the other can, and actually does, deliver as promised. Ideally, the patron and client would both have recourse to sanctioning methods. However, democratic polities are generally not explicitly designed for enforcing imperfect contracts which privatize public goods. Votes, the medium of exchange, are supposed to be free and secret, and state benefits universally available, not contingent upon private exchanges.

Information and monitoring are acute problems in clientelist relations. Contrary to conventional wisdom (Putnam 1993), clientelism may depend on trust as much as reputedly "civic" relations do. The client cannot be sure in advance that the patron is capable of delivering the promised goods; the patron cannot be sure the client has voted for him or her. Further, if the patron's political party is part of a coalition (multiparty) government, the patron may be able to blame his or her apparent malfeasance on the demands of the coalition, and the client may not even have access to information on whether the patron made a good faith effort to obtain the promised benefit. Only where a party can construct an effective

---

[6] See Verdier (1995) for an elaboration of possible conditions.

monitoring system is clientelism a feasible *and* efficient strategy for winning votes; only where the voter has no alternative to the party is the vote exchange rational for the voter. Adding to the cost of clientelism is the fact that the medium by which the client pays for the patron's services is clumsy: the client has only one vote but perhaps multiple needs and the patron can extract payment only at election time.

Clientelism also requires a supply of patrons: politicians willing to use patronage. It is on this point that the comparison between the French and Italian Christian Democratic parties is instructive. Institutional and ideological factors put clientelist relations at the constituency level in France, at the individual level in southern Italy, and at the interest group level in northern Italy. The comparison of the parties' use of clientelism also shows that clientelism is a strategic choice, informed by a party's values and goals, not merely by the external context.

After World War II, with the nationalization of multiple industries and the growth of administrative structures to regulate the activities of its citizens, the French and Italian states controlled vast economic and bureaucratic resources. Much of citizens' private lives depended on dispensations from the public sector. Civil servant appointments in both countries were governed by legal rules intended to create objective standards. What varied most between the two countries was *how* those institutions were used, whether the rules were observed, and the extent to which parties penetrated the public bureaucracies.

Historical Legacies

France: Bureaucratic History

> It is certainly unfortunate that too large a number of elections are due to monetary corruption, and also to a corruption more subtle, more difficult to pinpoint and punish, the corruption by the promise or concession of posts and favors. (L. Duguit, a French legal scholar, in Puech 1922: 195)

This complaint about the corruption of the democratic process through patronage was by a French, not Italian, speaker, in 1921. Contrary to the image of the strong, *dirigiste* state, France had a long tradition of patrimonialism (Ertman 1997) and its public administration between 1870 and 1940 had some of the characteristics commonly associated with that of

Italy. French politicians of the Third (1871–1940) and Fourth (1946–58) Republics did not face an impenetrable bureaucratic wall; in the Third Republic, in fact, they were able to use the state bureaucracy to favor their own clients. Personal recommendations mattered (Chagnollaud 1991, Sharp 1931; Suleiman 1974: 308–10). Civil servants were not protected from arbitrary, politically motivated firing. It was not until 1930 that the state passed a law (which it also enforced) which required municipalities to establish objective criteria for hiring employees, subject to approval by the state's prefect in the department (Chapman 1955: 97).[7]

For parliamentary campaigns, citizens sold their votes to the highest bidder. Candidates also would agree, for a price, to withdraw. Deputies were, in the words of Third Republic Prime Minister Raymond Poincaré, required to "use the largest part of our efforts in petty errands and unrewarding solicitations."[8] Distributing governmental largesse to one's constituency was the key to winning office; having friends and relatives in the ministries was critical to the deputy's ability to transfer resources to his electorate. Parliamentarians "formed groups of all sorts which cut across the official party labels they gave themselves" (Zeldin 1973: 577; cf. Weil 1895). At least until Vichy, France had a functioning patronage system of loosely organized parties.

Most institutional analyses of French politics remark on the French administration's apparent "strength" and/or independence from political intervention (e.g., Hall 1986). This view needs altering: it was the party leaders of 1945 who constructed the French "constituency for bureaucratic autonomy" (Shefter 1994: 39). It is the sense of a mission for the state (Catherine 1955), not the specific state structure, which distinguishes the "strong" French state from the "weak" Italian state.

The political class which came out of World War II was initially dominated by Resistance members who sought to alter the French administration so that it could no longer be tampered with by politicians (Bazin 1981, Charlot 1983, Gaïti 1987, Novick 1968). This restructuring effort included the successful creation of the École Nationale d'Administration

---

[7] The word "department" refers to the territorially based administrative structure which organizes France; there were approximately ninety-five departments in the Fourth Republic.

[8] Poincaré, speaking in 1926, was Prime Minister in 1912, from 1922 to 1924 and 1926 to 1929, and President from 1913 to 1920 (quoted in Zeldin 1973: 376, 581–82).

(ENA), France's elite civil service school. The operative command was that the "will of the State," the national interest, should prevail. *Fonctionnaires* (bureaucrats) were to be inculcated with a sense of national, not party, service: *service public* (Bonini 1987: 212–13, Chagnollaud 1991: 194, Williams 1964: 337).

Fourth Republic participants in the remaking of the public sector spoke not of change in the institutions per se, but of change in strategy and attitude. Politicians and bureaucrats set out to change administrative norms, creating an atmosphere and a set of operating procedures which were basically hostile to patronage (Gaïti 1987: 139). The previous French administrative structure offered latitude for individual level patronage; the postwar emphasis on renewal reduced it (Vinen 1995: 82–101).[9] More than institutional structure, it was the (new) organizational norms which hampered politicians' attempts to use the public institutions for patronage (Chagnollaud 1991: 167–86).

Why the dramatic change? The answer comes partly from the orientation of the dominant postwar parties: the Christian Democrats (MRP), the Socialists (SFIO), and the Communists (PCF). These parties, which together formed the early postwar governments, had been active in the World War II resistance. The MRP rejected anything that smacked of special interests (see below), the PCF had a closed structure and rigid ethos which did not allow for the individual-level negotiations which clientelism requires, and, for a while, the SFIO pushed universalist policies.[10] Though these parties stood to benefit substantially from reinstating certain features of the Third Republic, they instead sponsored a system which made individual-level clientelism more difficult (Shefter 1994: 58). French citizens came to expect fair treatment. While some institutions, such as l'Inspection des Finances, had a tradition of *service public* encapsulated in its *esprit du corps*, it took the general normative changes of the Fourth Republic to spread this attitude (Catherine 1955; Diamant 1957).

---

[9] Generally, getting a job in the French public sector, even at low levels, did not depend on voting for a particular party. Family connections could be helpful (Vinen 1995: 85), but most important for higher level positions was the locus of one's higher education. Admission to the Grandes Écoles was more a function of socioeconomic status (Armstrong 1973: 218–21; Rioux 1987: 110–12). That, in turn, did not depend upon a party affiliation. In 1946, resistance activity, not party label, characterized the personnel appointments to a number of the important government agencies.

[10] The SFIO was involved in every major scandal of the Fourth Republic (Williams 1964: 99, 391).

Italy: Bureaucratic History

> There happens frequently in Parliament a type of bilateral contract. The Minister mortgages the population to the deputy, so that the deputy assures him of his vote. The nominations of prefect, preceptor, police commissioners, are made in the interest of the deputy, in order that he maintains his local influence. You should see the pandemonium in Montecitorio [Italian parliamentary building] when the moment of a solemn vote approaches. The Minister's agents run for the rooms and corridors, where they corner votes. Subsidies, awards, canals, bridges, roads, everything is promised, and sometimes a long denied act of justice is the price of the parliamentary vote. (Crispi n.d.: 575)

It is well known that pork-barrel politics were rife in the pre-Fascist years of united Italy. As in Third Republic France, prefects were expected to rig elections. Prime Minister Giovanni Giolitti, for whom the period covering the years 1903–14 is named, and his immediate successors used patronage to form governmental majorities. Nineteenth- and early twentieth-century Italian patronage was similar to that of Hanover England, Spain of the *turno pacífico*, and Third Republic France. The plundering of the administration for the aggrandizement of a specific political party was introduced by the Fascists: Mussolini had made government contracts and jobs contingent upon membership in his Fascist party (Allum 1973a: 64–71). Yet, while Mussolini could staff the bureaucracy at his pleasure, he did not need to buy votes. Hence, until World War II, patronage, and not clientelism, characterized the Italian political system.

Things began to change after World War II when the political system was fully democratized. To fulfill the clientelist exchange, the operation and even the formal layout of the Italian bureaucracy was dramatically modified. The Italian bureaucracy grew in a haphazard fashion: the Italian state administration has been called "the only true Italian forest." In 1951, the secular Republican party (PRI) leader, Ugo La Malfa, heading a commission charged with compiling a report on the public administration, described the bureaucracy as "an uncharted jungle." Ten years later, a DC national secretary, Amintore Fanfani, rather like Dr. Frankenstein being disconcerted by the creature in the creation of which he had had a significant hand, commented that "the public administration is really a clandestine organization, no one knows anything about it."[11]

---

[11] For "forest," see Emiliani (1975: 5); on "jungle" and "clandestine," see quotes in Allum (1973b: 140).

Parties fought viciously over the top appointments to the ministries which allegedly oversaw the branches of the bureaucracy. These disputes frequently occasioned the collapse of a government (Mershon 1996). The obscure structure of the bureaucracy and its limited accountability actually gave politicians the opportunity to develop clientele by intervening on behalf of individuals in order to prompt administrative action. As Ginsborg notes (1989: 199): "The speed and efficiency, also the simple execution, of a bureaucratic act depended in large measure on the pressure a citizen could exert upon the administrator."

By the early 1950s, the state bureaucracy and its many subdivisions began to have the appearance of a make-work project: the south accounted for 38 percent of Italy's population, and 45 percent of Italy's state employees, with unemployment averaging 7 percent higher in the south than elsewhere in Italy.[12] By 1963, some 63 percent of the bureaucrats came from the south (only 38% of the population), 14 percent from the north, and 21 percent from the center (Cappelletti 1974: 145, 143, 139). Between 1946 and 1958, the number of people in state employment grew by 11 percent, or 100,000 (Demarchi 1967: 395). It needs to be stressed that in a country of 25 million voters, adding 100,000 to the state bureaucracy would hardly be enough for a party to gain more seats at an election. However, since the bureaucracy distributed allegedly universal resources, such as social security benefits, only at its discretion, politicians had ample opportunity to take the middleman's role, brokering the exchange of state resources for party favors.

Opportunities and Incentives for Patronage

If a party is going to use patronage, it needs a supply of resources. The scope for patronage in both countries was vast. Civil service laws, nationalized industries, the social security and municipal administrations, and auditing agencies all illustrate that similar institutional structures can be put to different uses. Both France and Italy had had a history of patronage politics; both altered that politics significantly after World War II, with France reducing the scope, and Italy increasing it. The source of the postwar divergence is found not in differing institutional arrangements but

---

[12] Calculated from Saraceno (1972: 102, table 1). The national yearly average from 1946 to 1959 was just over 10 percent (Hildebrand 1965: 157).

in the differing uses to which the respective state administrative apparatus was put.

Upon unification of the country, during the Risorgimento, Italy adopted the Napoleonic ministerial system, and did not alter it despite two world wars so that, even today, its administrative system strongly resembles that of France. Ministers had a chief of cabinet, who might be from the civil service, or not. Below this chief was the ministry's senior civil service agent, with the title of "director." In both countries there were semiautonomous agencies set up to run social security, the mails, trains, and numerous other public services. The relevant minister could set broad policy guidelines; the agencies had extensive discretion.

The ministries also had affiliated administrative commissions, which exercised some oversight. The French bureaucrats were represented on them by trade union members chosen by election. Whether the political parties got any mileage out of the *fonctionnaires'* affiliations depended upon how the party and union interacted (Catherine 1955: 128–31). Italy had the same arrangement; likewise for civil service hiring requirements. Administrative jobs were to go to applicants who had done well in a nationally competitive exam (Allum 1973b: 155, Benvenuti 1974: 115).

At the end of World War II, the major French parties (Communist, Socialist, and Christian Democratic), as well as Charles de Gaulle, supported the nationalization of major sectors and the creation of numerous significant semipublic, autonomous enterprises. These included an auto manufacturer (Renault), the central bank (Banque de France), the trains (SNCF), the airlines, coal, steel, gas, and electricity (GDF and EDF). Most nationalized companies had a monopoly on production and distribution, and were financially independent of, but overseen by, the Ministry of Industry. In addition, the prefectorial personnel in all departments, the tax revenue services, the road repairmen, and the 15,000 police agents became government employees (Nadal 1952). A large, though not easily quantifiable, section of the economy was in the state-held public economy (Caron 1979).

As the business scholar Henry Ehrmann has noted, most nationalized industries were "upstream from the most important economic activities of the private sector." In considering the extent of credit and investment controls, of price-fixing in agriculture and other areas, in wage regulation, "the most important decisions on the changing distribution of wealth are made on the administrative level" (Ehrmann 1957: 257–8; on agriculture, see Caron 1979: 221, Wright 1964). The commingling of government and business, rather similar to Japan and Italy, has long been remarked upon (Cohen and Gourevitch 1982, Ehrmann 1957, Levy 1999). The resources for patronage certainly existed.

France, like Italy, had a social security administration employing a significant number of people, another potential plum of patronage. The system under the Fourth Republic was decentralized, with financing being predominately subnational: "contributions" from workers and employers going to various department-level Caisses. As in Italy, workers voted for department-level governing boards. Each trade union ran a list of candidates, as did several social movements. A national agency reduced financing differentials between departments. The system, overseen by a general directorate, covered risks of illness, accidents, old age, and death, and subsidized childbirth and rearing (Galant 1955: 51, Laroque 1952, Rioux 1987: 118). The French social security system would seem to have provided room for manipulation and fraud to the benefit of political parties. In theory, auditors could have overlooked cases of bribery, selective withholding of payments, and kickbacks (Galant 1955: 40). Instead, the system operated efficiently and without interference from politicians. "Use" of it by politicians came from improving and extending benefits to large categories of the population – "sectors" and "factors," in Verdier's terminology (1995). Indeed, in the mid-1950s, conservatives and peasant party deputies pushed through a bill extending coverage to their constituency of independent farmers and their families.

In Italy, government ownership of industries and financial institutions was also extensive. Throughout the 1950s, nationalizations increased: rail service, utilities, and the Bank of Italy were nationalized; and most of Italy's steel mills and engineering firms were financed by a government holding company, the Istituto per la Riconversione Industriale (IRI).[13] Italy's gas company, AGIP, became the Ente Nazionale Idrocarburi (ENI), a huge conglomerate with a monopoly over Italy's natural gas resources and extensive investments in energy resources throughout the world. By 1962, at least 20 percent of the Italian economy was in the public sector. Clearly, in both France and Italy, state holdings in the economy were extensive.

The social security system was under the supervision of the Labor Ministry. The DC shared control over the system with the leftist Partito

---

[13] IRI was set up in 1933 to salvage banks whose financial connections with numerous heavy industries were about to render them bankrupt. It was not unlike the American Reconstruction Finance Corporation (Hildebrand 1965: 377; Posner and Woolf 1967: 23).

Socialista di Unità Proletaria (PSIUP), as both parties managed to hold the Ministry of Labor for part of the immediate postwar period. The Minister in turn was able to appoint new directors as he created new categories to be covered, and replaced those who left office (Cazzola 1976: 438, table 7). But even as the number of categories of workers covered by social security was rising, and with it the number of party-appointed directors, the DC's vote did not rise proportionately, because it could not restrict social security benefits to Catholics alone. Italian politicians, however, put this fact to creative use. Not only were benefits and coverage extended to specific constituencies, but management of the system was given over to politicians in exchange for support of the DC.

A political party, as Lipset and Rokkan noted (1967: 53), can build itself through the control and use of local resources. Besides the obvious point that people live in localities, drive on local roads, go to local hospitals and schools, and work in local shops and bureaucratic offices, local control was all the more important when televisions, telephones, faxes, and the like were not ubiquitous. In the early 1950s, over 43 percent of the French population lived in towns with a population under 3,000 people, and worked there or nearby. Over 58 percent of the French lived in towns of 10,000 or less. In Italy, the comparable figure for towns of 3,000 or less was 14 percent, rising to 45 percent for towns of populations of less than 10,000.[14]

The French and Italian municipal councils had limited powers. Municipal councils were elected by universal suffrage every six years and handled matters such as sale of municipal properties, road changes, bond issues, and creation of market areas.[15] The bureaucrats who worked for the French municipalities after the war were recruited by written exam. The municipal council could not, for a position requiring certain technical or administrative competencies, nominate to the post someone who did not have the appropriate qualifications (Chapman 1955: 97). Violations of these procedures were prosecuted by the Conseil d'Etat.

As in France, Italian municipalities had little discretionary power. Municipal funding depended heavily – upward of 60 percent – on the national government. That being the case, the political party which

---

[14] Data are from Institut National de la Statistique et des Etudes Economiques (1967: chapter 2, table 4, pp. 24–25) and Istituto Centrale di Statistica (1953: 25–27, table 19).

[15] On municipal powers in France, see Chapman (1955: 57–58); on Italy, see case studies and introduction in Rotelli (1981).

controlled the majority of ministries in the government was in a good position to dispense favors to local governments. In Italy, as in France, each municipality had a national government-appointed "municipal secretary." The secretary was recruited by competitive exam in the Interior Ministry; his career was controlled by the prefect and the Minister of Interior. The municipal secretary, with his legal and administrative education, was "often the deus ex machina of the situation." Municipal secretaries were thus "faithful and reliable watchdogs of the central government over the activities of the local governments" (quotes in Allum 1973a: 272–73, n. 3).[16]

Both France and Italy had auditing services designed to prevent and prosecute financial corruption within some of their administrations. It was the manner in which the French institutions were used which left less room for scandal and corruption in France. France's Inspection des Finances was an auditing service created when the monarchy was restored to power (March 25, 1816). Its bureaucrats spot-checked the expenditures of the departments (Lalumière 1959, Legendre 1968: 519, Waline 1958: 171). With the notable exceptions of banks and nationalized industries, all budgetary accounts of the French state are under its surveillance, as are the accounts of any entity receiving state funds. After 1945, inspectors were recruited almost solely from l'École Nationale d'Administration, untouched by political parties (Fayol 1952; Lalumière 1959: 35). The organizational culture was fairly apolitical.[17] The Fourth Republic had a Court of Budgetary Discipline and Finance which prosecuted budgetary errors and irregularities committed by administrators (Lalumière 1959: 405–6, 419–22). The funds which municipalities received for infrastructure improvements from the central and departmental governments were subject to that court (60 to 80% of total funds) and the court worked (Chapman 1955: 56, Williams 1964: 338–39).

Italy, too, had a regulatory agency called the Corte dei Conti. As in France, the Corte was barred from overseeing the nationalized industries (Posner and Woolf 1967: 35). The Corte "exercises a preliminary control

---

[16] On France, see Chapman (1955: 100). On the working alliances which nevertheless can develop in France between local elected officials and Interior Ministry personnel, see Kesselman (1967).

[17] The Inspection was a bastion of the Radical party in the Third Republic. In the Fourth Republic, its members ran the political gamut: about 20 percent MRP, 20 percent Socialist, 20 percent Radical, and 40 percent independent (Catherine 1955: 134 and 131, table 8).

over the legality of government acts, performs a post-audit on the budget and supervises the financial activities of enterprises to which the State contributes capital. The main problem is that it is ignored" (Allum 1973b: 189). Prior to World War II, another agency, INIGIC, was established to oversee the collection of the local excise taxes (imposed "on almost all goods sold within the communal boundaries"). As Allum notes, "In 1954, however, INIGIC itself became the subject of a scandal involving 1 billion 500 million lire contributed to party funds" (1973b: 218). It was the Italian parliamentary majority which did not insist on enforcement.

One cannot contend, therefore, that France had laws and other institutions which prevented abuses of the sort prevalent in Italy, whereas Italy did not. Italy all along has had the legal and other institutional means to enforce antipatronage, anticorruption laws. The Tangentopoli and Mafia prosecutions of the 1990s confirm that Italian laws can be made to have teeth. Yet Italian politicians had decided to render them largely harmless.

Clientelism in the Early Postwar Period

France

In France, with the postwar push for some bureaucratic autonomy, politicians had less access to the selective benefits on which clientelist relations depend. Due to new standards, service to specific individuals was more difficult than to constituencies as a whole. Generally, citizens approved of the protection and promotion of constituency interests.

The national budget was subject to extensive "politicking" but deputies were not able to attach district-specific riders. At best, deputies could propose private member bills for funding of public works projects (Williams 1964: 275–77). Once ministries had their budgets, government projects usually were evaluated and awarded on their technical, not political, merits. A helpful prefect could try to blur that distinction on behalf of a politician, and a politician on occasion could try to rescue a municipality from cost-benefit-calculating bureaucrats (Waline 1958). But, once a project was settled, the politician could not restrict employment or a contract to a particular person or firm. So while patronage was available for a deputy to develop a clientele, that clientele was typically a large collective actor or an electoral constituency.

Cabinet ministries were also potential patronage resources. However, in France a ministerial post did not necessarily improve a party's fortunes.

It was a double-edged sword: while it conferred prestige on its holder (he was seen as someone who could get things done), it rendered him and his party responsible, in the public's eye, for the maladies of the country. On the other hand, if the politician exploited his ministry's resources, he was sometimes able to offset any voter retribution.

In the Fourth Republic, French ministries were used more for pushing party programs than for party financing or for obtaining jobs for individual voters. Politicians did not blatantly interfere with government or private job appointments. They might have recommended particular candidates, but getting a job in the public sector did not depend upon the recommendation of a party or deputy (Williams 1964: 359). Unlike in Italy, ideological stance, rather than institutional structure, seems to have been an obstacle to using state resources to create clienteles.

Municipal council candidates who, as mayors, had run their communities well, or who had the support of such mayors, tended to defeat challengers. There were similar constituency service requirements at the parliamentary level: parliamentary candidates were in good shape if they had brought state services to their constituency. That often entailed working to the benefit of dominant economic interests. To be reelected or elected to a higher office, candidates needed to steer public works toward their electoral constituency.[18]

Bringing state resources to bear on a locality was what fostered an appreciative constituency and could earn the support of local organizations. As one scholar noted, "subsidyism" is "at the base of the electoral life in the countryside" (Aragon 1958: 512). Another noted that even in Paris, politicians would make local issues prevail in an electoral campaign. As the historian Philip Williams said, "the deputy who neglected his department was not lightly forgiven [by the voters], however worthy his reasons" (Williams 1964: 329; cf. Warner 1998: 570–71).

Typically, parliamentary candidates, including incumbents, had informal meetings with the municipal councilors and mayors of their constituency, learning the material concerns of the area, and promising to intervene, if (re-)elected, in the relevant state agency. If a deputy

---

[18] This was not a sufficient condition: candidates also needed to make frequent public appearances in their constituency, and cultivate local leaders. As allowed in French law, an individual could hold multiple elected offices. This phenomenon, known as the *cumul des mandats*, may have allowed some mayors/deputies to increase their clientelist potential merely by linking the central to local government. Evidence on the effectiveness of this on clienteles and electoral success is lacking.

performed a miracle (e.g., provided electricity to rural hamlets), he or she could count on votes of the municipalities served (Prieur 1957: 60–61; Wylie 1964: 223–26). If it were to be used to a politician's benefit, the state administration would have to be used to improve the public good of a constituency.

The French system did not guarantee reelection. While a mayor, appreciative of the work the incumbent had done, might encourage residents to attend the candidate's meeting in the locality, he or she had no means of controlling the votes of his citizens. The constituency as a whole benefited, not just those who voted for the deputy responsible for the action.

Italy

As Hopkin and Mastropaolo note (infra Chapter 7; also Warner 1998), the DC in 1948 owed its success (a parliamentary majority) to the Church and its anti-Communism ideology, not to extensive clientelism; virtually none of the national "patronage" agencies had been set up. The state bureaucracy was not yet its minion: in 1954, over 95 percent of the directors had been in service for at least twenty years – they owed the DC nothing (Cappelletti 1974: 124). The DC had to wait until it won the parliamentary majority in 1948 before it could control key patronage ministries.[19] It took the dethroning of De Gasperi and the arrival of a new party secretary, Amintore Fanfani, in 1954, to make clientelism a central strategy of the party – in part as an effort to lessen Church leverage over the DC, in part as an effort to block political competitors (Caciagli 1977: 64–65; Galli and Prandi 1970: 161; Mershon 1996; Walston 1988: 54).

Italian deputies had to occupy themselves with their constituencies, but not necessarily in the same way as their French counterparts. Particularly in southern provinces, deputies seldom worked to solve problems at the aggregate level of a constituency, they just targeted local notables, whose ties to bureaucrats and private businesses were used to parcel out resources to individuals (a job, military service waiver, emigration papers, building contracts). Italian deputies made an explicit deal with local party leaders, the "capi," as they were called, whereby the national deputies distributed governmental largesse and the local leaders parceled it out to secure votes

---

[19] Those include Post and Telecommunications, Public Works, Interior, Finance, Education, Agriculture, and Defense. For a listing of the cabinets and the ministers' party affiliations, see Allara (1989: 388–404).

and the reelection of the deputies. The DC, and other parties which had access to them, arranged to have public resources fragmented, not so much to complete a specific project as to touch as many hands as possible. If the finances were spread widely, a huge net of obligations was cast. How thinly they were spread did not matter.

The DC worked with interest groups to create an intricate clientelist system. The party used its control of state agencies to steer resources to favored employers. In return, employers agreed to hire only that party's members, while the party guaranteed that the employees would not be unruly ("proper people ... people who gave no trouble"), and that the employer would not be held responsible for various infractions.[20] Given the information and monitoring costs of such an arrangement, parties had an incentive to rely on an interest group of which the workers were members in order to get information and supervision. In the DC's case, this function was filled by the Catholic Church and the Catholic trade union.

The DC created a clientele of interest groups by letting the groups influence ministry job appointments in exchange for their logistical support and campaign endorsements (Warner 2000: chapter 8). An administration official explained, "Catholic Action [a Church ancillary organization] can and does determine who will be the higher civil servants in many of the ministries. It may also be in a position to determine to some extent which members of the Christian Democratic party are chosen as ministers and as under-secretaries in certain ministries" (in LaPalombara, 1964: 308). Politicians who served large clienteles were rewarded with higher placement in the party's electoral lists; the more extensive the network, the more likely the politician would be granted (or could wrest) control over a resource-rich state agency (Zuckerman 1979). The DC and its coalition partners plundered the bureaucracies for patronage. The southern development agency, Cassa per il Mezzogiorno (Cassa), is just one example. In the region of Calabria, from 1950 to 1976, all the directors of the main Cassa office, called the Opera per la Valorizzazione della Sila (OVS), were Christian Democrats. In the words of one report, "Over the years OVS has grown heavy and become a Christian Democrat 'emirate' and electoral bandwagon at the service of the party; the DC has

---

[20] Interview with a Neapolitan DC activist, by Istituto Carlo Cattaneo n. 4B (1963), pp. 1–3; quoted in Allum (1973a: 167).

used the OVS for its own clientelistic and electoral interests by giving jobs to party militants and the greater part of the party apparatus."[21]

Electoral clients rewarded patrons. Incumbents were far less often driven out by a dissatisfied electorate than by candidates from their own party or a rival party who had more patronage, or more skillfully used it. What is particularly striking about the Italian system was the low level of performance which clients received from their patrons (Chubb 1982). Only in a context in which other alternatives (nonclientelist parties, market means of obtaining necessary resources) were absent would it be rational for clients to tolerate malfeasance.

The DC's clientelist system relied on an organizationally expensive monitoring system: interest groups and private enterprises were paid with patronage in return not just for supporting the DC but for ensuring that their members fulfilled their end of the bargain, voting as instructed. Sometimes their end of the bargain was rather hollow. In the Reggio Calabrese municipality of Trunca, the inhabitants abstained from voting in the 1958 legislative elections to protest the lack of basic services (electricity, telephones, roads). Their parish priest verbally crucified them for this; they revolted. The regional bishop supported the priest, and, thus, the DC.[22] Through a corruption of voting procedures, and selective enforcement of campaign laws, DC politicians were able to monitor the voting behavior of their clients. The cost was that at each step in the monitoring process, each DC politician had to pay what was, in essence, a transaction fee to the "broker" or agent who did the monitoring (Walston 1981: 429).

The Parties' Views and Strategies on Clientelism

Shefter's argument would lead us to expect that, since both the MRP and DC were "externally mobilized parties," neither would turn to patronage. Yet, while it also used ideological appeals, the DC relied heavily on various types of clientelism. For the most part, instead, the MRP rejected that strategy. The MRP wanted people to vote for it, and secondary organizations to support it, because those individuals and groups believed in the

---

[21] *Calabria Oggi* 2/7, March 20, 1963, p. 10.
[22] ACS, MinIntGab., 1957–60, fondo Clero, f. 15326/66. b. 206, Reggio Calabria, rapporto del prefetto, no. 4587, June 7, 1958, and Questura (police headquarters) report of June 1, 1958.

MRP's cause. Material interests were not to be the factor motivating actions or decisions in French politics. For the MRP, catering to specific individuals would be at the expense of national policy and the common good. Only in some regions did the MRP employ constituency and group patronage.

MRP's Clientelist Practices

The MRP's declared goal was to reform French society, to "awaken" the French to their "civic responsibilities." It rejected the clientelistic practices of the Third Republic, stating that the former Republic was like "a woman of easy virtue, without principles and without dignity" (MRP leader, quoted in Yates 1958: 428). The party did not want material interests to be the basis of voter support for the MRP. Its tenure in the Ministry of Agriculture is a good example. The MRP held the Ministry of Agriculture from November 1947 through August 1951 and had a policy of consolidating and modernizing agriculture. It used that office to enact those "politically explosive" policies (Wright 1953: 543). The MRP wanted to reduce the number of family farming operations, farms which tended to hinder the international competitiveness of French agriculture. Just as the 1951 electoral campaign was to begin, an irritated agricultural leader in Catholic Action published a statement in the Catholic press by a "prominent social Catholic agronomist." The latter's statement that "France has a million too many peasants" was associated with the MRP. The Communist and Conservative parties attacked the MRP, saying it was "aiming to destroy the little peasant." Its price support policy was, in fact, designed to consolidate farms; there were no special clauses protecting inefficient family farmers. Ironically, as the MRP did not miss noticing, MRP agricultural policies benefited those large-scale farmers who were at odds with the MRP for other reasons, and who voted for (de Gaulle's) Rassemblement du Peuple Français or conservative candidates (Wright 1953: 548). As Wright notes, it was the MRP leaders' "conviction that France needs change" which prevented them from catering to peasants.

Traditionally, ministers attempted to assist deputies from their own party; the MRP did not. One party deputy complained that "many deputies do not obtain what they demand of an MRP Minister. In the other parties the organization of services rendered works fully. But in order to see an MRP Minister, it is better to go by way of the intervention of a deputy of another [political] tendency. . . . It is often legitimate to demand assistance in relevant cases. . . . it has been impossible to obtain an appointment with our Ministers."[23] The MRP did not even make use of what the French norms of holding office allowed. The MRP evaluated cabinet positions in terms of programmatic content and consequences: would the party be able to implement its concepts? As with the other parties, the MRP "colonized" some of the ministerial departments, notably, Foreign Affairs, but, unlike several other parties, did not use its "colonies" to extract votes from constituencies (Williams 1964: 418–19; Wright 1953).

DC's Clientelist Practices

It was not the case that the DC had access to more ministerial positions than did the MRP. The DC (and other parties) used the ministries they had to coopt interest groups and local leaders. Technically, ministerial powers were like those in France, but the DC used the ministries to provide selective incentives (side-payments) to interest groups. Letting Paolo Bonomi of Coltivatori Diretti organize and plunder rural agricultural cooperatives kept an able politician within the DC circle (Ginsborg 1989: 230–2; Rossi-Doria 1963). The DC's clientelist system grew not so much from staffing the public bureaucracies under its control, but from distributing the financial largesse of which the state agencies were in possession, and from bureaucratic problem-solving on behalf of individual constituents. When Prime Minister Amintore Fanfani took over, the DC made itself, as Ginsborg (1989: 209) states, "one of the principal centers of economic power" in the country (Calandria 1978: 343). Insulated from market forces, the DC opted not to use its power for the common good, but to extract votes and party infrastructure from the electorate.

The DC operated in several different contexts. In southern Italy, where potential voters were disaggregated and interest groups existed more on paper than in reality, DC politicians developed clienteles by targeting individuals or a lower-level patron, who then targeted individuals. In the conditions of extreme scarcity which prevailed in southern Italy, it might seem inevitable that a party would build itself on the basis of discretionary resource distribution, eschewing ideology and universalist policies. The southern DC federations seemed to meet such expectations, welcoming as

[23] AFS, Groupe Parlementaire du MRP, Jan. 26, 1946.

activists even laic and Masonic movement members (Cingari 1988: 378). The party became selective only when one faction, gaining control of the provincial or section offices, attempted to weaken a rival faction by refusing membership to the latter's supporters. Feuding became the party's dominant trait. As early as 1945, the prefect of Reggio Calabria noted that DC activists in the province were "evincing jealousy and personal ambition for preeminence."[24] In the 1952 provincial elections, the prefect reported that the results could have been better for the DC in some municipalities if it were not for tactical errors and the factionalism of exponents, including some priests, who posed their personal interests against the interests of the party and the collectivity.[25]

Lest one think that the Reggio Calabrian DC's behavior was just a reflection of the socioeconomic and political structure of the Italian south, of a lack of "social capital," one might consider that in the neighboring Calabrian province of Cosenza, public initiatives by DC representatives were undertaken and the party was not split into myriad self-interested factions (see also Piattoni 1998). The DC in Cosenza, however, lost far fewer votes in the 1953 election. The same could be observed of another southern region, also noted for its poverty and lack of social capital, Basilicata. An in-depth study of Basilicata concluded that the DC's success there was due to the fact that the DC had presented itself "with the face of a modern, reformist and democratic party" (Ciranna 1958: 109).

In northern Italy, many potential voters were already encapsulated in various Catholic interest groups and DC candidates had to win the support of the local leaders of those groups through selective benefits. The Brescian DC federation was successful in the 1950s at making itself into an effective accomplisher of public works. In this Lombardian province, the prefect observed that for the 1957 municipal elections, the DC won the majority in five sixths of the municipalities because "in face of the growing uncertainty with the minor parties of the center-left and the nostalgic ideas of the parties of the right, the DC appears, to the Brescian electorate, [as] a guarantee of the defense of democracy and of social development." As the prefect's remarks indicate, DC voters were considering not just anti-Communism, but also social benefits, universally distributed.

---

[24] ACS, MinIntPS, 1944–1946, fondo Relazioni Mensili, Reggio Calabria, f. 365, b. 24, no. 797bis, March 10, 1946.
[25] ACS, MinIntPS, 1953, Relazioni, Reggio Calabria, b. 17, May 31, 952.

Why Is There a Difference between the MRP and DC?

As we have seen, while in France and Italy the institutional scope for clientelism was relatively similar, French norms limited (but did not prevent) its use. Within that more restricted context, the MRP's conception of itself further reduced its use of clientelism as an electoral and party-building strategy. In contrast, the DC was willing to rely on clientelism. Since it was the first party to control the Italian government, it was able to structure a system wherein almost no party could survive without availing itself of patronage.

The MRP

The MRP was reluctant to use patronage, no matter how good it was for the local constituency and for electoral results. It did not want to base French politics and society solely upon the satisfaction of material needs. That was subsidiary to its vision of society as "a collection of human beings united for the conquest of the common good, which they pursue by light of reason" (Gilson 1948: 24). The MRP had deplored the "passivity and egoism of citizens" in the Third Republic (quote by MRP's François de Menthon, in Yates 1958: 428). The party's principles militated against its politicians working the political opportunity structure for electoral advantages.

The MRP tended to view the holding of office in idealistic terms. Honesty was not just a "phase" any new party might go through; it persisted even years later, after severe electoral defeats in municipal and senatorial elections. In 1950, an MRP deputy, Patrice Weil, summarized the party's view: "One often laughs at our scruples, and at our honesty which for us is neither a political issue nor a publicity item."[26] The MRP was trying to do away with the pork-barrel politics which had marked the Third Republic, proudly declaring: "We are the representatives of the general interest and have to be concerned with special interests only in order to arbitrate conflicts."[27]

It was not French culture or French voters which compelled the MRP to adopt such a position. Even when pressured to do so by some party activists, the MRP leaders refused to accept certain ministries which had

---

[26] AFS, Congrès Fédéral, 1950, Rapport sur la Politique Générale, p. 25.
[27] On the Third Republic, see Izard (1937: 738). Quote in Ehrmann (1957: 237).

constituency or interest group patronage potential. An open "spoils system" was not condoned in France, but political parties could and did colonize the ministries. The MRP took one of the least electorally useful: the Foreign Ministry (Williams 1964: 340–41). It also took Labor and Industry, both for four years, and did with them what the party had done with Agriculture, taking the politically unpopular path (Irving 1973: 106–29; Letamendia 1975: 374–78; Movement Républicain Populaire 1946a,b).

Not many French voters supported "the politics of the general interest," as the MRP was wont to put it. Rather, they rewarded politicians who catered to the interests of their particular electoral constituency (Stoetzel and Hassnor 1957; Williams 1964: 275–76, 342). The MRP politicians had a different idea, which was to "prepare the people for the actions which [they] intend[ed] to undertake."[28] While seeing itself as a response to the true desires and needs of the people, and claiming the party formed "a permanent line between the people and power, in order to construct a humane democracy," the MRP ignored the desires and needs which could motivate peoples' votes.[29] Indeed, as noted earlier, the MRP's vision of modernizing France ran headlong into the sacrosanct French peasantry.

In a few regions, mainly in Brittany, the MRP did develop local clienteles through constituency and group patronage. One example was in the department of Morbihan, where the MRP deputies had close organizational ties to the important groups of the region, and where the candidates made an effort to improve conditions for their constituents. One of the area's party leaders had been a Parti Démocrate Populaire (PDP) deputy from 1936 to 1940 (and prisoner of war for four years); another was editor of major daily paper in Brittany, the Catholic oriented *Ouest-France*; a third had been a deputy for the Jeune République, a Catholic oriented prewar party. A fourth was president of the FDSEA (the agricultural union), and the party's female candidate had been active in local charitable organizations (Velain and Nadin 1990: 19–27). Early on the MRP organizers recognized that being on, and active in, municipal councils would be important to building the party. The MRP did well in areas where it was warmly welcomed or assisted by the mayor and where its candidates had stressed their accomplishments on behalf of the department.

[28] AFS, Georges Queste, *Les Problèmes du Mouvement*, report presented to Congrès Fédéral de Clichy (Fédération de la Seine) du M.R.P., Oct. 27–28, 1951, p. 5.
[29] Ibid., p. 2.

Unlike the MRP at the national level and in some other Catholic departments, the Morbihan MRP federation stressed its support for state subsidies to private schools. In this heavily Catholic department, the prefect noted that the issue "more than ever constituted the criteria permitting one to fix the orientation of the vote."[30] The clergy actively supported the MRP-Peasant list, so too did the dominant agricultural organization in the region, the FDSEA. Its president was third on the party list. The party leaders had been careful to solicit agrarian groups' support, through clerical pressure and constituency service. The lead MRP candidate, Paul Ihuel, an undersecretary of agriculture in the late 1940s, was active on behalf of the department. Ihuel worked on increasing the funding available to farmers for equipment. This work enabled Ihuel to dissociate himself in his constituents' eyes from the MRP's Minister of Agriculture.[31] Ihuel cultivated his constituency: every week in Berné, the municipality of which he was mayor, Ihuel had an open-house meeting with constituents. By being elected president of the departmental Conseil Général, Ihuel acquired a powerful, respected position, giving him more leverage over Parisian and departmental bureaucrats. This increase in his access to patronage increased his electoral appeal.[32] MRP mayors had made a point to be visible with the Catholic hierarchy in religious festivals, and to attend fairs and other local events. As the prefect noted, "supported by the ecclesiastical milieu, the agricultural and commercial organizations," the party list was able to canvass the department, carrying the authoritative weight of those organizations with it.[33]

The MRP was something of an exception in French politics: other parties often used constituency patronage to establish their electoral base. The French Radical party, a loose grouping of disparate laic politicians, was a good example. Radical party politicians were solicitous of their constituencies, and catered to important secondary organizations. The party had been the linchpin of the repudiated Third Republic, and many of its candidates had voted to give the French government over to the dictatorship of the Maréchal Pétain. Abandoned by the electorate in 1946, Radical candidates implanted themselves on municipal governments by careful cultivation of local organizations, administrative officials, and voters. From

---

[30] AN, FI CII Dr. 150 Morbihan, Rapport du Préfet, Feb. 4, 1950; ibid., Dec. 19, 1950.
[31] AN, FI CIII Dr. 150, Morbihan, Rapport du Préfet, Feb. 26, 1951.
[32] AN, FI CII Dr. 150, Morbihan, Rapport du Préfet, Jan. 9, 1956.
[33] AN FI CIII Dr. 1301, Morbihan, Rapport du Préfet, July 10, 1951.

there, they climbed back into parliament.[34] As a Radical deputy stated, "We are not among those who proclaim: perish France rather than a principle."[35] As if to prove his point, the MRP criticized the Radicals for obtaining success by abandoning universalist principles.[36]

The various conservative and peasant party politicians who challenged the MRP for the Catholic vote also operated similarly. So too did the small, center-left grouping led by (future Fifth Republic President) François Mitterrand, the UDSR. The Communist party (PCF), until forced out of the government, was similarly blatant about packing the public economic sector with sympathizers (Einaudi et. al. 1955: 100–101; Williams 1964: 391, 340).

The DC

By defining itself as a Catholic party, and as *the* anti-Communist party, the DC was able to dominate the first regular, post-fascism legislative election (1948). DC leaders argued that Italy was the font and keeper of Christian civilization. That claim enabled the DC to turn governing into a "just war," in which the ends justified the means. Pragmatically the DC hooked up electorally with many local notables of unquestionable anti-Communist faith. These, in turn, resorted to traditional patronage methods, thus importing exchange tactics into the DC electoral tool kit.

The DC, then, based its strategy upon a complex interweaving of programmatic appeal (Catholicism and moderated capitalism), threat (anti-Communism), and patronage. The party's first main leader, Alcide De Gasperi, was determined to prevent a reenactment of 1922, when the Catholic Church turned its support toward Mussolini and fascism, and preventing a Communist revolution. To forestall those outcomes, and to recover from the war's damage and build a liberal democracy while preserving "Christian civilization," the DC's dominant bloc saw it as essential to bring together in one party all strands of Catholicism. Were the Catholic left to form its own party, De Gasperi and other centrists feared the Catholic right would follow suit. In such a situation, the Church would

[34] On the Radical party, see Berstein (1980/82), de Tarr (1961), and Loubère (1974).
[35] François Delcos, deputy from Pyrénées-Orientales, at Radical Party Congress of 1949, Toulouse (in de Tarr 1961: 155).
[36] AFS, Georges Marec, report of Oct. 27, 1951, regarding a risk that if MRP ministers and parliamentarians responded to political exigencies, the MRP would "slide onto the slippery slope of radicalism" in the "worst sense of the word."

ally with the right, and perhaps lead a return to fascism, or precipitate a civil war leading to a Communist takeover. The DC wanted to demonstrate to the Church that Catholicism could coexist with democracy (Scoppola 1977: 128–29, 114–15, 153, 242).

The other traditional source of political opposition in Italy was the southern notables. They could have tilted the delicate balance that the DC was trying to strike by throwing their weight toward the extreme, monarchist right. Evading those constraints through patronage was particularly important since De Gasperi would not define the DC as an explicitly clerical party, and since the DC's agrarian reform laws had gone against the interests of southern *latifondisti*.

Clientelism, thus, was a means of implanting the party and of giving it a base beyond the Catholic Church and within those social groups that would have otherwise sided with the Communists or the Monarchists. By utilizing patronage, the DC created incentives and coercive mechanisms for voters and interest groups to continue supporting the DC. In large areas of Italy, particularly in the south, politicians used the municipalities for individual-level clientelism and for some constituency patronage. DC politicians sought to get into a position whereby they controlled the distribution of a scarce resource, and could select the recipients. It was in locales where the DC was slow to use or did not use patronage that it met with electoral defeats. This, of course, rationalized its use to the party.

A national-level DC official stated in 1958: "[T]he DC is the party of government, and as such it exercises a clear monopoly of power, of the opportunities for acquiring and exercising it, and, more important, of its distribution in Italian society. . . . It may well be that every group or individual within the party cannot enjoy the same opportunities for the control or exercise of power. But at least they have no intention of cutting themselves out of the power game – that is, they would not cut themselves out of the major instrument through which power can be secured, exercised, and generally controlled" (LaPalombara 1964: 316–17). For a political entrepreneur, the DC offered the easiest access to power and resources (Caciagli 1977: 65, 76–81).

The DC, like the MRP, faced a choice about developing as a clientelist party. The DC, unlike the MRP, opted for the use of patronage as one of the means by which it maintained its electoral and governmental dominance of Italian politics, and by which it held together the broad coalition which gave the DC a "center-right" character. The DC's choice had a critical impact on maintaining its initial electoral success. When it became, with the extensive aid of the Church, the dominant party in 1948, the DC began making sure that DC membership was important to one's life chances (education, employment, housing). Clientelism was part of the DC's strategy of distancing itself from dependence on the Church, while making the party more attractive, even essential, to the Church, to Catholics, and to many who were religiously indifferent. In contrast to the MRP, adhering to the DC did not require material sacrifice; very often, DC voting and membership involved, instead, rewards which were denied to those outside the DC.

The DC also created strong incentives for politicians to operate within the DC. Encouraging party members to create and staff public agencies was an effective means of retaining activists and, potentially, a means of stabilizing the party's electoral market share. The sharing out of patronage also enabled the DC to construct "centrist governing coalitions against opponents who were both skilled and determined" (Cazzola 1976; Tarrow 1990: 319).

Structural conditions may have contributed to the different forms of clientelism. Societal organizations and the state were more present and important in the central and northern parts of Italy; the southern areas were characterized by individual, hierarchical links (Sabetti 1984; Warner 1994: chapter 11). More of the DC's organizational structure in northern Italy was supplied by corporate groups which actively elicited the participation of their members (Chiarini 1985). In one Lombardian province, Brescia, the DC federation pursued, rather successfully, a strategy of winning votes from the working class. The key difference appears to be the support the DC received from the Catholic union, from Azione Cattolica's labor organization, and from the Catholic Church. The DC federation got such support without resorting to individual-level patronage. Prefects, ever alert to the problems arising from self-serving abuse of office, found instead that the DC used its majority of seats in 125 out of 161 municipalities responsibly.[37] The DC "developed an intense capillary propaganda in residences and in factories, using all the methods at its disposal: priests, monks, ACLI, technicians, teachers, etc." Azione Cattolica groups organized retreats and pilgrimages; they undertook this "to galva-

---

[37] Results calculated from Istituto Centrale di Statistica e Ministero dell'Interno (1946: table 5, p. 22). "Responsibly" in ACS, MinIntGab, Brescia, f. 24201.244, no. 9393, March 26, 1946.

nize their force and prepare themselves for the capillary work. Another initiative is that of 'consecrating' houses . . . it is intended to be an instrument for penetrating all houses, and with the excuse of the religion, oblige the family to vote DC."[38] The DC became "the obligatory passage for diverse social sectors and groups who intended on maintaining and extending power in society" (Bragaglio 1981: 172). The DC's clientele were collective actors.

In southern Italy, membership in most such organizations existed on paper only, and links were coordinated by local notables or officials in the Church. In describing the socioeconomic structure of a large southern area, a noted authority characterized it as being rather unstructured. Society in the province was fragmented, lacking in social cohesion, and had no "lasting coagulations within each [socio-economic] class" (Bragaglio 1981: 172). Other researchers have also commented on the fragmented society of southern Italy and the strong potential for extreme political fragmentation (Bevilacqua 1985; Calamandrei 1950; Cappelli 1985; Walston 1988). The Fascists had not tried, let alone succeeded in, knitting together the numerous atomized sociopolitical entities of the region.

The Italian Christian Democrats need not have acted as they did. There are provinces in Italy in which the governing party did not abuse the public administration, yet was electorally successful (Falivena 1957: 127; White 1980). In Piacenza, a province bordering Lombardy in the north, prefect reports on the DC focus mostly on the contribution made by the clergy and by the DC having an effective "capillary" organization. In that province, some within the DC accused fellow (read "rival") candidates of "opportunism" as a way of discrediting the latter.[39]

Conclusion

We have seen that clientelism is one tool in a party's kit of strategies. Emphasizing choice, rather than constraint, in a party's use of it raises the

[38] ACS, MinIntGab, 1953–56, fondo Relazioni Mensili, Lombardia, Comando Generale dell'Arma dei Carabinieri, f. 16996/8, b. 374, no. 98/3, April 9, 1953.

[39] ACS, Pubblica Sicurezza (PS), 1946, fondo K2 Azione Politica del Clero, f. 17, b. 216, Piacenza, no. 01250, Jan. 23, 1945; ACS. MinIntGab, 1953–56, fondo Relazioni Mensili dei Prefetti, f. 6995/60, b. 362, Piacenza no. 980/2/2, March 31, 1953; on opportunism, ACS, MinIntGab. fondo Partiti Politici democristiana, 165-P-60, b.34 bis, Piacenza, prefect report on the Nov. 9, 1952, Congresso Provinciale della Democrazia Cristiana, Nov. 10, 1952.

question of why one party's leaders choose clientelism and another's do not. While it is tempting to credit "culture" – and culture may deserve some of it – the founding circumstances and ideals of the party may play a formative role (Locke and Thelen 1995; Panebianco 1982; Shefter 1977). A party's ideological orientations often outlive the circumstances that gave rise to them. Events and relationships create memories which actors carry and respond to (Rousso 1991). Certainly the feasibility of setting up a clientelist system, including whether its costs can be externalized (as in Italy), is a consideration. The system, to work with any efficacy, requires monitoring capabilities. Monitors must be found and their work paid for; if the norms of a political system frown on clientelism, a party may not be able to "pay," or even find, monitors.

In France, the opportunities and incentives for constituency-level clientelism were greater than is commonly thought. Even though the French deputy could suggest but not direct public works toward a particular constituency, he or she had influence in that area and could use the office to coopt interest groups. Electorates rewarded politicians who brought public benefits to their particular department. The MRP opted to ignore that signal and paid a heavy electoral price for its unwillingness to use constituency clientelism and for its idealism in general (Warner 1998). One might be tempted to conclude that clientelism is thus a "profitable" strategy for parties. Yet it exacts high costs on the autonomy of the party, its ability to act collectively, its ability to implement coherent public programs, and its ability to control the activities of its activists and politicians, who can become free agents or establish a monopoly of control in a geographic region or in the state bureaucracy (Warner 1997). While clientelism enabled the DC to dominate the Italian state for almost fifty years, the party was eventually consumed by its own politicians.

This chapter has downplayed the role of culture, the chief component of conventional "demand side" explanations of clientelism, and, rather, emphasized that of economic conditions and organizational capacities in accounting for an electorate's "demand" for clientelism. When prompted by secondary organizations and the parties, culturally diverse electorates respond to ideological or programmatic incentives. The parties have choices: indeed, it is their strategies which set the tone of the relationship between the bureaucracy and political parties. Politicians have an important and independent role in creating the constituency for patronage or for bureaucratic autonomy. The materials might be there, but it is the politicians who must arrange and activate the system.

In the end, the MRP rejected and the DC embraced clientelism. Max Weber wrote that "[a]ll party struggles are struggles for the patronage of office, as well as for objective goals" (in Gerth and Mills 1948: 87), and Léon Gambetta stated that "[o]ne governs with a party; one administers with skills."[40] It seems that the MRP never listened to Weber, and the DC never bothered with Gambetta.

[40] Léon Michel Gambetta (French Prime Minister Nov. 1881–Jan. 1882, deputy 1869–82), quoted in Sharp (1931: 75).

7

From Patronage to Clientelism: Comparing the Italian and Spanish Experiences

JONATHAN HOPKIN AND
ALFIO MASTROPAOLO

Introduction

Italy and Spain are often seen as "natural" comparators. The apparent similarities in their cultural, social, economic, and even political development have not escaped the attention of social scientists, and in Spain in particular Italy has been seen as a useful model for speculating on future developments (see, for example, Linz 1967). In this chapter the justification for comparison is the apparently striking parallels between the development of clientelism in the recent history of the two states. In both cases, a passage from patronage to clientelism (Weingrod 1968) can be traced, and the contemporaneous emergence of corruption scandals in the early 1990s provides a further reason for investigating parallels between the two cases. The aim of this chapter is therefore to chart the evolution of clientelism in Italy and Spain, to examine the similarities and differences between them, and to offer tentative explanations for those similarities and differences.

We argue that to look at the "supply side" of clientelism alone is not enough. While rejecting, like Shefter (1994: xi, 22–25), an analysis of the "demand side" that blames clientelism exclusively on the "ethos" of given populations or given social classes, we still think that it is important to pay attention to the autonomous and induced transformations of society and, hence, to its greater or lesser vulnerability to the clientelist bid from party politicians. What the comparison between Italy and Spain tells us is that, even within similar historical-institutional contexts, the scope for clientelism can vary according to the receptivity of society to selective methods of electoral mobilization. The politics of personalistic, divisible benefits – the very essence of clientelism – may just happen to be "out of sync" with society.

Patronage and State-Building

Although Italy became a nation-state almost four centuries later than Spain, the weakness of the Spanish state in the nineteenth century allows parallels to be drawn between the two cases. Both Italian unification and the centralizing impulse of the liberal elites in nineteenth-century Spain represented serious threats, in part externally imposed, to the premodern societies of these two countries. The political threat of the nation-state was accompanied by the threat of economic liberalization, which also challenged traditional networks of relations. These twin challenges provoked twin responses from Italian and Spanish society, both of which were provided by tradition: on the one hand, clientelism (*caciquismo* in Spain), on the other, localism (which in the Spanish context has meant regionalism and substate nationalism).

The durability of these responses is a reflection of the weakness of the threats that provoked them. In both cases the aim was to implant a centralized and homogeneous state on the French model; in neither case were the centralizing elites capable of integrating heterogeneous subnational elites into such a project of modernization. Similarly, the patchy nature of industrialization and marketization in the two countries (modern capitalism scarcely developed outside the Northern industrial triangle in Italy, and Catalonia and the Basque Country in Spain) meant that subnational elites in less economically advanced areas had little interest in the modernization project.

In consequence, modernizing elites were faced with little option but to make a pact with the representatives of a society resistant to the notion of a centralized state. In both cases, the forces of localism and substate nationalism were marginalized as the central state used patronage to bind the center to the periphery. Local agrarian notables protected local interests from the forces of change, and the state apparatus left them to exercise local power without undue interference. The representatives of the central state, rather than agents of centralization and homogenization, as in the French case, instead adapted to local custom; as Franchetti concluded, in the Italian case "the government [people] were the first people to be corrupted by local influences" (Franchetti 1992: 240). The results at the national level were remarkably similar: the gentle and artificial alternation of government power known in Spain as the *turno pacífico*, and the rather less structured turnover of government personnel in Italy known as *trasformismo*.

Although there are important differences between the two cases – the relative stability of the Italian liberal state contrasting with the reiterated interventions of the military in Spain – the parallels between them at this stage of development are striking. However, political developments in the first part of the twentieth century sent the two states down diverging paths, which account for a number of differences in the way patronage has evolved and persisted. The polarization resulting from the emergence of left-wing movements representing the industrial working class and landless peasantry ushered in authoritarian responses which differed in their ideological characteristics and, most important, in their duration. Liberal democracy was firmly established in Italy at the conclusion of World War II, while Spain had to wait until the death of the dictator Franco in the mid-1970s to begin its transition to democracy. This chapter therefore examines the evolution of patronage in the two countries in turn.

Christian Democracy and the "Modernization" of Italian Patronage

The establishment of the Italian Republic after World War II saw the persistence of the model of governance followed since unification, with clientelism widely used by government as an *instrumentum regni* (particularly in the south) and localism (most characteristic of the north and center), often consigned to opposition. Democrazia Cristiana (DC), the dominant political party in the postwar period, was quick to see the electoral potential of clientelistic networks, particularly in the south, and reluctant to develop the model of regional government suggested by the constitution. The DC became a successful clientelistic mass party, while the parties of the left, the Socialists (PSI) and Communists (PCI), were pushed into opposition, pressing for a regional reform which would give them some access to political power.

Although some observers (for example, Pizzorno 1992, 1994, 1996) have seen the relationship between these parties as a form of consociationalism, with party elites overcoming social antagonism and distributing state resources among themselves, this seems to underestimate the depth of the ideological divide which characterized much of the postwar period (Mastropaolo 1996). The ideological and organizational divide between Christian Democrats and Communists was the foundation of an original "two-headed" model of governance, under which Italian democracy was stabilized and important economic and social advances were made (Mastropaolo 1996). The two parties, by articulating collective identities based on class and religion through the development of mass organizations, were able to absorb the particularistic tendencies of clientelism (the DC) and localism (the DC and the PCI) and integrate them into national politics. In particular, the DC's extensive use of patronage succeeded in binding the southern periphery conclusively to the nation-state, and provided the party with the electoral resources to maintain its essential control over the government machinery for over forty years.

In the south, the DC succeeded in equating the state with clientelistic resource distribution. It rejected the path followed by its predecessor, the Partito Popolare, which had attempted to compete with clientelism by latching onto the movement for municipal and regional autonomy. Instead, the DC adopted existing clientelistic networks, signing up local notables who had often been closer to the parties of the right, converting them to Christian Democracy, and offering them opportunities for political advancement (see also Chapter 6). In the immediate postwar period, this took the form of old-time patronage, with the traditional agrarian notables sometimes using their personal contacts in the state structures to obtain resources for clientelistic distribution (such as jobs in the public administration), but most often distributing their own resources or those of other notables (such as agricultural work). These clientelistic networks were able to show the benevolent face of the state, which not only made few demands on citizens, but could even help resolve their private difficulties. As far as the less benevolent face – taxation, military service, bureaucratic inefficiency – was concerned, the state's deference toward local notables allowed them to offer their clients help and protection.

Notables' autonomous control over resources, characteristic of traditional patronage, limited the DC's authority over its social base in areas such as Sicily, where local bosses could win elections independently of any assistance the party could offer. In this sense the changes in the DC's organizational structure (after 1953) and its use of government power are important. The role of local notables was gradually restricted and ultimately substituted by a new generation of professional politicians, as the DC introduced the technology of *machine politics* (Shefter 1994) to Italy. While the clientelism which was developing did not allow the party to "encapsulate" local society in the way patronage had, it did have substantial resources at its disposal. Local party leaders and coopted traditional notables not only offered services and favors to their clients in exchange for the vote, but could also call on the resources of a mass political organization which controlled the executive and the most important ministries, banks and public companies, bureaucratic recruitment, the judiciary, local government, and the allocation of public works. As state intervention in the economy grew in the postwar period, particularly in the south through the establishment of the Cassa per il Mezzogiorno, Christian Democrat clientelism could show increasing generosity toward clients in return for only the rather abstract and infrequent request for the vote. The emergence of a capitalist market in southern Italy was also conditioned by state intervention in the form of public works and state-led investment, which under the DC's direction became intertwined with the clientelist system.

The development of clientelism based on state resources was accompanied by rapid social change. The weight of agriculture in the southern economy declined in favor of industry and in particular the tertiary sector, and economic transformation brought urbanization, mass education, secularization, and a significant improvement in material living standards. However, the economy remained dependent on state money, and local capitalism was not strong enough to survive without such help, a situation described variously as "modernization without development" (Schneider and Schneider 1989) and "development without autonomy" (Trigilia 1992). In this context, to use Fantozzi's (1993: 61–62) typology, the "popular-familistic" model of clientelism, in which patrons and clients engaged in a direct exchange of favors and votes – patronage, in the terminology of this book – was replaced by two new forms of clientelism: the "network" model, in which public jobs and opportunities of various kinds are distributed to strategically placed clients in exchange for electoral support, and the "category" model, in which the clients are collective actors – associations, trade unions, professions – able to deliver en bloc their members' votes. Although southern Italy's modernization process faced many obstacles, it did ultimately undermine traditional community and personal solidarities, accentuating the fragmentation of southern society and permitting the new generation of political mediators to construct a new, more flexible set of relationships.

These new variants of clientelism were introduced by changes within the main governing party. Amintore Fanfani, elected DC secretary in 1953, was determined to reduce the party's dependence on external forces, such as the economic powers (particularly the business association Confindustria), and the Church hierarchy and Catholic associations which had played a major role in the party's initial efforts at mobilization (Tarrow 1972: 270–318). Fanfani's internal reforms transformed the DC from a party of notables dependent on the Catholic Church for its mass presence into a genuine mass party with a centralized organization and a flexible approach to ideology, which quickly descended into "network" clientelism as a means of maintaining its political and electoral position. The resulting transformation of clientelism was also conditioned by changes in public policy. The PSI's entry into the governing coalition in the 1960s brought policy changes of which perhaps the most relevant is the expansion of welfare spending. The emergence of a welfare state in Italy brought a massive growth in the resources to be distributed, and a corresponding updating of clientelism into "category" clientelism to respond to the political opportunities this provided.

Although most of our attention up to now has been focused on the south, this is not the only part of Italy where clientelism has prospered. Certainly, the DC's electoral strength depended largely on the south, but the party also had an important base in the "white" areas of the north (particularly in the Venetian region). Moreover, the southern party elites did not enjoy a dominant position inside the DC, and even when the Campanian Ciriaco De Mita took over as party secretary in the early 1980s he did so with the support of the Base faction, which was mainly implanted in the north. The DC was very much a factional party and the factions had most of their support in different, well-defined geographical areas, so that the party's internal dynamic reflected a balance between the interests and resources of various personalistic or localistic interests. The party leadership rarely interfered in the internal affairs of party factions, and candidates were usually selected locally, with little central intervention. Only with the most clamorous cases of corruption and Mafia connections in the 1980s did the central party authorities take over local sections to weed out malpractice. Given these structural constraints, the DC's involvement in clientelism in the north cannot be explained in terms of a simple "contagion from the south."

Instead, the "nationalization" of clientelism is due in part to the characteristics of the north's own process of economic modernization. Italian business has historically enjoyed significant support and protection from the state, even though the state has formally respected business autonomy (Amato 1974). In a country where the state bureaucracy has traditionally lacked autonomy from politicians, this has provided the political parties with the opportunity to use their control over the state apparatus to generate political support through economic intervention. The DC was particularly skillful in using the state's economic resources for partisan ends. Italy's economic transformation brought massive social change in the postwar period, with the decline of the primary sector in favor of the secondary and tertiary sectors. This had electoral consequences, as the DC had initially drawn much of its support from the Italian peasantry in the north and south (though not in the center), while the working class had favored the left. It therefore became all the more important for the DC to secure the support of the middle classes: small landowners, the petty bourgeoisie in both the public and private sectors, and the independent middle classes, such as artisans, and professional categories. Clientelist generosity – in the form of regulation to protect small business, a lax approach to tax collection for the self-employed, and so on – was systematically directed at these groups, so successfully that they actually grew as a proportion of the Italian population (Pizzorno 1974; Sylos Labini 1975).

This new, "category" kind of clientelism grew exponentially in the 1980s, accompanied by an equally exponential growth in political corruption. This is reflected in the increase in the number of investigations carried out by the magistrates in this period, which demonstrated that such practices were present throughout the country and involved all the governing parties. The case of the PSI, the target of the first investigations by the Milanese Mani Pulite (Clean Hands) magistrates, illustrates with particular clarity the characteristics of this form of clientelism. The PSI was originally territorially rooted in the north, with an electorate mainly composed of industrial workers and sectors of the lower middle class. On entering government in coalition with the DC in the 1960s, the party lost support in these areas. In the seventies, in order to recover support in the historical northern strongholds and to further strengthen its southern following, the new northern leadership – Bettino Craxi was elected party secretary in 1976 – put into practice the clientelar techniques learned from the DC, which had already earned the PSI electoral growth in the south.

The PSI's increasing reliance on clientelism can be explained in terms of the loss of both its ideological identity and its class identity. Craxi's internal reforms and reliance on short-term tactics led to a deemphasis on ideology within the party organization, removing an important constraint on clientelism and corruption (see also Hopkin 1997a). The collapse of class-based collective identities was a more general phenomenon. The passing of the mobilizations of the late 1960s, the trauma of terrorism which led the PCI to identify itself unequivocally with the state, the failure of the strategy of the "historic compromise," as well as the broader social and economic changes affecting the productive system and the differentiation of the social structure, brought the dispersal of the collective identities which had previously articulated Italian society and the decomposition of the system of interests. The decline of the two dominant ideologies – Catholic and Communist – led to a decline in party membership and activism, weakening the party organizations. The parties, faced with increasingly complex demands (amplified by the proportional electoral system), responded by allowing clientelism to pervade every corner of political and social life. This included the field of industrial relations, where the state failed to manage effectively the conflicts between unions and business, and of interest groups, each separately seeking satisfaction for their demands from an equally fragmented political elite, using the threat of electoral punishment to press for concessions.

In the 1970s the costs of resolving social and economic conflicts had been passed on to public spending and prices, with the result of an exponential increase in inflation and public debt. The governing parties' success in maintaining their electoral support by these means meant that in the 1980s – with the largely symbolic exception of the abolition of the *scala mobile*, the mechanism by which salaries were automatically adjusted for inflation – they were unwilling to rein in this profligacy. On the contrary, as the DC's electoral decline continued, the electoral market became increasingly competitive, and the growing threat to DC hegemony presented by the PSI and the other lay parties made the discontinuation of clientelist practices unfeasible. In this competitive environment, the parties' loss of activists and the increasing costs of political campaigning (through the growth of television propaganda) provided Italian party leaders with greater incentives to use clientelism to acquire financial resources from firms seeking public works contracts. Clientelism thus evolved into outright corruption. Neither was a line drawn at taking bribes to finance politics: the money was often partly dedicated to personal enrichment of the politicians involved. In parts of the south, politicians developed close links with organized crime, which had always been close to clientelist networks and in a position to influence the vote in the areas under their control.

The 1980s also brought remarkable changes to the composition and behavior of the political elite. The expansion of clientelistic negotiation led to the rapid growth of the "political class," as a breed of professional

159

political mediators emerged to mobilize votes and resolve conflicts. These individuals held party offices and positions in the public administration, or were elected as representatives, but also placed themselves in strategic social positions so as to profit economically or politically from their activity as mediators. In the new political market of the 1980s, politics became increasingly personalistic. Impersonal and bureaucratic party organizations with elected leadership were substituted by clientelistic networks formally attached to a political party, but in practice dependent on a specific individual. Such individuals, sometimes members of parliament, ministers, or regional or local councilors, were effectively "freelance" mediators, who would rarely distinguish between economic resources raised to finance electoral campaigns and their own personal finances. A new figure was emerging – the "business politician" (Pizzorno 1992: 23–24) – which developed and managed clientelistic exchanges in collaboration with other opportunists, often from outside the parties and the representative institutions, who acted as intermediaries with businesses and interest groups, themselves closely connected with politicians and prepared to recruit their own intermediaries, from politics or public enterprises, to represent them (Gribaudi and Musella 1998).

It was suggested in the 1980s by authoritative observers such as Joseph LaPalombara (1988) that this form of "democracy Italian style" was compatible with political stability and social and economic progress. In fact, the deterioration of the governing parties into an extreme form of "the political machine" can be seen as the proximate cause of the collapse of the system in 1992–94 under the weight of a state financial crisis, growing protest in the economic powerhouse of the north, and a determined drive on the part of a sector of judiciary to expose politicians' unrestrained involvement in clientelism and corruption. The costs of the governing parties' attempts to secure electoral support through clientelism were unsustainable. The decline of the country's infrastructure, the poor quality of public services, the lack of international competitiveness of Italian businesses, and the costs of servicing the public debt were all factors which contributed to the discrediting of the governing class. Most Italians were certainly well aware of the extent of corruption, but many – in particular the Christian Democrat and Socialist electorates – saw it as a by-product of a form of government which offered a number of advantages. In the 1990s, however, the limitations of this way of running the country became evident and the complex network of clientelistic relations effectively collapsed.

Clientelism and the Restoration of Spanish Democracy

While in Italy the DC established a durable power structure based in part on the development of clientelism, the moderate right in Spain failed dramatically to consolidate its own position. The Union of the Democratic Center (UCD), a factionally riven organization occupying a political space similar to that of the DC in Italy, was initially successful in taking control of the government machinery, but quickly descended into infighting and ultimately disintegrated, leaving the Socialist (PSOE) opposition as the only feasible party of government (Hopkin 1999). The potential for alternation in the Spanish party system – the PSOE itself was dislodged from government in 1996 – and the possibility of single-party government has meant that the stability and even stagnation of the party system in Italy until the 1990s has not been repeated in Spain, with important consequences for the development of clientelism.

In some respects, however, the circumstances of the transition to democracy after Franco were favorable to clientelism. The transition strategy followed – a "negotiated break" with the institutions of the dictatorship – quickly succeeded in establishing a formally democratic political system, but refrained from carrying out a comprehensive renewal of political and administrative personnel. A line was drawn under political responsibilities in the period of the dictatorship, and a generation of new converts to democracy was able to survive in the new context. To this extent, the traditional patronage which had prospered under the dictatorship had the opportunity to adapt to the new democratic environment and capitalize on the local resources it controlled, much in the same way local notables in southern Italy had been allowed to maintain their power structures intact as a result of the weakness of the Italian central state (Tarrow 1977).

At the same time, the emphasis on elite negotiations in the transition process (Gunther 1992), which required all the emerging parties to make significant concessions in order to secure broad acceptance of the new democratic institutions, further demobilized a society which forty years of authoritarianism had rendered politically apathetic (Sastre García 1997). Although it has been argued that the success of the democratization process in 1970s Spain owed much to the emergence of a form of civil society in the final phase of Francoism (Pérez Díaz 1993), there is evidence to suggest that the defining feature of Spanish society in the 1970s was its low level of associationism and political participation. Even the most

161

electorally successful political parties had paltry memberships (Spain still has the lowest levels of party membership in Western Europe), and union membership was also low, particularly after 1980. It seems more accurate to talk of a society lacking the kinds of horizontal solidarity and collective action structures which provide the best defense against clientelism. The isolation of most Spaniards from formal political and social organizations in the new democracy was comparable to that of the postwar Italian south, constituting a further incentive for the persistence of clientelism into the new context.

On the other hand, party competition reemerged in Spain in a social context quite different from that of postwar Italy. Spain in the 1970s was, in key respects, a "modern" society with social and economic characteristics similar to those of its democratic European neighbors. Rapid economic growth in the 1960s had brought a massive shift in population from rural to urban areas, the creation of a large middle class employed in service industries, a decline in religious practice, and access to consumer goods and mass media for the majority of Spaniards. As a consequence, electoral behavior in the initial period of the new democracy was characterized by low levels of "class voting," and the important impact of national party leadership (mediated by state television) on voting decisions (Barnes et al. 1985; Gunther 1992; Gunther et al. 1986; Linz and Montero 1986; McDonough et al. 1981). General elections were fought on national issues, and political parties made use of modern mass communications techniques in order to mobilize the large numbers of undecided voters (Hopkin and Paolucci 1999).

So unlike southern Italy in the immediate postwar period, traditional notables' patronage was not viable in most areas of post-Franco Spain. Voters may have been politically inactive and lacking horizontal ties, but they were also well educated, relatively prosperous, and mostly integrated into a "modern" urban culture. The social conditions which had favored clientelism in southern Italy in the 1950s – a politically atomized and underemployed class of agricultural laborers – were absent from most of Spain in the 1970s, although unemployment in general was to rise to serious levels in the post-Franco period. Patronage was therefore restricted to a small number of economically backward regions. The UCD, created hurriedly immediately before the first democratic elections in 1977, recruited individuals of prestige and authority in the provinces who could generate votes for the party on the basis of the clienteles they had established through their exercise of political power under the previous regime.

Many UCD candidates were mayors, local and provincial councilors, members of Chambers of Commerce and Agriculture, or members of provincial delegations of the various ministries (all political appointments under the Franco regime). The most extreme case of this was the UCD's formation in Galicia, a region well known for the strength of *caciquismo* (De Juana et al. 1995; Núñez Seijas 1995; Jáuregui 1987: chapters 5 and 10). UCD obtained twenty out of the twenty-seven seats in the Congress representing Galicia, an indication of the potency of these networks. Other areas where clientelistic structures appear to have been absorbed by UCD were the Canary Islands (Hernández Bravo de la Laguna and Millares Cantero 1995) and some provinces in Castile (Gunther et al. 1986: 102).

In contrast, the PSOE, in its initial phase of development, could claim to be largely free of clientelistic activity. Its very small membership was largely composed of trade unionists, and some intellectuals and minor professionals (lawyers, functionaries); a cursory examination of the profiles of PSOE parliamentarians in the transition period reveals that the party recruited few of the kinds of prestigious local figures which abounded in the UCD parliamentary elite. Indeed, what is striking about the PSOE parliamentary elite in the transitional period is the number of young individuals with indifferent professional status representing the party (see the biographies of parliamentarians in Díaz Nosty 1977). Such people, elected in areas where clientelist networks could be expected to exist, are not obvious candidates for the label of *cacique*. This is hardly surprising. Local notables seeking to position themselves in the new environment emerging after Franco's death were obviously unlikely to attach themselves to an organizationally fragile opposition party, of formally Marxist inspiration, whose electoral prospects originally appeared fairly modest. Most *caciques* instead opted for UCD and the conservative formation with Francoist sympathies, Alianza Popular (Gunther et al. 1986). This in itself is evidence of the weakness of clientelist networks in electoral terms. While UCD performed well in the 1977 elections, Alianza Popular, which consciously sought to use clientelism to mobilize what it saw as a depoliticized and pro-Francoist majority (*el franquismo sociológico*), failed dismally, winning only 8.9 percent of the vote.

The UCD's extraordinary electoral collapse in 1981–82 (Hopkin 1999: chapter 6) provides compelling evidence of the limited impact of clientelism in Spain's electoral evolution in the immediate post-Franco period. The party's unexpectedly crushing defeats in the Galician regional elections in 1981 and the Andalusian regional elections in 1982 have been cited as examples of local notables shifting their clienteles from one party to another in response to the governing party's poor performance (Cazorla 1995: 41). However, close analysis suggests that the role of clientelism in determining the realignment of the Spanish party system in 1982 was fairly limited. In both Galicia and Andalusia, UCD lost most votes in the most economically advanced and urbanized provinces, while its vote remained more stable in the backward rural areas where evidence of clientelism could be found (González Encinar 1982; Porras Nadales 1985). In the 1982 legislative elections where UCD's vote collapsed from 35 percent to under 7 percent, ten out of the eleven deputies it elected represented precisely those areas where UCD's cooptation of clientelist structures has been most documented (five deputies were elected in Galicia, two in the Canary Islands, and three in New Castile). The UCD's electoral fragility is testament to its limited success in establishing stable electoral clienteles.

The research on Spanish electoral behavior in the post-Franco period would tend to reinforce the impression that clientelism was restricted to a relatively small proportion of the electorate, largely concentrated in a handful of provinces. Local notables were mostly unknown to voters: in the 1982 elections, fewer than 20 percent of voters outside Madrid, Catalonia, and the Basque Country could correctly name the number one candidate on the list they had voted for (Gunther 1991: 56). Although this does not in itself suggest the elimination of clientelism, it does indicate that such personalization of electoral politics that existed was largely confined to the national level. The popularity of national party leaders such as Suárez, González, Fraga, and Carrillo were major factors in explaining election results, and voters in the various Spanish provinces voted largely in terms of national personalities and issues. This appears to be confirmed by analysis of local politics: municipal election results largely mirrored preceding national election results (Delgado Sotillos 1997), and the 1983 municipal elections saw a very high turnover of local representatives in response to the UCD's collapse at the national level the year before (Márquez Cruz 1992). The kind of "old clientelism" in which the local notables generated support on the basis of personal loyalties appears to have had a limited impact on elections in post-Franco Spain, in contrast to the well-documented impact of clientelism on postwar Italian elections.

One reason for this was Spain's "modern" social structure: whereas 42 percent of the Italian labor force in 1952 worked in the agricultural sector, in 1980, 15 percent of the Spanish labor force worked in the same sector (Gunther 1991: 57). Clearly, the emergence of democratic party competition in Spain was unlikely to mirror the initial phase of electoral politics in postwar Italy. The characteristics of poverty, isolation, and illiteracy, which provide the ideal context for the development of patronage (Cazorla 1992: 5), had been eliminated from much of Spanish society by the time democracy was reestablished. At the same time, the potential for clientelism to take root was undermined by the limited spending power of the Spanish state in the aftermath of the Franco dictatorship. Public spending accounted for only 25 percent of GNP in 1975, considerably below average Western European levels. Although spending was significantly increased in UCD's period of office, funds were distributed in terms of the need for political consensus on key issues such as education and social security. To this extent, the beneficiaries of increased spending under the UCD were often not UCD voters, nor even potential supporters of the party of government: the spending was aimed at reducing the tensions among the labor force in order to avoid politically dangerous social conflict. Such a strategy would appear to be the opposite of the clientelistic forms of "occupation of the state" and fiscally driven "social engineering" in the Italy of the DC.

However, developments after 1982 pushed Spain in the direction of the Italian model. The Socialist governments of 1982–96 both increased state spending and targeted it in more obviously partisan ways. State spending, which was 38 percent of GDP in 1982, had risen to 44 percent in 1994, and most of this increase in spending was accounted for by capital investment and social protection (Gunther 1996: 38). Although this spending can certainly be justified in terms of economic and social rationality, and to an extent the PSOE merely took over where the UCD had left off, it is also clear that spending priorities had significant implications for the party's electoral support. First, state capital investment had the dual purpose of improving the competitiveness of the Spanish economy and distributing work and infrastructure to areas where the party's support was strong. The south of Spain (Andalusia and Extremadura), where the PSOE had its most reliable electoral base, was particularly favored by infrastructure investment, the most striking example of which was the Madrid–Seville high-speed rail link. Moreover, state subsidies and credits to ailing industries also had an electoral rationale, favoring regions such as Catalonia, Andalusia, and Asturias, where the PSOE vote was strong. It is, of course, questionable whether this kind of territorial bias in the distribution of state resources amounts to clientelism. However, there does seem to be an element of exchange and reciprocity involved, and such policies could fall into Fantozzi's "category" type of clientelism, as local party bosses have been able to convert their electoral resources into a means to pressure their own "patrons" at the highest levels of the party machinery for the distribution of resources.

Perhaps the clearest example of clientelism in post-1982 Spain revolves around the distribution of subsidies to agricultural workers in the south. The PER (Plan for Rural Employment) grants wages to agricultural workers provided they have worked a minimum number of days in the year. Given that the local mayor is responsible for certifying the number of days worked, the potential for local politicians to ensure electoral support in exchange for approving the payment of these subsidies is obvious, and it appears that the PSOE, the majority party in the areas covered by the PER, has made use of this power to secure a faithful electoral clientele (Cazorla 1994, 1995; Martín de Pozuelo et al. 1994: chapter 16). Along similar lines, the PSOE also established noncontributive pensions and increased expenditure on unemployment benefits, both decisions which can easily be defended on universalistic grounds, but which have also had the happy consequence of rewarding groups which have provided the party with reliable electoral support. The PSOE has distributed resources to rather diffuse "categories" in exchange for political backing, in much the same way as the DC's policies favoring shopkeepers and the self-employed brought the party electoral advantage.

There is less doubt over whether the PSOE's approach to public sector employment constitutes an example of "network" clientelism. The PSOE entered the transition period organizationally fragile and lacking in grassroots support: the party essentially consisted of small groups of ambitious young politicians in a handful of cities. Even after the party's electoral successes in 1977 and 1979, and its extraordinary victory in 1982, the PSOE was still a very top-heavy organization with a membership of little over 100,000, a ratio of one member for every 100 voters. Control over the government machinery provided the opportunity to remedy this organizational weakness through a significant expansion of employment in the public administration. Again, this policy could be defended on rational, universalistic grounds: the social democratic strategy of state-driven economic growth and the development of a welfare state required a better resourced administration, so an expansion in state personnel was necessary. Moreover, given the PSOE's massive popular support in the early

1980s, it would be surprising if a large number of the beneficiaries of this expansion in state employment were not Socialist supporters. Between 1982 and 1994, more than half a million state jobs were established (Beltrán 1996: 269), and there seems little doubt that many of these jobs were given to party sympathizers in exchange for material help in the party's activities. In this way, the Socialist leadership – with deputy leader Alfonso Guerra particularly active in the process – established "a clientelistic network that has thrived in the Spanish political culture and through the power the electoral list system gives to party elites" (Gillespie 1994: 57). The party acquired human resources, and the families of those who found jobs through their party links were likely to reward the party with their votes.

As in Italy, these practices became enmeshed with plain corruption. In one emblematic case, Guerra's brother Juan, appointed as assistant in the vice-president's office, developed a role as an intermediary in classic practices of corrupt party financing. Through his illegally occupied office in government buildings in Seville, Juan Guerra arranged for Socialist local representatives to make decisions in favor of certain business interests who would then pay commissions to the party (Martín de Pozuelo et al. 1994: chapter 8). The Socialist party was not alone in this: similar practices in other areas implicated the main opposition party, the PP (Popular Party), and the Catalan nationalist formation, CiU (Convergence and Union). The political class in Spain grew to include a range of professional mediators, similar to the *faccendieri* in Italy, able to capitalize on their proximity to decisionmakers for private enrichment as well as the illegal financing of the parties which offered them protection. Remarkably, this situation became politically unsustainable in the early 1990s, at broadly the same time as the emergence of the Tangentopoli scandals in Italy, and for much the same reasons: the electorate's weariness of a political class which had enjoyed uncontested political power for too long, the economic pressures emerging from the Maastricht treaty, and the stark contrast between the increasing hardship facing most citizens and the accumulating evidence of embezzlement of public funds by politicians and their parties.

The close coexistence of clientelism and corruption present in Italy was therefore repeated in Spain. While the differences between the two phenomena must be recognized (see Caciagli 1996), it can be hypothesized that they share similar origins. The kind of nonideological, often particularistic distribution of resources characteristic of clientelism encourages the creation of a political class characterized by its opportunism and electoralism, and perfectly willing to sacrifice principle for political expediency. The same kind of reasoning which justifies skewing the distributional effects of public policy to favor narrow party interests can also justify the connivance between politicians and business at the expense of the public purse for the financing of political campaigns. The "deideologization" of the PSI charted earlier bears uncomfortable resemblance to the evolution of the PSOE after the abandonment of Marxism in 1979. Ideology was deemphasized in favor of governmental pragmatism and the need to attract electoral support from outside the traditional working class. In both cases, internal party power was centralized around the leadership, and local interests assuaged with opportunities for the distribution of public offices. The evidence of close cooperation between the two parties as the PSOE built its organization in the 1970s and 1980s suggests that organizational practices may even have been directly transferred.

Conclusions: The Present and Future of Clientelism

All regimes founded on the selection of political elites through free electoral competition are exposed to the risk of clientelism. Aspiring politicians have two basic tools for winning citizens' support: the distribution of symbolic, and particularly ideological, incentives; and the distribution of material incentives, which take both universalistic and particularistic or selective forms. Political scientists have generally analyzed the latter in terms of the concept of clientelism, used by anthropologists to describe the networks of interpersonal solidarity which articulate traditional societies. Clientelism has often been regarded as a function of social and cultural backwardness: in a fragmented social context lacking the conditions for ideological mobilization, politicians tend to act as patrons, offering benefits and protection to their clients in exchange for political and electoral support. A second important condition for the development of clientelism is the organizational and cultural weakness of the state administration, and its inability to infuse citizens with commitment to the universal principles of the *Rechtsstaat*.

However, it has been shown that the particularistic distribution of benefits to voters is not exclusive to less advanced contexts, and is compatible with mass party politics. In fact, this form of mobilization has often competed with, and even substituted, ideological mobilization. This is what Shefter (1994) describes as *machine politics* and what we called simply clientelism in this chapter: the particularistic allocation of benefits not only to individuals, but also to groups, organized interests, professions, and local communities. For Shefter the role of the state is equally decisive here: where the state administration is weak and unable to resist the encroachment of elected politicians, clientelism prospers.

The Italian and Spanish cases clearly confirm this hypothesis and show striking similarities. In both Italy and Spain the collapse of dictatorships brought the reemergence of patronage to the least developed areas: the south in Italy, and Galicia and the Canary Islands in Spain. In both cases it can be suggested that patronage, despite its negative consequences, can have positive effects, the most important of which is its contribution to democratic socialization in contexts unfavorable to the consolidation of democracy. In postwar Italy, for instance, patronage networks were absorbed and controlled by a mass party with a clear ideological dimension – the DC – which was able to substitute local Fascist elites with the help of traditional notables. In the Spanish case, a significant sector of the Francoist local elite was resuscitated by the parties of the center and right, which would otherwise have had difficulty in establishing a presence in rural and peripheral areas, despite the Spanish transition to democracy taking place in much more modern social context than the Italian postwar transition. In the mid-1950s the Italian DC began to "modernize" patronage and export it from the south to the rest of Italy, and in the 1980s the Spanish Socialists adopted similar techniques.

However, these apparent similarities disguise important differences in the motivations for adopting clientelistic strategies. In the Italian case, clientelism allowed the DC from the 1950s on to become a genuine, centralized mass party, independent of both the Church hierarchy (with its associational base) and the most powerful economic interests (principally the southern landowners and the business peak organization Confindustria), which had provided its initial organizational backbone. As the DC concentrated on exploiting state resources to build its own organizational structure, its ideological vitality declined, encouraging the extension of clientelistic practices outside the south. The responsibility for these developments must be shared between the party and its voters (as individuals or organized groups), who increasingly conditioned their electoral support on the distribution of particularistic benefits.

The Spanish case is somewhat different: while the DC had a stable electoral base and used clientelism to increase its organizational autonomy, the Spanish PSOE used clientelism in order to help build an organization and, to a lesser extent, a core electorate. The PSOE was a structurally weak party which emerged as a political force in a period of decline of class identities, and adopted clientelism as a substitute for ideological mobilization. In Shefter's terms, the DC and the PSOE were both "externally mobilized parties," which initially relied on ideological incentives to attract voters and activists and which only later caved in to the expediency of clientelism as a means to strengthening their electoral following. However, while the DC made the shift soon after gaining access to power positions, the PSOE held onto ideological appeals a little longer and did not become very dependent on clientelist electoral mobilization. Although both were initially "externally mobilized parties," it can be argued that "at the moment when they first undertook to acquire a mass base, these parties for all intents and purposes stood in the same relationship to potential supporters as do internally mobilized parties" (Shefter 1994: 34).

Clientelism does not only have negative consequences: as in Italy, clientelism often acts an obstacle to development (Trigilia 1992), but can on occasion bring economic benefits (Piattoni 1998), as well as absorbing conflict and promoting social integration. The PSOE model was adopted in Italy, in the same period, by the PSI, which was able to arrest its electoral decline by installing itself as a governing party in coalition with the DC, and competing ferociously with the DC for control of the resources for expanding electoral support. The DC and PSI's overreliance on clientelistic techniques for winning support was demonstrated by their electoral collapse after sectors of the judiciary launched an anticorruption drive in 1992. This raises the delicate issue of whether this collapse was the result of voters' moral outrage at politicians' corrupt behavior, or rather of their realization that the indebted Italian state could no longer finance the parties' clientelistic activities.

Of course, clientelism is not automatically accompanied by corruption, and it is worth considering why the two phenomena have coexisted in the Italian and Spanish cases. Three conditions for this coexistence can be identified. First, the weakening of state bureaucracies and their "colonization" by parties remove one potential obstacle to the abuses of clientelist politics. Second, the weakening of party organizations, and the ideological atrophy that is associated with it, provide a strong incentive for the exploitation of state resources: some of the Italian and Spanish parties in the 1980s acted as political "firms" composed of competing factions whose principal aim was to capture state resources and generate political support for materialistic objectives (Hopkin 1997b). Third, the decline of ideologies can undermine the moral quality of political personnel. Ideologies have often constituted a brake on personal ambition, encouraging individual politicians to put the collective interest – the interest of the party – before their own private interests. Although acts of corruption in the name of the party are not uncommon, the systematic embezzlement of public resources at the height of Tangentopoli rested on the abandonment by many politicians of any collective rationale for their actions.

To conclude on a speculative note, the Italian and Spanish cases suggest a further hypothesis, which it would be interesting to apply to other cases. If clientelism prospers in conditions of weak state bureaucracies and social fragmentation, and if the particularistic distribution of material incentives is a natural feature of politics in pluralistic democracies, a curious scenario can be imagined. The postmodern age, characterized by the absence of ideological mobilization, the decline of the great social cleavages and collective identities of class and religion, a growing social differentiation, and an exaggerated emphasis on particularistic interests, would appear to provide fertile ground for the reemergence of clientelism. It could even be provocatively suggested that in such a context, clientelism may constitute a valuable source of social integration in the most advanced societies, a far cry from the classic interpretations of clientelism as a phenomenon characteristic of social, economic, and cultural backwardness.

8

Clientelism in a Cold Climate: The Case of Iceland

GUNNAR HELGI KRISTINSSON

Introduction

Clientelism in Iceland is in some respects a rather surprising phenomenon. Scandinavian politics are assumed to be, for the most part, free from clientelism. European clientelism is usually studied in its "Latin" or Mediterranean settings, indicating a cultural boundary which has existed at least since the time the Protestant churches rebelled against corruption in the Catholic Church. Icelandic clientelism, however, is solidly Protestant and North European. Clientelism, moreover, is supposed to thrive on asymmetric power relations, where clients seek the protection of powerful patrons (Blok 1969). Icelandic clientelism, instead, takes place in a cultural context characterized by egalitarianism and the absence of social deference or great inequalities of wealth. The Icelandic constitutional, legal, and administrative structures rest on Scandinavian foundations, imported in large measure from the mother state of Denmark. Yet, unlike their Scandinavian cousins, the Icelanders are richly experienced in clientelism (Kristinsson 1996).

The Icelandic experience provides a unique opportunity for studying the development of clientelism outside the cultural context with which it is more commonly associated. The present chapter seeks to do this using Martin Shefter's (1994) theory as its point of departure. The great advantage of Shefter's theory in this context is its attempt to explain the emergence of clientelism without relying too much on cultural variables. Institutional factors such as the state bureaucracy and party organizations, instead, take center stage. It emerges that, while Shefter's thesis offers a convincing interpretation of the rise of Icelandic clientelism in the twentieth century, it does not do quite so well in accounting for its subsequent decline. Despite Shefter's prediction that clientelism, once established, is difficult to get rid of, Icelandic clientelism has in fact shown strong signs of decline in recent decades. The second half of the chapter deals with this problem.

Democracy before Bureaucracy

Unpropitious conditions for clientelism, according to Shefter, exist where a strong state bureaucracy developed before the emergence of mass mobilization and democracy. The bureaucracy, in such instances, is sufficiently strong to shield itself from the attacks of the emerging mass political movements aiming at making the bureaucracy a servant of party organization. Instead, where a strong bureaucracy does not develop before the advent of democracy, the emerging parties can use access to administrative power to build party organizations (Shefter 1994: 25–36).

The emergence of clientelism in Iceland can basically be understood within this broad framework, even if some of the particulars are peculiar to Iceland. With only distant memories of an independent commonwealth, Iceland remained a dependency of the Danish state until the twentieth century. Domestic legislative power was established in 1874, but the executive was essentially Danish until 1904, when Home Rule was introduced. Iceland obtained sovereignty in 1918 and became a republic in 1944, when the joint kingdom with Denmark was abolished.

While Denmark fulfilled Shefter's condition for escaping clientelism – bureaucracy before democracy – the same does not hold for Iceland. The Danish administration in Iceland – even if mostly manned by Icelanders – was not an autonomous body and hence highly restricted in its political maneuvering vis-à-vis domestic society. The officials of the Crown were perhaps the only substantially privileged class of society above the peasant farmers, and their privileges were widely resented. As the Icelandic nationalist cause gained momentum during the second half of the nineteenth century the position of the officials became rather difficult, caught as they were between loyalty to their administrative masters and the demands from domestic society, represented by the Icelandic legislature, the Althingi. The legislature represented popular opinion, whereas the executive represented foreign rule and privilege. When Home Rule and parliamentary government were granted in 1904, as a consequence of a change of regime in Denmark three years earlier, the administration stood defenseless against parliament, lacking both popular support and stable political allies. A series of changes were made in the structure of the administrative system and its leadership retired. The new administrative system was broadly based on a Danish model, but its leading personnel and major institutions were new, lacking also the political strength and traditions on which the Danish system was based. Iceland at this time was basically a democracy without a strong bureaucracy.

Mass clientelism did not set in immediately. To use the distinction between patronage and clientelism made in Chapter 1, the weakness of the state bureaucracy was reflected in several instances of patronage – basically the handing out of offices on political grounds – rather than clientelism on a massive scale. At this time, the Icelandic party system was in a state of flux and the political parties did not have formal membership organizations. The demand for particularistic services had not found effective channels to the administrative apparatus. The underlying weakness in the position of the bureaucracy did not become apparent until the 1930s, when the parties had stabilized and began to organize their membership.

The Development of Clientelism

If political parties need members, they also need to provide good reasons for joining. There may of course be any number of reasons why people should join political parties, but as far as rational motives go, they are primarily of two kinds. One is selfish, individual gain, such as career opportunities, access to contracts, grants, services, or any other values which the administrative system can provide for the party member. The other is a function of the party program, the reward of working for a cause. Each type of reward can exist along with the other, but obviously the dominance of the former type of motive will have far-reaching consequences for the behavior of a political party (Wright 1971). Clientelist parties, where such motives are dominant, are likely to be nonprogrammatic. Strong principles can get in the way of what is the essential objective of the party, namely, gaining control of the administrative apparatus. Nonclientelist mass parties, by contrast, offer their programs as the main reward for the members and must of necessity devote greater attention to their programmatic functions. They cannot allow themselves to be as transparently office-seeking as the clientelist ones, since programmatic compromises may cause unease, demoralization, or open revolt among their members.

Clientelism in a Cold Climate: Iceland

The major parties of twentieth-century Iceland emerged between 1916 and 1930. Formal membership organizations, however, really developed only in the 1930s. The only party with a membership organization prior to that was the Social Democratic party, but its organization was an indirect one, the labor unions formally being divisions of the party. Apart from this, there existed a few organized political societies prior to the 1930s, but they were without formal ties to the parties in parliament. Political parties were essentially groups of parliamentarians, sometimes associated with a particular newspaper. Candidates emerged through an informal process of consultations between the parliamentary groups and local notables, but nonetheless candidates identifying with the same parliamentary group sometimes competed against each other.

In an atmosphere of intensified political competition, during the 1930s, the parties, for the first time, felt the need to organize their followers. The main party alternatives had been stabilized during the 1920s and the competition for governmental power, as a consequence, had increased. In the early 1930s, party competition was further intensified through the effects of the Depression and the emergence of extremist political movements. Membership organization made the parties more competitive. The parties organized so as to solidify their following among the electorate and to gain increasing campaigning efficiency. To a certain extent, party organizations also served the function of strengthening the central leadership and improving its strategic position in the competition for governmental office.

With the rise of partisan membership organizations, clientelism spread rapidly. By the late 1940s it had permeated most spheres of society. Each of the parties had its particular clientele. The largest party, the conservative Independence party, served the interests of the private sector and parts of the farming population, and operated a highly effective party machine in its main stronghold, Reykjavik. The rural Progressive party served the agrarian interests and especially those of the rural cooperative movement, which was also strong in many of the provincial towns. The Social Democrats served the labor unions, but after the organizational ties between party and unions were severed in 1940–42, the Social Democratic organization was probably the weakest among the major parties. Of the major parties, the left socialist People's Alliance was least integrated into the clientelist system. Being to a certain extent an outsider to Icelandic politics, it had less access to materialistic rewards than the other parties and consequently had to build its membership organization on the idealism of its members more than on private gain.

The strength of the party organizations reached its zenith in the 1940s and 1950s. In those years it was difficult to get anywhere without the right party connections. Public employment, from the most routine manual jobs to senior civil service positions, was distributed on a partisan basis. Hardly any senior public positions were within reach of those outside the clientelist networks. Services provided by the public sector played an important role in the clientelist organizations, particularly those which had in one way or another to do with housing. Lack of housing was a major problem in postwar Iceland, and consequently housing, subsidized loans, building sites, and permits were goods in high demand among the clientele of the parties. The financial system was more or less completely nationalized and overseen by political commissioners, whose role was to secure a fair share for the clienteles of their respective parties. In foreign trade and commerce, government licenses were required for almost any transaction that took place. Here a "split-even" system existed between the Progressive party, serving the cooperative movement, and the Independence party, serving the mainstream private sector. Almost all spheres of life were party political. Innumerable stories are told of how this complicated life for the party supporters. A strong Progressive party supporter unfortunate enough to run out of gas in front of a Shell station (Shell in Iceland was associated with the Independence party) stubbornly declared: "I'd rather drive without gas. . . ."

Pork-barreling became an advanced art form at this time. The rural constituencies were greatly overrepresented in the electoral system and took advantage of their position by obtaining various favors from the legislature, especially with regard to basic infrastructure. This included items such as electricity, telecommunications, roads, harbors, hospitals, and schools. There existed a strong expectation in the rural constituencies that the MPs would bring public funds and projects to their constituencies. They were also expected to oil the state machinery in Reykjavik whenever their constituents needed it and even to sign personally loan guarantees for their constituents when needed. The necessary forms were available in the House of Althingi.

Many old-style politicians still defend clientelism as a perfectly natural way of doing politics. One, former government minister Matthias Bjarnason, put it like this when discussing his political career:

All things were difficult in these years and both parliamentarians and local government leaders had to put up a struggle to get things moving. Now they call this pork-barreling [literally from Icelandic "constituency-poking"]. I'm not impressed by this sort of nonsense or calling others clientelist politicians as if that were an abusive word. What are members of parliament for? Shouldn't they take care of their constituents in any way they possibly can? (Arnason 1993: 103)

In some cases, the role of the parliamentarian was merely that of a broker, advising his clientele on how to get the best results from the various state agencies they dealt with. This role was created through lack of communications and lack of knowledge of how the public sector worked. But the role of parliamentarians went far beyond that, including activities such as securing financial support, jobs, roads, and various other desired goods for their clienteles. Former prime minister Steingrimur Hermannsson in a recent memoir maintains – while in no way denying his own role in it – that this arrangement is neither fortunate nor normal.

Improved communications, professionalism and a strong administrative system should have replaced such practices through new and improved procedures. In the seventies, however, access to loans was even more tied in with the political system than it is now and it was well nigh impossible for businessmen not to become part of it. I tried to support those from the Western fjords [his constituency] whom I believed in and who needed assistance. (Eggertsson 1999: 107)

More or less every provincial politician had to take part in the clientelist system if he was to remain in favor with his constituents. Those who did not generally did not last long in Icelandic politics. This, however, was less true of Reykjavik. Although the conservatives operated an effective clientelist machine in Reykjavik, this never reached all sections of the population to the same extent as in the provinces. In Reykjavik, many of those who were outside the Independence party orbit felt that the clientelist system put them at an unfair disadvantage.

The clientelist system was not viewed equally favorably by all sections of the population. From the 1960s onward clientelism met with an increasingly negative response in public life, and by the turn of the century it was only a shadow of its former self. Pork-barreling is still practiced by parliamentarians, and former government ministers sometimes retire into high administrative posts, but clientelism can hardly be said to be the driving motor of party life to the extent that it used to be.

The Decline of Clientelism

Unlike the emergence of clientelism in Iceland, which fits nicely with Shefter's theory, its decline sits uneasily with some of his themes. This applies in particular to his "critical experience" thesis. The way political parties originally mobilized popular support, according to Shefter, was a "critical experience" in the sense that it established patterns which subsequently were difficult to get rid of. Shefter's thesis in this respect has more than passing resemblance to Lipset and Rokkan's (1967) "frozen cleavages" thesis, whereby the way political mobilization originally takes place is seen to determine the subsequent format of the party system. But just like party alternatives may have been less solidly frozen than Lipset and Rokkan assumed, so clientelism may also stand on weaker ground than Shefter assumes.

To be fair, Shefter does not maintain that the way political parties originally organized utterly determines the way they subsequently operate. He merely maintains that it weighs the dice toward one outcome or the other (Shefter 1994: 29–32). Thus, Shefter discusses two cases – France and the United States – which produced mixed results with regard to the crucial factors of his theory. Sections of the French state and the western states of the United States escaped the fate of clientelism during the original phase of mobilization and subsequently provided a home base for the opposition to such practices. Clientelism or opposition to clientelism became not only a question of organizational strategy but a political issue in its own right. Thus, clientelism in the early stages of democratic development does not mean that a country is irreversibly condemned to clientelism.

The predicted outcome can be reversed, but any effort to reverse it engenders a crisis of the regime and requires the total reorientation of the nation's politics – perhaps even a revolution – to succeed. If and when such a crisis occurs, the challengers to the old order and the defenders of that order mobilize their forces, and the outcome of the struggle depends upon the breadth of the popular support and the character of the institutional backing enjoyed by each side (Shefter 1994: 56–57).

The problem with Shefter's contention from an Icelandic angle is the stress on a radical break and "total reorientation." The decline of clientelism in Iceland is in itself certainly an important change, but it has occurred without sudden or dramatic changes in other spheres of political life, let alone a revolution. Instead, it has happened in a piecemeal fashion, step by step, sometimes forward and sometimes backward, in a protracted death struggle of both traditional party organizations and clientelism.

Clientelism in Iceland was a diffuse phenomenon affecting most spheres of society. Trying to simplify matters somewhat, we review the principal ambits of Icelandic clientelist intermediation to appraise the pace and mode of its retrenchment.

Jobs

Public employment was always a major reward for political support in the Icelandic system. This applied not only to senior administrative posts but to any job within the public sector. In fact, majority coalitions in local governments sometimes break down over the hiring of personnel for routine manual jobs (e.g., swimming-pool attendants, foremen, maintenance people). Within central government – which includes the larger part of the public sector – previous practice of this nature has been abandoned to a larger degree. There remain jobs which still tend to be used in this manner (in particular, directors of the Central Bank and ambassadors) and the occasional government minister still tries his hand at old-style clientelism, but for the most part jobs in the public sector are filled on the basis of professional criteria. Thus, professionalism has played a part in driving out clientelism. It has been helped by an increasingly effective legal environment protecting the rights of applicants for public employment.

Contracts and Procurement

State contracts and public procurement have always been in great demand by the private sector. Political connections were often crucial. The best-known example was probably the use of contracts with the U.S. government for servicing the U.S. military base in Keflavik, which created a fortune among favored supporters of the major parties (except of course the People's Alliance, which was against the military base). Everyone knew that favoritism played a large role in contracts and procurement. International pressure has made this type of clientelism increasingly difficult to practice. Regulation has to a considerable extent replaced arbitrary decisions in this respect. Through membership in the European Economic Area (which includes the European Union, Norway, Liechtenstein, and Iceland) Iceland has adopted competition policies and relatively autonomous control mechanisms which make a continuation of the old-style politics much more difficult, except by breaking the law. Breaking the law, however, was never a substantial part of Icelandic clientelism – clientelism thrived on the ambiguity of the law and legal vacuum rather than outright law-breaking.

Licenses

Foreign trade and anything that had to do with foreign currency used to be strictly controlled by the Icelandic authorities. There existed a "split-even" arrangement between the two largest parties, the Independence party and the Progressive party, whereby each would secure for their clients a fair share in foreign trade. This applied to both imports and exports. The right to use foreign currency to import goods was distributed between the cooperative movement (served by the Progressives) and the mainstream private sector (served by the Independence party). Since the Icelandic krona tended to be valued unrealistically high (especially prior to 1960), currency licenses were of considerable value and created a grateful clientele for the major parties. A similar system existed in exports. The major export product of the economy was fish, but exports required licenses, which in theory were intended to strengthen export organizations among producers. In effect, the licenses went partly to the mainstream private sector firms associated with the Independence party, and partly to the cooperatives, associated with the Progressive party. Icelandic participation in free-trade cooperation since the 1960s has gradually undermined this type of clientelism. Trade was freed from excessive licensing, and the cooperative giant, the Association of Cooperatives, as a result, has broken down. Trade, by the turn of the century, has become a thoroughly non-politicized business.

Financial Services

In the nationalized Icelandic financial system access to loans was also politically apportioned. Financial institutions were governed by boards manned by representatives of the parties, and their managers were usually de facto politically appointed. Loans were highly valued because inflation was endemic and ate away the real value of what had to be paid back. This was unavoidably a very wasteful system, where political clout determined investment profitability and firm viability. Favorable loans were decided in a thoroughly politicized manner until liberalization was introduced in the financial sector, primarily in the 1980s and '90s. Liberalization of the financial sector was to a significant extent brought about as part of the more general liberalization of the economy following Iceland's (still limited) participation in European integration. Today, a politicized financial sector is rapidly being replaced by a professionalized one.

Social Services

Iceland never developed a welfare state to quite the same extent as the Scandinavian states. At the margins of the welfare state there were always the "little men" (so called by a leading clientelist politician) in need of particularistic services. There were families in need of special support, queues which did not move fast enough, and special favors which put the clients forever in debt to the politicians. The housing system was an important link in the services provided by the parties to their clientele and politicians cultivated their links to the agencies which provided housing support. In the 1980s the housing system became bureaucratized and the direct interference of politicians more or less disappeared. The same seems to apply to other social services, at least those provided by central government. Local government, on the other hand, has not been affected to the same extent by the decline of clientelism.

Pork-Barrel Politics

There continues to be a strong demand for legislative favors in the provinces outside the Reykjavik area. Politicians are sensitive to these pressures and try to accommodate them in the budgetary process (Kristinsson 1999). Constituency pressure has strongly influenced government expenditure in the past, and still does to some extent. But the parliamentarians' room for maneuver in this respect is not what it used to be. Although the Icelandic parliament is still an influential legislature by international standards, its role and position in Icelandic politics is declining. Its legislative initiative has been declining steadily over decades and its budgetary role has decreased in the 1990s as a result of reforms in the budgetary process. Both legislative initiative and the budgetary power of Althingi have declined largely as the result of increasing professionalism and expertise in the executive branch of government, which the legislature can no longer compete with.

Thus, the retreat of clientelism has followed many parallel paths. A number of different variables seem associated with its decline, among them globalization, regulation, professionalization, and liberalization. But none of these different factors seems to provide an adequate explanation on its own. Globalization is a global phenomenon but it has not purged the globe of clientelism. Professionalization is also a general trend but it has not had the general effect of putting an end to clientelism. If clientelism could be extinguished by regulation, this would of course simplify matters considerably. Unfortunately, regulation is scarce enough. And there is no direct or obvious relationship between the amount of government intervention and the degree of clientelism, as a superficial glance at the cases covered by this book tells us. Scandinavia, with its large public sector, is more or less free of clientelism, whereas the United States, with their liberal traditions, is not.

The problem remains of finding a convincing explanation of the decline of clientelism in Iceland. To analyze the decline of clientelism we follow the lead of Bernard Silberman (1993), who maintains that in order to understand the type of bureaucracy which developed in modern states it is necessary to start out from the position of the political leadership, and in particular the extent to which this position was characterized by uncertainty. In the Icelandic case, we maintain, the decline of clientelism and the growth of professional administration is best understood from the position of weakness of the political leaders.

Leaders and Followers

In a programmatic party, the organization is valued as a forum for democratic participation and as the ultimate source of the party platform. In a clientelist party, instead, the organization is valued principally for its instrumental value, particularly its role in winning elections. In the clientelist party organization, both leaders and followers are motivated by power and material rewards, rather than by idealism. Hence, the party leadership deals with the party organization in an instrumental way, weighing the costs and benefits of involving the organization at each turn of events. Shefter (1994: 81–86) maintains, for example, that this type of attitude characterized the relationship of Roosevelt and the Democratic leadership to the party machines in the 1930s.

In the Icelandic case, the initial effects of establishing membership organizations were mainly beneficial to the parties. While the party organizations were often highly informal – networks of individuals rather than orderly democratic institutions – they managed well what the leadership primarily needed from them, namely, to provide support during elections. The party members performed various duties during campaigns – from providing transportation to marking the electoral register with guesses on their neighbors' political sympathies – and were expected to turn up at meetings and to support their candidates. The party network was also the major source of funding for the parties, since – as membership fees were not very common – party activities (especially lotteries) and direct contributions from individuals, firms, and organizations in the network kept the parties out of financial difficulties. Characteristic of the informal nature of the parties was that membership files were often nonexistent or highly inaccurate and the members themselves would sometimes not even be sure if they were formally registered (although receiving the annual lottery ticket was a clue). Similarly, in many smaller localities, organizations of the national parties were nonexistent and local elections were contested by purely local lists.

In the 1940s, the four major parties monopolized the political agenda, and in the parliamentary election of 1949 not a single outsider was able to come forth – something which has never happened either before or after. The parties managed exceptionally well to mobilize the electorate, and in 1956 turnout reached an all-time high of 92 percent.[1] Dissenting voices were easily ignored and, apart from one minor party breakthrough in 1953, the parties were firmly in control. In the mid-twentieth century, the party organizations were stronger than they had ever been before.

The costs and benefits of membership organizations to the party leaders, as Scarrow (1994) points out, are not self-evident and need to be analyzed in each instance. In the Icelandic case, it seems, the advantages were primarily electoral. The networks were strongest in the provinces, which were especially important to the parties because of the over-representation given to them through the electoral system. Thus, in the summer of 1959, the 57 percent of the population living in pure town constituencies elected merely 44 percent of the parliamentary representatives.

Clientelism, however, was not without disadvantages. The membership organizations and clientelist networks not only placed constant demands on the time and energies of their representatives, but also increasingly became an electoral liability. Gradually, the party leadership became willing to sacrifice the clientelist organizations in favor of a looser and less costly form of organization. This process, roughly speaking, involved four major steps.

---

[1] Bearing in mind that although voting is not compulsory in Iceland, electoral participation is very high. It rose above the 70 percent mark during the 1920s, above the 80 percent mark in the 1930s, and was normally around 90 percent from the 1950s. In the 1980s and 1990s there has been a slight drop in turnout.

First Step: Changing Electoral Arithmetic

As noted before, not all sections of the electorate were equally well served by the clientelist organizations of the parties. A survey conducted in 1987 gives an indication of which sections of the electorate were most favored by the system and which were least favored by it. Following a public debate on clientelism the following question was put to a national sample of voters: "Do you agree or disagree with the contention that clientelism is justified on account of those who are at a disadvantage in dealing with the political system?" In the national sample, 26 percent supported clientelism, 38 percent were against it, while 37 percent were undecided. The proportion against clientelism among selected groups is given in Table 8.1.

Table 8.1 shows that opinions were divided on clientelism and probably indicates which groups of voters had been well served by the system and which had not. The provincial constituencies were well served by the clientelist system, as were the primary industries and the Progressive party clientele. Reykjavik, on the other hand, was not so well served, nor were the supporters of the People's Alliance, which, as we indicated before, was partially an outsider in the clientelist system. The opposition of the highly educated and the professionals is easily understood. Shefter notes at one point that "[T]he leadership of America's constituency for bureaucratic autonomy is drawn from roughly similar groups in all regions of the nation – from the professional upper middle classes and from those elements of the local nobility and business community that do not enjoy privileged access to the locally dominant party . . ." (Shefter 1994: 59). Having

Table 8.1. *Opposition to Clientelism Among Selected Groups of Icelandic Voters in 1987 (% of all respondents)*

Least opposed to clientelism (% opposed)		Most opposed to clientelism (% opposed)	
Provincial constituencies	31	Reykjavik	46
Least education	30	Most education	63
Workers in fish processing	20	Teachers	63
Fishermen	31	Specialists	60
Farmers	35	Nursing professions	47
Progressive party voters	32	People's Alliance voters	55

Source: Data from the national election study archives.

184

devoted a considerable number of years to acquire formal qualifications in order to improve their competitiveness in the labor market it is easily understood why professionals find the prospect of such qualifications being ignored less than appealing. They have a direct self-interest in maintaining formal standards of qualifications for public office (or indeed any job). Professional standards and respect for correct procedure, moreover, tend to make them skeptical of the modus operandi of clientelism.

From the point of view of clientelist organization this was a potentially harmful situation. The groups best served by the clientelist system tended to be in structural decline, whereas those most skeptical of it were gaining numerical strength. The population is becoming increasingly educated and professionalized, living in ever greater numbers in Reykjavik and its vicinity.[2] This created an electorate increasingly receptive to criticism of the clientelist system.

A change in the electoral system occurred already in the autumn of 1959, when proportional representation and a greater (although far from complete) equality in the weight of votes were introduced. The change itself was brought about by the parties which would gain the most from it, in order to increase their competitiveness for office. But apart from that, it had various unintended consequences. For one thing, it increased the electoral weight of those sections of the electorate least happy with the clientelist system. From then on, the parties had to become increasingly attentive to the sentiments in Reykjavik and its vicinity. After all, in 1959, Reykjavik alone contained 55 percent of the electorate.

Equally important, the change lowered considerably the representation threshold for insurgent parties. New parties have emerged regularly after the introduction of proportional representation, and splinter candidacies from the established parties have also become more common than before. Almost every new party since the 1970s[3] has made ethics in government an issue, thus making the practice of clientelism riskier for the older ones. While none of these parties has survived, their impact on the practice of clientelism has been considerable. They provided an opening through which dissatisfaction with clientelism could be channeled. The established

---

[2] The proportion of the electorate living in Reykjavik and the surrounding Reykjanes was 68 percent in 1999. The corresponding figure in 1959 was 55 percent and 41 percent in 1942.

[3] These include the Union of Liberals and Leftists (1971), the Social Democratic Alliance (1983), the Women's Alliance (1983), and the People's Movement (1995).

parties have therefore had to be much more careful than before of not offending the groups of voters dissatisfied with clientelism. This even played a role in the Independence party split in 1987, when a clientelist politician of great renown, Albert Gudmundsson, left his old party, partly as a consequence of an attempt by the party to enforce stricter standards. Gudmundsson quickly mobilized his personal network and within a matter of weeks managed to obtain 10.9 percent of the national vote for his new (but short-lived) party, the Citizens' party, which openly favored clientelism.

Since the 1960s, the parties have been facing an increasingly skeptical electorate. They could have tried to respond by integrating broader groups of voters into the clientelist organizations. Instead, they decided to downgrade the role of the membership organizations.

Second Step: Responding to Criticism

During the 1960s there were various signs of an undercurrent among voters against the party organizations. The term "party rule" (*flokksraedi*) was used to denote the situation where closed party caucuses could make key decisions in most realms of social activity. Since the parties had never developed particularly democratic organizations, they were rather sensitive to this kind of criticism. The parliamentary parties had always been the real decision-makers within the parties, while the general membership organizations had played a marginal role. The complaints against "party rule" actually had some basis in reality: the party power structure was highly elitist (cf. Grimsson 1976).

In an attempt to appear more open and democratic, around 1970 the parties began to change their methods of candidate selection. Instead of drafting candidate lists from within the party organizations, they adopted primaries as their main method of selection. The primaries varied in the extent to which they were open to nonmembers of the parties. In some instances they were completely open to anyone who wished to take part, although more often they were open to an undefined group of party "supporters" – anyone, of course, could claim to be a supporter. Only the People's Alliance limited participation in party primaries to party members – but even so, there was a tendency in some cases for the membership files to swell before the primaries. Many nonsupporters would vote in the primaries; some even voted in the primaries of more than one party, for example, to support a candidate from a particular locality. In a few cases, the number of voters in a party's primaries actually exceeded its votes in the subsequent elections. What the primaries did to the parties was to take away one of the major prerogatives of party membership, namely, the right to select candidates (Kristjansson 1994).

Strangely enough, the membership organizations did not resist the introduction of primaries, except perhaps in the case of the People's Alliance. The primaries were actually a welcome solution, in many cases, when there were conflicting views on the order of candidates on the party lists. They were a way of making decisions without the party elite deciding everything. The happy welcome which the primaries received by the Icelandic parties is indicative of the lack of democratic legitimacy enjoyed by the party organizations.

The primaries, however, undermined the party organizations in a significant way, affecting both the rank and file – which became little more than party fan clubs – and the party leadership in some cases. Candidates entering the primaries were dependent not so much on the goodwill of the party leadership or even the party membership but on their ability to bring out their own personal votes during the primaries. In some cases a certain amount of independence from the party leadership may in fact draw attention to candidates and enhance their chances in the primaries. This made parliamentarians, to some extent, more independent than before. In the Reykjavik primary of the Independence party in 1983, party leader Geir Hallgrimsson competed for first place with Albert Gudmundsson. Gudmundsson had a considerable personal following and commanded a strong clientelist network. He obtained first place on the party list, while Hallgrimsson ended up seventh, losing his seat in parliament and eventually the party leadership as well.

Gradually the parties adapted to having a much lower dependence on the membership organizations. They installed a generous system of public funding for political parties, which replaced the membership activities as a major source of finance. Firms, moreover, were offered tax exemptions for contributions to the political parties.[4] Campaigning techniques changed so as to make the general membership organizations more or less pointless. Election posters have to a large extent disappeared, leaflets play only a marginal role, and election meetings are much less common than they used to be and their significance is greatly reduced. The parties no longer mark the electoral register and only the Independence party still

---

[4] Other than that there was no general legislation on party finances.

keeps its representatives at polling stations to watch over the attendance of its believed supporters. The parties, as membership organizations, are withering away. Campaigns, instead, are designed on the basis of professional advice, mostly utilizing commercial advertising, and the only persons likely to come into contact with voters on behalf of the parties are the candidates themselves. In particular, every front-row candidate is expected to attend a large number of workplace meetings and to travel extensively to share with the electorate their particular versions of the political agenda. The role of the general members, on the other hand, is by now insignificant.

Step Three: The Parties Lose Control of the Political Agenda

During the 1960s, the political parties were still firmly in control of the political agenda. All the newspapers were party political and the national radio and television were supervised by a political watchdog committee which severely restricted significant attempts at independent journalism. Independent inquiry and evaluation in the media was in short supply; the news was basically partisan.

In the late 1960s the antiestablishment feelings that ran through Europe and the United States reached Iceland as well, and some attempts were made by younger politicians and journalists to challenge the stagnant public debate. Attempts by the elite to repress this only added fuel to the fire. Then, in 1975, the first really independent newspaper emerged, the *Dagbladid*, offering nonpartisan news coverage, an antiestablishment attitude, and an open forum to people of all political persuasions to raise issues which could not find expression through other channels. The paper thrived on scandal and disclosure and soon became a favorite forum for some of the crusaders against the old clientelist system.

Other media inevitably followed suit. "Investigative journalism" became the phrase of the day and gradually journalism became professionalized. A journalistic career, which previously was more or less confined by political boundaries, could now involve working on various different media. The press became less partisan in its news coverage and even the party papers would distinguish more clearly than before between their political coverage and their news coverage. A new kind of journalism emerged in the state-run radio and television, far less subservient to the political parties than before. The emergence of private radio and television in the 1980s – based on commercial considerations – further meant that the parties no longer had control of the media. By the 1990s the established party organs had all disappeared and – although the papers may still have a partisan bias – the media essentially competes on a commercial basis.

All of this was of course bad news for the clientelist type of organization. A small industry emerged thriving on the disclosure of scandal, corruption, and the questionable methods of clientelism. Voters have become much less loyal to their parties and electoral volatility has increased substantially (Hardarson 1995). Hence, continuing the practice of clientelism would have involved substantial electoral risks for the parties. The Independence party, to take an example, used to operate a strong clientelist machine in Reykjavik. In 1978 it lost control of the city for the first time since its foundation in 1929. Upon returning to power in 1982 the party was much more careful than before of the way it operated the city administration.

The changing ways of doing politics in Iceland in the 1970s and early 1980s were personified by Vilmundur Gylfason. Literally born into the Social Democratic party – he was the son of social democratic leader Gylfi Th. Gislason – he received his political education in the weakest of the party organizations. From the pages of the *Dagbladid* he started a crusade in the 1970s against the established methods of Icelandic politics. He drew his strength from the primaries and was among the first to use unconventional campaigning methods, such as workplace meetings, to reach the public. Gylfason had little patience with the rank and file of his own party and wished to introduce various organizational changes to break up the traditional organizational concepts of the parties. He maintained that the abolition of parliamentary rule in Iceland was a necessary step to block the control of parliamentarians over the administration. In the end he split from his old party and formed the Social Democratic Alliance in 1983. The new party had considerable success in its first election, obtaining 7 percent of the vote, but Gylfason felt this was insufficient to bring the established party system to its knees. He committed suicide shortly thereafter.

Step Four: Regulating the Public Sector

By the mid-1980s a considerable amount of change had taken place in the way Icelandic politics were conducted. Some old-style politicians had difficulties in catching on to the change and some were simply opposed to it. The party leaders, however, had an interest in appearing modern and reformist in the way they ran the administrative system. From the mid-1980s a series of changes were instigated concerning the regulation and control of the public sector, which together amount to the greatest changes in Iceland's administrative history since the introduction of Home Rule in 1904. The net effect of the change was to empower the public with the legal tools to effectively fight the injustice created by clientelism in the administrative system – or indeed any kind of misconduct in office.

The first phase of the change, beginning in 1987, involved the strengthening of parliamentary control of the administration. The state audit was transferred from the ministry of Finance to parliament, where it became much more effective than before. More important, the office of Parliamentary Commissioner for Administration – the ombudsman – was established that same year to hear complaints against the misuse of administrative power. The ombudsman – although without formal judicial power – quickly established his authority and has become a major channel for complaints against questionable administrative practices, reviewing several hundred cases each year (in a state with 280,000 inhabitants).

Second, Icelandic participation in the European Economic Area has created a more complex legal environment where regulatory agencies, particularly with regard to competition policy, provide an additional instance where the citizens and firms can have their cases heard. The judiciary, at the same time, has tended to take a more independent line vis-à-vis the executive and to take increasing notice of international law and agreements in its rulings. Thus, globalization adds one more weight to the scales against clientelism in Iceland.

Finally, the legal environment of the administration changed drastically in the 1990s with the passing of the Public Administration Act of 1993 and the Public Information Act of 1996. Based essentially on similar Danish legislation, both had been on the agenda for some time but were postponed because the administrative system was too primitive to cope with them. There seems no doubt that both have had an enormous impact on public administration in Iceland. In particular, the Public Administration Act has transformed the standards of what is acceptable within the public sector.

The political parties at the turn of the century operate in a manner and environment different from that in which they operated thirty years ago. Competition for votes and offices has gradually led them away from the clientelist type of organization to a new kind of relationship where, instead of patrons and clients, there are political representatives and fans of the parties. Politics has become almost entirely a spectator sport. The interesting question is whether the parties can survive the demise of clientelism. One of the parties, the Independence party, shows no significant signs of decline. Its organization is still strong on paper, although its vital signs are actually quite weak, and the party has been reformed to some extent from the heyday of clientelism. The Progressive party organization seems much weaker and probably has not been reformed to the same extent as that of the Independence party. Any revival of clientelism would most likely have to be based on either or both of these parties. The old Social Democratic party and the People's Alliance have disappeared. They entered the election of 1999 in an electoral alliance (along with the Women's Alliance) and formally merged in the spring of the year 2000. Both organizations were essentially weak – that of the Social Democrats for historic reasons, and that of the People's Alliance on account of severe internal strife throughout most of the 1990s. In fact, part of the People's Alliance broke away before unification and formed a new party, the Left Greens, which seems a likely heir to the People's Alliance traditions.

Conclusion

We started out on the basis of Shefter's theory of clientelism and found that it offered valuable insights into the reasons for the development of clientelism in Iceland. Essentially, Iceland seems to conform to Shefter's thesis that where democracy emerged before bureaucracy, political parties are likely to utilize administrative goods to build party organizations. In a democratic and programmatic mass party the rank and file organization may be valued on the basis of its intrinsic democratic value. In a clientelist party, which is less democratic and less programmatic, the organization is mostly valued for its instrumental value.

On the other hand, we found Shefter's "critical experience" thesis less useful. We have seen how, in Iceland, the assessment of the usefulness of clientelist membership organizations changed over time. Organizations were initially an electoral advantage improving the electoral fortunes of the parties and their chances of getting into office. By the 1960s, these organizations were growing increasingly unpopular and the practice of clientelism riskier than before. The risk increased in the 1970s and 1980s when the parties lost control of the media, becoming themselves agenda-takers instead of agenda-setters. The party leaders responded by downgrading the role of the organizations, first in the nomination process and later also in the general conduct of politics and electoral campaigns. At the end of the twentieth century, the decline of both clientelism and party membership organization has advanced to such a degree that a return to old-style politics seems unlikely. Although the remnants of clientelism can be found in local politics and in the way some provincial members of Althingi cultivate their constituencies, the opportunities for being useful in the same way as before are much smaller and the risks involved much greater.

The lesson, as far as Shefter's thesis is concerned, is that the fate of clientelism – like that of any political phenomenon – is not given once and for all but depends on a number of factors. We have seen that key in the Icelandic case was the position of the party leadership and the uncertainty and risks which clientelism created. Changes, both domestic and global, forced the parties to abandon the old clientelist networks. It is, perhaps, a tribute to Shefter's insight that, in Iceland, party organization itself is in danger of extinction along with clientelism.

9

Clientelism, Interests, and Democratic Representation

SIMONA PIATTONI

Particularistic Politics

Real democracies, as opposed to idealized ones, do not operate only on the basis of categorical interests represented through territorially elected representatives and through functionally selected spokespersons. The interests which are worthy of being represented and supported are not necessarily only those broad enough to claim to represent "the general interest" of society or to be harmonized, with other equally broad interests, to yield "the general interest" (see, e.g., Pizzorno 1981: 255).

Citizens often do not ask from their representatives the elaboration and implementation of political programs for the improvement of the whole society, but rather quite specific policies for the improvement of their personal lot. Workers and other categorical interests often do not ask of their associations the protection and promotion of their broad functional interests, but rather immediate advantages for their fairly narrow categories. Religious, ethnic, and language groups often do not fight for religiously tolerant, multiethnic, and multilingual societies, but for the defense of their own religious, ethnic, and language traditions. Single-issue movements may not care about the wider repercussions of the policies they favor but about the advancement of their (sometimes narrowly defined) interests. While particular interests may be more effectively promoted if couched in universalistic terms – as furthering the welfare of the whole society or as redressing the faulty implementation of universal rights – often they are simply promoted for their own sake, without much concern for competing interests or for the society-wide consequences that their promotion may engender. Hence, the inputs of politics are often, probably inherently, particularistic.

The theory of democratic government prescribes that these particular interests be recomposed into "the general interest" or, at least, into compromise solutions everyone can live with. In deeply divided polities, such compromises may take the form of carefully balanced packages of mutual concessions, with only minimal areas of joint decision-making (consociationalism). In more homogeneous countries, the interests of one broadly defined class may be assumed to represent the interests of society, but judicious self-restraint is expected in return (corporatism). In fragmented democracies, political decision-making often takes the form of ceaseless bargaining, with only minimal agreement on the rules of the game, and decisions often have the quality of horse-trading (pluralism). While the inputs of politics may be particularistic, the output is still supposed to have universal applicability. Yet this is often not the case. Although couched in general terms, policy outputs often benefit only rather selective interests.

According to Martin Shefter (1994), it is party leaders who decide whether to elicit support through broad programmatic appeals or narrow divisible benefits. In a similar vein, Daniel Verdier (1995) argues that whether interests are aggregated along class, territorial, functional, or individual lines depends on how politicians decide to allocate rents – which groups treat as their own "clienteles." Both have a supply-driven view of politics. In the short term, when the rules of the political game and most variables that can independently shape the demand are fixed, politics appears to be dictated, and society appears to be molded, by the strategies of the suppliers of representation alone. In the longer term, however, when the demand side can change – because of independent external developments, because of competitive mobilization through nonpartisan agencies, or simply because of the unintended effects of past policy decisions – politics starts to look much more like the product of the interaction of supply and demand – a sort of recursive model of successive approximations toward an equilibrium that may well never be attained. With another powerful image, social, economic, technological, and political dynamics could be seen as disparate "wheels of fortune" (see Chapter 2), whose radiuses and speeds vary and which combine into constantly changing configurations. To explain why certain modes of interest representation become possible or even dominant in given times and places, both the supply and the demand sides must be taken into account.

This is what we tried to do in this book by focusing on one such mode of interest representation and promotion, clientelism. We argued that clientelism is best seen as an exchange relation – a strategy whereby the politicians (the patrons) try to gain and maintain power by distributing divisible benefits to the voters and the voters (the clients) try to obtain selective access to state-administered goods (without much concern for, and even at the expense of, other clients) by granting their vote to the patrons. Whether or not such exchanges occur on a systematic basis depends on whether the structures of public decision-making – elected government and nonelected bureaucracy – are, respectively, interested in and available for this kind of exchange and whether the citizens have ways of obtaining access to desired goods other than entering such exchange relations.

We took as our point of departure for our historical, comparative exploration Martin Shefter's thesis which, maximally simplified, states that the relative timing of bureaucratization and democratization explains why, in some countries, patronage became an entrenched mode of political mobilization,[1] and found that only in a handful of countries can the supply side alone explain the absence of clientelism from the established repertoire of a country's mobilization strategies. To make sense of most of the other cases, we needed to consider also the demand side.

Among the countries studied in this book, only Sweden managed to forgo altogether the experience of clientelism (even though positions of authority, as Apostolis Papakostas notes in Chapter 2, have been for long the perquisite of a selective stratum of the population). Similar fates have been shared by Germany, Denmark, and Norway, which, however, have not been analyzed in this book.[2] With these exceptions, all European countries have, at some point or another, known some form of patronage and clientelism.

Three countries covered by this book – England, France, and the Netherlands – have known extended periods of patronage, but have nevertheless managed to expunge it from their repertoire of mobilization strategies or to recycle it into more acceptable – because operating at higher levels of interest aggregation – forms of (particularistic) politics:

---

[1] For a more accurate rendition of Shefter's thesis, see Chapter 1; for the full account, see Shefter (1994: 3–14, 25–36).

[2] It turned out to be impossible to include in this book a chapter covering what would have been a most interesting comparison between Germany and Austria. That two countries, in which bureaucratization preceded democratization, should have such diverging experiences with clientelism in the postwar period strongly suggests that Shefter's "critical experience" thesis (1994: 29–32) is far from foolproof.

"constituency service" (England and France) and "consociational democracy" (the Netherlands). A fourth country, Iceland, may be in the process of purging itself from widespread clientelism. In all of these cases a deeper look at the demand side proved necessary.

England is the country in which the ruling class has probably shown the greatest capacity for self-reform. The reform of "corrupt practices" has been a slow, gradual process, certainly prodded along by radical pamphletists and opposition representatives but mostly implemented by government representatives determined to equip themselves with more efficient and economical administrative structures (Chapter 3, by Frank O'Gorman). France has trodden a more tortuous path from early eighteenth-century patrimonialism to twentieth-century technocratism. In France, as shown by Carloyn Warner in Chapter 6, it has been the political costs of rent-seeking which have prompted some postwar political formations to adopt a reformist stance and to embark upon an almost messianic drive for modernization, which even ignored the demand for "constituency service" that was present in society. However, how deeply and how extensively these efforts have succeeded needs to be carefully assessed. In the case of the Netherlands, examined by Nico Randeraad and Dirk Jan Wolffram in Chapter 5, demand-side factors weighed even more heavily. The central and local ruling classes had engaged in patronage for a century as a way of keeping together an otherwise divided country, but once the independent Dutch provinces united under a common monarchy, institutional solutions were found to compose the otherwise explosive internal tensions. Institutional reforms and the reorganization of society into "pillars" had the effect of eliminating all room for patronage.[3] In Iceland the reform of clientelism seems to be pushed along even more forcefully by independent developments on the demand side. According to Gunnar Helgi Kristinsson (Chapter 8), social, economic, and technological developments are equipping the carriers of new professional skills with convincing arguments for a reform of the public administration and the system of political representation. While Iceland's overall dynamics confirm Shefter's theory of the likely formation of a "constituency for bureaucratic autonomy" under such circumstances, the smooth manner in which the transformation is taking place in Iceland

---

[3] This does not seem to apply to Switzerland, as Walston (1988) and Vitali (1996) reveal. On Austrian clientelism, see Müller (1989) and Kitschelt (2000).

indicates a certain capacity for self-reform on the part of the suppliers of political representation.[4]

For a third group of countries – Greece, Spain, and Italy – the interplay between supply and demand is absolutely crucial to understand the diffuse and systematic presence of patronage and clientelism, as well as their particular character and geographic distribution. In these countries, a widespread system of patronage was established at the dawn of political mobilization. *Caciquismo* and *trasformismo* are the terms used in Spain and Italy to denote the nineteenth-century systems of limited representation in which governmental majorities were based upon the distribution of patronage to a restricted class of local notables. What is most striking about these countries is not so much that the interests represented were socially narrow – for this was also true of other countries at similar stages of political mobilization, such as Sweden, England, and the Netherlands – as that patronage reached the ultimate receivers through chains of personal relations, rather than through membership in a social group or a local community.[5] So, while the supply side in these countries is not dramatically different from that in other countries, the demand side is.

The Greek, Spanish, and Italian peasants were considerably less empowered than their Swedish, English, and Dutch counterparts: they were poorer, less literate, and less organized. In part this has to do with the hegemonic position, in these countries, of religious organizations – the Catholic and the Orthodox churches – which did not put a premium on literacy or, for a host of different historical reasons, acted as an organizational catalyst alternative, but not opposed, to the state.[6] For the bulk of the Greek, Spanish, and Italian population the only way to protect and

---

[4] It would be interesting to speculate whether a greater exposure to international pressures and an increase in the level of education of the population is not exerting similar effects also in Ireland, a country arguably similar to Iceland in many ways. On Irish clientelism, see Higgins (1982) and Komito (1984).

[5] The term *trasformismo* was coined by a Prime Minister of the liberal Right, Francesco Crispi, who encouraged his opponents on the liberal Left to "transform" their self-serving ideological stand into a more public-regarding position and to grant their support to government. Paradoxically, the expression ended up denoting the habit of switching all too easily one's position and of granting one's support to *any* governmental majority is exchange for patronage.

[6] For example, even though in Italy Catholic associationalism was, in some areas, very vibrant, it did not become a source of political mobilization until after World War I.

promote one's interest was to strike a personal deal with (become client of) a patron.

All these countries experienced a long period of autocratic government. This is clearly not the place to engage in an analysis of the causes of Fascism: one possible reading is that it was an attempt, on the part of the ruling classes, to handle mass mobilization while avoiding sharing power with the "externally mobilized parties," as Shefter suggests (1994: 9, 53). Fascism put a halt to the exchange of votes for favors for the simple reason that there were no free elections, though exchanges of centrally distributed benefits for party membership and other services continued. What is more interesting for us is to speculate why, with the return of democracy in these countries, patronage was revived and expanded into full-blown clientelism. In line with our view of patronage and clientelism as strategies, the authors do not endorse a facile cultural-ist explanation nor do they subscribe to a developmentalist argument. They rather point, once again, to the situation on both the supply and the demand sides.

Apostolis Papakostas does not cover, in his analysis in Chapter 2, con-temporary Greece, but gives us the elements of a possible answer. He emphasizes how economic modernization and urbanization did not break family and village networks, which ended up being recomposed within Greek cities. As long as the organizational capacities of the citizens restrict them to the use of networks of friends and relatives and until state-admin-istered goods, and particularly jobs in the public administration, remain the most secure strategy for social advancement, clientelism is likely to be reproduced by the encounter of supply and demand. Georgina Blakeley, who in Chapter 4 studies Spanish political development before, during, and after Francoism, points to the weakness of the liberal democratic project enacted during the Second Republic. While the Spanish state did try to empower its citizens by granting them liberal rights and imple-menting some economic reforms, these reforms did not penetrate deep enough into the structure of Spanish society. An inherent flaw, she sug-gests, was contained in that "liberal project," which presumed to empower the citizens, so to say, only "on paper." Yet, as Jonathan Hopkin argues in Chapter 7, society evolves also independently of state action, carried along by international developments. Spanish society did modernize also during the Francoist period. With the return of democratic elections, Spaniards proved to be rather uninterested in entering the clientelist bid of the conservative parties and, rather, opted for the more ideologically oriented

Socialist party. Yet, as predicted also by Shefter, once "externally mobilized parties" have gained power, they may discover the convenience of also using patronage for power consolidation purposes. The supply of clientelism may increase and become more attractive: it is to be hoped that the demand remains low. The rather optimistic scenario drawn by Hopkin contrasts with the darker one sketched by Carolyn Warner in Chapter 5 and by Alfio Mastropaolo in Chapter 7. Italy returned to democracy under two particularly unpropitious circumstances: a still rather backward society and the cold war. The first circumstance implied that Italians, particularly in the south, mostly lacked the cognitive and organizational capacities to articulate their demand, with the exception of personal networks. The second pressured the anti-Communist parties into gaining and keeping power almost by all means, clientelism included. In Italy, the encounter of demand and supply was fateful: clientelism developed into a veritable system, engulfing also initially ideologically oriented parties, such as the Italian Socialist party. The political developments of the nineties seem to confirm Shefter's prediction (1994: 12–13) that, when the economic and political costs of clientelism become unbearable, mobilization against it may be sudden and dramatic.

The empirical material presented in this book should have shattered structural explanations of clientelism, whether culturalist or developmentalist, and invited a more open-ended view of both the "inevitable" fate of given political systems and the "pathological" nature of clientelism. For what exactly should be "pathological" about clientelism? That it gives uneven political access to citizens with different social and economic status (injustice), or that it produces decisions which benefit individuals and groups selectively (particularism)? As shown, neither trait is exclusive to clientelist political systems.

A certain degree of particularism in politics cannot be suppressed. Institutional, impersonal channels of political representation and interest promotion may not fully satisfy the citizens' need that their interests as individuals, groups, or communities be protected and promoted quite regardless of competing interests. Clientelism may act as an additional and parallel channel for the promotion of particular interests. As Ayşe Güneş-Ayata underscores, referring to Carl Landé's thesis of clientelism as addendum (Landé 1977): "institutional forms and clientelism are not only compatible but also complementary. . . . constitutional forms do not provide for all the needs of the community and its individual members. Dyadic relations provide the additional framework necessary to meet individual needs in the form of affect-laden voluntary, selective relation-ship" (Güneş-Ayata 1994: 20).

In this book, we have questioned whether these relations must necessar-ily be "affect-laden"[7] and, rather, have proposed to see them as strategic. We have presented a picture of European political development in which the promotion of particular interests is the rule, rather than the exception. Interest politics is often particularistic: it is the task of political institutions to ensure that particular interests are weighed, ordered, and aggregated. Different political systems achieve this goal differently, with important consequences in terms of the policies enacted and the values propounded.

In this chapter I engage the normative dimension of the debate on clien-telism and ask, What are the specific costs and benefits associated with this system of interest representation and promotion, compared with other systems which have received better review from political scientists (albeit not unqualified approval), such as (interest group) liberalism, corporatism, and consociationalism?[8]

What Is Wrong with Clientelism?

Clientelism can be usefully conceptualized as the lowest rung of a ladder that climbs upward according to the level at which particular interests are aggregated. This is the ladder of "interest politics" which has, at the lowest possible level, the interests of individuals and families (*clientelism*); at a higher level, those of villages and constituencies (*localism* and "*constituency service*"); at yet higher levels, those of religious or ethnic groups (*consocia-tionalism*) and functional and professional groups (*interest group liberalism* and *corporatism*), and, at the very highest level, those of the national com-munity (*nationalism*) and the international community (*internationalism*).

---

[7] Yet some such relationships seem to remain "affect-laden," indeed. *The Economist*, in com-menting on the worldwide reaction to Princess Diana's death, noted that "this week's emo-tions actually illustrate one of the monarchy's greatest strengths. That is that it focuses on human beings rather than on the more abstract world of political institutions or docu-ments" ("The Tragedy of Diana" 1997: 15).

[8] "Interest group liberalism" is the name that Theodore Lowi (1979) gave to the system of interest representation that had developed in the United States from the 1930s onward. He was critical of this system, which he considered a corruption of true liberalism. The classical reference on consociationalism is Lijphart (1968); those on corporatism are Rokkan (1966) and, in particular, Schmitter (1974). In many ways, this book seeks to "rescue" the concept of clientelism and make it into an acceptable term of the political scientific discourse, just as Schmitter (1974) did for corporatism.

Clientelism, Interests, Democratic Representation

What is the crucial difference among these well-known types of interest politics? How pliable are they to solving democracy's capital problem – arriving at a workable definition of "the general interest"? "The general interest" is a fiction which describes a compromise among particular interests that most members of a society can live with: is it true that the higher the level at which the particular interests are aggregated, the most likely the attainment of such a workable compromise?

Theorists of liberalism, corporatism, and consociationalism give a positive answer. For liberal thinkers, on the one hand, the interests that are particular to a given group are already the result of a process of internal articulation and aggregation of individual interests, and hence already reflect, at least to some degree, the search for a workable compromise. The composition of the interests of many such groups is, therefore, relatively easy. For the theorists of corporatism and consociationalism, on the other hand, the search for compromise solutions among few encompassing functional organizations or "pillars" is prompted by the need to coexist peacefully in hostile environments. For all, then, the composition of the interests of secondary associations, functional organizations, and "pillars" appears more conducive to democratic accommodation and stability than the composition of less internally aggregated interests, such as those of local communities and individuals.

Because the group members need to find a common ground for the promotion of their individual interests, they correspondingly need to shift the level of discourse. They thus learn how to think of their individual interests as particular instances of the interests of the group: in this process, the individual interests are redefined and the costs connected to upholding the group are exacted.[9] These same basic processes of interest redefinition and cost-bearing also characterize the aggregation of group

[9] The liberal theory of group formation has been criticized for failing to explain why rational individuals would want to contribute to the costs of creating and maintaining a group when they can enjoy the public goods provided by the group irrespective of their contribution (Olson 1971). Olson suggested that the problems of collective action can be solved when the group is small, and hence each member's contribution counts, or when selective benefits are attached to being members of the group and bearing the costs of its maintenance. This line of reasoning would then make clientelism into a highly rational system of interest representation from the point of view of the maximizing patron or client (cf. Warner 1997). In this section, however, I take a more benevolent stance toward liberal group theory and assume that the problems of collective action can be solved thanks to the moral rewards that individuals receive from being members of a group. For a similar approach, see Pizzorno (1981).

interests into "the general interest." Once learned at the group level, these operations are more easily performed also at the societal level. This seems to be the reason why interest group liberalism, corporatism, and consociationalism, despite their flaws, are normally considered "superior" to clientelism.

In other words, the exercise in interest aggregation which occurs within the groups has an impact both on the number and kinds of interests which get promoted at the societal level and on the attitudes and expectations of the group members. With clientelism, instead, individual interests are promoted without further elaboration and aggregation, and the level of discourse is never lifted up. What is worse, clientelism runs the risk of making a mockery of public discourse, as it often operates to "privatize" decisions, structures, and goods which are presented as public.[10] Yet clientelism has advantages of its own, which should not induce us to dismiss it as just a "pathological" form of interest representation: it is simple, it is open, and it defuses conflict.

This latter aspect is certainly the most appreciated by incumbent political leaders: the "mobilization of bias" which comes with the extension of conflict (Schattschneider 1960) spells danger for current representatives.[11] But citizens too may like a system which gives something to each without much mobilization effort. Individual cost–benefit analysis may make clientelism look convenient. The social externalities of the system may not be felt until much later. Clientelism is also simple: a vote for a benefit. Democracy, with its complicated rules of the game – which become all the more complicated the more democratic the game needs to be – may be rather impenetrable and opaque to the average citizen. It takes a certain amount of cognitive and organizational empowerment to be able to understand the rules and play successfully by them. Finally, clientelism, at least in its twentieth-century version, is a remarkably open system: it takes just one vote to become a client, and all can apply. Clearly, individuals who, thanks to their social and economic status, can put pressure on others and

---

[10] For an exhaustive list of clientelism's ills, see Landé (1961: 118). Yet clientelism comes rarely in its most naked and instrumental guise. Patrons often justify their role with reference to general principles, for example, the protection of local communities from an exploitative center, not so much to cover up their repressive rule as to set the terms of the "clientelist exchange." See Silverman (1977b), and the instances reported by Briquet (1997).

[11] This aspect is underlined also by Shefter when he argues that the incumbents prefer to collude with the opposition or buy electoral support through divisible benefits, i.e., patronage, than to engage in competitive mobilization and full-scale conflict (Shefter 1994: 6–10).

deliver whole packets of votes become "preferred clients"; however, all voters have potential access to the favors of a patron. Even the role of patron, in contemporary polities, is easily accessible to anyone: with "clientelism of the bureaucracy" what counts is service to a party and capacity as mediator rather than social and economic status, as it used to be with the "clientelism of the notables" (Tarrow 1967).

Interest group liberalism, consociationalism, and corporatism, on the contrary, can be criticized for leaving unrepresented those interests which do not fit through the dominant channels of representation. Economically and culturally disempowered members of society cannot take full advantage of interest group representation, nor can individuals whose identity is not encompassed in any of the existing "pillars" receive sufficient attention for their needs, nor again can marginal or unemployed workers find adequate protection in functional organizations.

To better see the relative pros and cons of each system, I propose to think of them as posing two types of barriers to interest representation and promotion. The first barrier acts by defining only certain interests as worthy of protection and, consequently, by leaving unrepresented all other interests: let us call this the *barrier to citizenship*. The second barrier acts by granting selective access to the goods that should come with citizenship rights: let us call this the *barrier to distribution*. To understand the relative strengths and weaknesses of the different systems of interest representation, it may be useful to create a two-dimensional space (Table 9.1), whose axes are given by these barriers, and to position in it both real-world and idealized systems of interest representation (the idealized systems are in square brackets).

It may be argued that clientelism and liberal democracy, in their idealized forms, represent two opposite forms of interest representation: the former very closed and selective and the latter very open and accessible. In terms of both citizenship – which interests are considered worthy of protection – and actual access to distribution, *ideal-typical clientelism* is a closed and selective system: oppressive rule in disguise.[12] To the contrary, *liberal democracy* is supposedly open to all citizens who feel that they bear an interest worthy of protection and promotion, and grants to all equal access to the goods that come with citizenship: both citizenship and distribution barriers are ideally extremely low.

---

[12] It could be argued that real-world systems that come close to this "negative ideal-type" are patrimonialism and nepotism.

Table 9.1. *Classification of Idealized and Real Systems of Interest Representation*

		Barriers to citizenship		
		High	Medium	Low
	High	[Clientelism]	"Continental" patronage	Clientelism
		Nepotism		Machine politics
Barriers to distribution	Medium	Patrimonialism	"English-style" patronage	
			Interest-group liberalism	
	Low	Consociationalism	Corporatism	[Liberal democracy]

Real-world situations may be rather different. We argued, in the introductory chapter, and illustrated, in Chapters 2–5, that nineteenth-century *patronage* came in different forms in different countries. While erecting everywhere medium to high barriers to citizenship – suffrage normally being conditional on the fulfillment of certain wealth and literacy requirements – nineteenth-century patronage opposed barriers of different heights, in the different countries, to access to the goods distributed through this system. Therefore, while in England and the Netherlands, access to "the spoils" was granted fairly evenly to members of given constituencies and, often, of given social classes, in Spain, Portugal, Italy, and France it was further restricted only to those who voted for a given party. While citizenship was similarly limited in most European countries, access to the goods of citizenship was granted in more or less selective ways.

Twentieth-century *clientelism* poses relatively low barriers to citizenship: it takes only a vote to be "entitled" to interest promotion. It is, however, fairly selective when it comes to access to the goods generated and distributed through this system.[13] An interesting contrast can be made with *interest group liberalism*, another real-world system of interest representation. In this case, the range of interests which are granted citizenship

---

[13] Plentiful examples are contained in Allum (1973a), Caciagli (1977), White (1980), Chubb (1982), Lyrintzis (1984), and, more recently, Farelo Lopes (1997) and Mavrogordatos (1997).

can be, de facto, rather low, as many legitimate interests are excluded for want of organizational capacity. However, once the interests have been acknowledged and promoted, everyone is entitled to the goods thus generated.

Consociationalism and *corporatism* also make for an interesting comparison. On the one hand, they pose fairly high barriers to citizenship, variously defined in terms of religion, ethnicity, language, or professional profile; on the other, they come very close to the ideal of universalism and impersonalism with regard to the access to the goods generated through the system. In this sense, they are mirror images of (real-world) clientelism.

Some will no doubt be taken aback by the treatment of clientelism as a system of interest representation (yet not Kitschelt 2000). After all, the phenomenon that strikes most people's attention and arouses their indignation is selective access to the goods to which citizens are entitled – the output of the political process. However, in order to understand why clientelism has revealed such surprising resilience, one cannot forget that it does grant everyone access to citizenship – the input of the political process. We may be led to conclude that, in some political systems, particularism on the input side of politics elicits fewer concerns than particularism (or selectivity) in the distribution of the output. What Landé predicated of postwar Philippines may apply to other political systems as well:

While skeptical of the practicality of achieving a general increase in wealth through collective action, and dubious about the possibility of achieving exact justice through the equalization of benefits, Philipinos realize that no important individual or group will accept permanent exclusion from access to benefits, and that peace within the community requires that none be permanently excluded. Inclusion is achieved not through equalizing policies but through the rotation of benefits over time. Letting other people "have their chance," like redistributive sharing, is thus seen to be essential to social harmony. (1961: 115)

While it is arguable that each real-world system of interest representation has its own strengths and weaknesses, it cannot be argued that these systems are equivalent. In particular, we cannot ignore that clientelism provides only very weak bases for the attainment of any workable definition of "the general interest" and that tends to generate economic and political externalities which may accumulate with devastating effects. It is probably for this reason that clientelism is an illegitimate system of interest representation, which draws from the rules that it breaks and the institutions that it undermines the life-line for its subsistence. For this very reason, clientelism is also unstable, showing a tendency to evolve into something else. At one end, clientelism can degenerate into corruption; at the other end, clientelism can also sublimate into more aggregated forms of interest representation (Piattoni 1998). Evidence of both kinds of transformations can be found in Chapters 6–8.

The above discussion of the normative implications of clientelism for democratic representation alerts us to the different normative status of several political phenomena that are commonly denoted as "clientelism." It should be now clear that the atomizing, exploitative type of clientelism that we know from traditional societies is largely disappearing in Western Europe and that new kinds of clientelist exchanges have set in. The approach to clientelism as strategy allowed us to make sense of variants of clientelism which operate personally, through dyadic chains, as well as of variants which operate impersonally, often involving entire groups.

One last point needs to be made in this regard. In some countries, the promotion of the narrow interests of a given constituency or corporate group, without regard for or even at the expense of the interests of other constituencies and groups, is considered not pathological but, rather, a normal state of affairs.[14] In other countries, instead, the promotion of the narrow interests of local communities and corporate groups is considered as pathological as the selective promotion of individual interests.

Attention to political development, once again, may help us understand why some countries are more sensitive to barriers to citizenship while others are more concerned with selectivity in distribution. Political development leaves a trace not only in the political institutions – the specific arrangements for the formation and the implementation of public decisions – but also in the norms and values that are embodied in these institutions.

Back to Political Culture?

Several chapters in this volume raised the question of whether the ideas and values which make up a country's political culture do not by any chance have an impact on the diffusion and forms of particularistic politics that

---

[14] It is enlightening to read the examples from Britain and Switzerland reported by Walston (1988).

we find in each country. The approach to clientelism as strategy discourages acknowledging political culture as having a direct and unmediated impact on the systems of interest representation. It rather leads to emphasizing the influence of the contextual circumstances in which actors choose their strategies. In this view, norms and values are subject to multiple interpretations and do not represent unequivocal scripts for action. Actors are seen as capable of defining and manipulating their own interests in creative ways. In the assessment of the situation and in the formulation of their strategies, actors are certainly guided by ideas and values, but the ways in which cognitive templates and normative considerations orient action are highly contingent and, ultimately, understandable only ex post. It is for this reason that, in explaining macro-phenomena, we have put an emphasis on the contextual circumstances, while allotting to micro-level strategic decisions the power to supersede and alter these circumstances.

There is one way, however, in which culture – ideas and values – have a systematic impact on individual choices and thus become part of the context which influences choice. While not exerting a determining impact, the ideas embedded in the existing institutions and the values expressed by their activation send powerful messages which influence the assessment of the situation on the part of the actors and inspire their strategies. I discuss here one such set of ideas and values which plays an important role in shaping actors' choices in several countries: ideas about the legitimate source of political authority and judgments about which interests must be considered "particularistic" and which ones can be considered "universalistic."

Without presuming to engage a debate for which different analytical tools would be needed, I propose here to use once more historical and comparative evidence from European political development to put forth a hypothesis about the impact that the systems of local administration have had on the prevailing notions of the legitimate source of political authority and on the assessment of which interests are worthy of promotion and which are not. Following Thomas Ertman (1997), I interpret statebuilding as a process through which public institutions for the extraction of resources for state use were created by granting particular groups the right to make a profit from this activity (rent-seeking). Two were the dominant strategies and two the outcomes: the construction of a proto-bureaucracy and the establishment of patrimonial institutions. While proving to exert unexpectedly long-term consequences, it was not the existence of bureaucratic or patrimonial institutions per se which appears to have had the most durable impact on future developments (Ertman 1997: 322). Rather, the presence of traditions of local self-government proved the key factor in both the construction of functioning bureaucracies and the later reform of patrimonial institutions. Countries with a tradition of political local representation were more successful than countries with a tradition of administrative local representation in building, eventually, a modern bureaucracy.

... constitutionalist (power-sharing) regimes like those found in Britain and Sweden would seem to have an advantage over their monocratic counterparts with regard to the construction of modern bureaucracies. As these two European cases suggest, such regimes are capable not only of building non-proprietary administrations under favorable circumstances (Sweden), but are also able to eliminate patrimonial practices already in place (England). (Ertman 1997: 323)

Absolutist regimes can also succeed in upholding a bureaucratic system without compromising with rent-seeking groups, as the German case shows. However, "under monocratic rule a lasting defense against patrimonialist tendencies depends almost entirely on the degree of vigilance and the quality of supervision exercised by the executive, a condition subject to a high degree of contingency in such a system" (Ertman 1997: 323) – and to obvious democratic shortcomings, one may add.

What, then, explains the rise of bureaucratic constitutionalism? Ertman points to the organization of local government during the early period following state formation.

As the patrimonialist fate of Hungary and Poland illustrates, the mere presence of participatory government is in itself not enough to ensure the triumph of bureaucratic constitutionalism. It is only the combination of participatory local government with a strong center equipped with independent capacities of rule that, the British case implies, can assure such an outcome. This is so because only a strong center is capable of intervening to prevent the oligarchization of local government by the community's most powerful elements. (Ertman 1997: 324)

Ertman thus offers a convincing account of how given state structures acted as constraints on particularistic deals or as stimulators of universal practices; in other words, he gives us the "objective" aspect of the supply side. The ideas and values that were embedded in these structures, however, operated also as subjective bounds.

In the absence of traditions of local self-government, the citizens of many absolutist regimes came to conceive the absolutist monarch and the central government as the only source of legitimate authority. Even though exemptions and privileges were granted to local communities and corporate groups to regulate themselves – the very essence of patrimonial administration – these were centrally determined "exceptions." While, in all European countries, absolutism later gave way to constitutionalism and democratic governments replaced the will of the monarch as legitimate source of authority, individual-, group-, and community-level particularism remained, in these countries, delegitimized. Hence, structurally as well as cognitively and normatively, the citizens of these countries (France, Italy, Spain, and Portugal) could not turn to any source of legitimate authority other than that of the central, national government for the promotion of their own interests. The articulation of interests at intermediate levels between the national community and the individual and her family has a particularly difficult existence in these countries. Whenever local or corporate interests are acknowledged as legitimate levels of interest articulation, this is still perceived as an "exception" granted from above than a right springing from below.

In those countries, instead, where local self-government has a long and honorable tradition, other levels of interest articulation, local as well as corporate, are acknowledged as legitimate sources of authority on a par with the central government. Indeed, it is this latter which is considered legitimate only insofar as it acknowledges and respects the local and corporate sources of authority. In these countries, such as Britain, Sweden, the Netherlands, and Switzerland, other levels of interest articulation, for example, the local and the corporate, are not only structurally available but also cognitively and normatively legitimate. The citizens of these countries, then, are cognitively and normatively free to articulate their interests at these intermediate levels and do not perceive the systems of interest representation that aggregate interests at this level as infringements of universalistic principles.

Lest this, too, should read as a deterministic account of how ideas and values are distilled through the course of time and come to exert a limiting influence on actors' choices, let us remember that ideas and values keep changing and are subjected to the same type of strategic manipulation that has also the power to shape institutional and structural circumstances. Cultural and normative traditions can be kept alive or allowed to fall into oblivion. Levels of interest aggregation can be legitimated by "rediscovering" past traditions as well as delegitimized by pointing to fateful events.[15] While being powerful pointers for action, values and ideas in no way constrain strategic choice.[16]

Globalization, European Integration, and Particularistic Politics

Particularism can manifest itself in several guises and serve different goals: its variation in kind and intensity in times of state-building and mass politicization has occupied the body of this book. In this closing section, I suggest that we may be facing a new upsurge of particularism.

It is possible to hypothesize that, while a certain degree of particularism is always present, it becomes stronger in times of transition. When the institutional landscape becomes more uncertain and a gap opens between the level at which decisions are felt and the level at which decisions are legitimately made, citizens may turn in greater numbers to particularistic channels. Rather than considering particularism as a trait of modernizing societies alone – as the culturalist-developmentalist approach would have us believe – I suggest that we might consider it as a permanent trait of societies, which becomes more intense in times of transition: for example, but not only, the transition to modernity.

Patronage may have been the shape that particularism took during the period of state formation and *clientelism* may have been the shape of particularism in times of mass mobilization. In some countries, these forms of particularism were successfully recycled into systems of interest representation which granted differential interest promotion and protection as citizenship rights: for example, *constituency service*, *consociationalism*, and *corporatism*. A certain degree of particularism is, therefore, to be expected in all societies at all times.

---

[15] Taking inspiration from Hopkin and Mastropaolo's discussion (Chapter 7) of how Italian postwar DC leaders decided to disallow the regional level as one of the levels at which interests could be legitimately aggregated while the leftist parties attempted the opposite operation in an effort to gain a legitimate level of interest aggregation in competition with the governmental parties, one could further speculate that Italian citizens are truly "starved" for levels of legitimate interest aggregation as even the national community and the corporate interests have been delegitimized by their use under Fascism. Italians were thus left with little else than the individual and her family: fertile ground, indeed, for clientelism. More recently, though, things have started to change again, and in Italy as well as in Spain and France, the regional level is acquiring growing legitimacy, as documented by Keating (1998).

[16] For an inspiring discussion of how individuals can manipulate their preferences, see March (1978).

In times of transition, when objectively as well as subjectively the confidence in the capacity of political institutions to protect and promote individual and collective interests decreases, individuals may prefer to turn to real persons who, for one reason or another, manage to command such confidence. Hence, *particularism* – the demand for the protection and promotion of particular interests and values – can become associated with *personalism* – the delivery of protection and promotion on the part of individual politicians.

Globalization, by rendering national institutions relatively powerless to steer economic transformations that have a clear impact on citizens' lives or even simply to protect them against the negative impact of such transformations, is shaking the citizens' confidence in national institutions. A rift is thus opened in the citizen–institution relationship at the national level that cannot be quickly and simply recomposed.

European integration, in turn, contributes to widening this rift in two ways. First, given the pro-liberal bent of much European politics, governments are encouraged to take a hands-off stand toward many social and economic issues, thus adding to their image of powerlessness – be it forced by external events or freely chosen. Second, the process of European integration entails creating additional levels of institutions which interact with existing national institutions in unprecedented ways. While national and European institutions slowly adapt to one another, individuals can more easily travel across the interstices thus created and shape the new institutions in their making. The space for personalistic politics is thus objectively enlarged.

It cannot be excluded then that Europe may be entering a phase of momentous transformations, comparable to those which surrounded state-building and mass political mobilization. While then people's allegiance had to be redirected from the local communities to the emerging state-building centers, we may now be witnessing the beginnings of a new reconfiguration whereby people's allegiance may begin to be shifting again in unknown directions. Like drops of quicksilver broken up by a sudden shock will tend to recompose, however probably in different lumps than the original ones, so will the interests and allegiances of European citizens recompose around new structures of political representation and interest promotion. And as the surface on which quicksilver lands will largely determine the shape of the new lumps, so will the historical and institutional traditions of each country determine the new legitimate channels that will emerge. In the meantime, old forms of interest representation may be granted a new lease on life and traditional forms of particularism may become widespread again.

The objective space for particularism which is opening up under the double impact of globalization and European integration, then, will be filled differently depending on the historical and institutional legacy of each country. Some institutional settings – those characterized by a tradition of local self-government and a notion of legitimate power as stemming from the "common wealth" – may be able to fill the gap by intensifying the "service" that representatives give their constituencies. Constituency service, in these settings, has a long and legitimate tradition which may be conveniently revived in times of transition. Other institutional settings – those with a tradition of centralization and a notion of legitimate power as stemming from the absolute sovereign – will instead probably witness a resurgence of personalistic politics (cf. Theobold 1992). Clientelism in these settings has long functioned as a counterbalance to rigid and often clogged institutional channels.

That old patterns may be revived is what Güneş-Ayata also seems to refer to when she writes about a strange convergence between pre- and postmodernism: "Although in principle postmodern forms of participation are vastly different from their premodern counterparts, both stand in sharp contrast to modern institutional forms. Both search for flexible solutions oriented towards individual needs, taking private concerns into consideration and integrating everyday concerns as public issues" (Güneş-Ayata 1994: 26).

Bibliography

Abers, Rebecca (1998). "From Clientelism to Cooperation: Local Government, Participatory Policy, and Civic Organizations in Porto Alegre, Brazil." *Politics and Society* 26, no. 4: 511–537.

Ahrne, Göran (1989). *Byråkratin och statens inre gränser*. Stockholm: Rabén & Sjögren.

Ahrne, Göran (1990). *Agency and Organization*. London: Sage.

Ahrne, Göran (1994). *Social Organizations*. London: Sage.

Ahrne, Göran, and Apostolis Papakostas (1994). "In the Thick of Organizations." In Göran Ahrne, *Social Organizations*. London: Sage.

Allara, Giovanni (1989). "Le istituzioni dello stato: Parlamento, governo, elezioni nell'Italia del secondo dopoguerra." In *Storia della Democrazia Cristiana*, vol. 5: *Dal delitto Moro alla Segreteria Forlani, 1978–1989*, edited by Franceso Malgeri, pp. 371–478. Roma: Cinque Lune.

Allum, Percy A. (1973a). *Politics and Society in Post-War Naples*. Cambridge: Cambridge University Press.

Allum, Percy A. (1973b). *Italy: Republic without a Government?* New York: Norton.

Amato, Giuliano (1974). "Introduzione." In Giuliano Amato, ed., *Il governo dell'industria in Italia*. Bologna: Il Mulino.

Aminzade, Ronald (1992). "Historical Sociology and Time." *Sociological Methods and Research* 20, no. 4: 456–480.

Amodia, José (1990). "Taxonomía e inestabilidad del sistema de partidos en España." *Association of Contemporary Iberian Studies* 3, no. 1: 39–48.

Aragon, Charles d' (1958). "Le village et les pouvoirs." In Jacques Fauvet and Henri Mendras, eds., *Les paysans et la politique dans la France contemporaine*, pp. 487–516. Paris: Armand Colin.

Arango, Ramon E. (1978). *The Spanish Political System: Franco's Legacy*. Boulder: Westview Press.

Armstrong, John (1973). *The European Administrative Elite*. Princeton: Princeton University Press, 1973.

Arnason, Ornolfur (1993). *Jarnkarlinn. Matthias Bjarnason raedir um aevi sina og vidhorf*. Reykjavik: Skjaldborg.

Artola, Miguel (1991). *Partidos y Programas Politicos, 1808–1936*, vol. 1. 2ⁿᵈ ed. Madrid: Alianza Editorial.

Balfour, Sebastian (1989). *Dictatorship, Workers, and the City: Labour in Greater Barcelona since 1939*. Oxford: Clarendon Press.

Banfield, Edward (1958). *The Moral Basis of a Backward Society*. New York: The Free Press.

Barnes, Samuel H., et al. (1985). "The Development of Partisanship in New Democracies: The case of Spain." *American Journal of Political Science* 29, no. 4: 695–720.

Barnes, Samuel H., et al. (1986). "Volatile Parties and Stable Voters in Spain." *Government and Opposition* 21, no. 1: 56–75.

Bazin, François (1981). "Les députés MRP élus les 21 octobre 1945, 2 juin et 10 novembre 1946: Itinéraire politique d'une génération catholique," vols. 1 and 2. Ph.D. thesis. Paris: Institut d'Études Politiques.

Beltrán, Miguel (1996). "La administración pública." In Javier Tussell et al., eds., *España entre dos siglos*, pp. 265–294. Madrid: Alianza.

Bendix, Reinhard ([1964], 1996). *Nation-Building and Citizenship*. London: Transaction Publishers.

Benvenuti, F. (1974). "Evoluzione della disciplina del pubblico impiego." In Sabino Cassese ed., *L'amministrazione pubblica in Italia*, pp. 109–122. Bologna: Il Mulino.

Berstein, Serge (1980/82). *Histoire du Parti Radical*, vols. 1 and 2. Paris: Presses de la Fondation Nationale des Sciences Politiques.

Bevilacqua, Piero (1985). "Uomini, terre, economie." In Piero Bevilacqua and Augusto Placanica, eds., *La Calabria*, pp. 115–362. Torino: Eiunadi.

Binney, John E. D. (1958). *British Public Finance and Administration, 1774–1792*. Oxford: Clarendon Press.

Black, Jeremy, ed. (1984). *Britain in the Age of Walpole*. London: Macmillan.

Blok, Anton (1969). "Variations in Patronage." *Sociologische Gids* 16, no. 6: 365–378.

Blok, Anton (1974). *The Mafia in a Sicilian Village, 1860–1960: A Study of Violent Peasant Entrepreneurs*. Cambridge: Polity Press.

Blomqvist, Hans (1992). "The Soft State: Making Policy in Different Context." In Douglas E. Ashford, ed., *History and Context in Comparative Public Policy*, pp. 117–150. Pittsburgh: Pittsburgh University Press.

Boissevain, Jemery (1966). "Patronage in Sicily." *Man* 1, no. 1: 18–33.

Boissevain, Jeremy (1974). *Friends of Friends: Networks, Manipulators and Coalitions*. Oxford: Blackwell.

Bonini, Francesco (1987). "L'Histoire d'une Institution Coutumière: Le Secretariat Général du Gouvernement de la République Française (1934–1986)." Ph.D. thesis. Paris: Institut d'Études Politiques.

Bragaglio, Claudio (1981). "Riflessioni sul blocco politico-sociale a Brescia." In Roberto Chiarini, ed., *Brescia negli anni della Ricostruzione 1945–1949*, pp. 149–184. Brescia: Micheletti.

Brewer, John (1989). *The Sinews of Power: War, Money and the English State, 1688–1783*. London: Unwin Hyman.

Brewer, John (1994). "The Eighteenth Century British State." In Lawrence Stone, ed., *An Imperial State at War: Britain from 1689 to 1815*, pp. 52–71. London: Routledge.

Bibliography

Briquet, Jean-Louis (1995). "Les pratiques politiques 'officieuses': Clientélisme et dualisme politique en Corse et en Italie du Sud." *Genèses* 20 (September): 73–94.

Briquet, Jean-Louis (1997). "Potere dei notabili e legittimazione: Clientelismo e politica in Corsica durante la Terza Repubblica (1871–1914)." *Quaderni Storici* 32, no. 94 (April): pp. 121–154.

Briquet, Jean-Louis, and Frédéric Sawicki, eds. (1998). *Le clientélisme politique dans les sociétés contemporaines*. Paris: Presses Universitaires de France.

Burn, William L. (1964). *The Age of Equipoise: A Study of the Mid-Victorian Generation*. New York: Norton.

Caciagli, Mario (1996). *Clientelismo, corrupción y criminalidad organizada: Evidencias empíricas y propuestas teóricas a partir de los casos italianos*. Madrid: Centro de Estudios Constitucionales.

Caciagli, Mario, et al. (1977). *Democrazia Cristiana e potere nel Mezzogiorno: Il sistema democristiano a Catania*. Firenze: Guaraldi.

Calamandrei, Piero, ed. (1950). "Calabria." *Il Ponte* 6, nos. 9–10.

Calandria, Piero (1978). *Storia dell'amministrazione pubblica in Italia*. Bologna: Il Mulino.

Calice, Nino (1976). *Partiti e ricostruzione nel Mezzogiorno. La Basilicata nel dopoguerra*. Bari: De Donato.

Cappelletti, Luciano (1963). "Local Government in Italy." *Public Administration* 41 (Winter): 262–263.

Cappelletti, Luciano (1974). "Caratteristiche strutturali dei quadri direttivi dell'amministrazione." In Sabino Cassese, ed., *L'amministrazione pubblica in Italia*, pp. 123–146. Bologna: Il Mulino.

Cappelli, Vittorio (1985). "Politica e politici." In Piero Bevilacqua and Augusto Placanica, eds., *La Calabria*, pp. 495–584. Torino: Eiunadi.

Carlsson, Sten (1953). *Lantmannapolitiken och industrialismen*. Stockholm: Lantbruksförbundets tidskriftsaktiebolag.

Caron, François (1979). *An Economic History of Modern France*. Translated by Barbara Bray. New York: Columbia University Press.

Carr, Raymond (1980). *Modern Spain, 1875–1980*. Oxford: Oxford University Press.

Carr, Raymond (1982). *Spain, 1808–1975*. 2nd ed. Oxford: Clarendon Press.

Cassese, Sabino (1983). *Il sistema amministrativo italiano*. Bologna: Il Mulino.

Catherine, Robert (1955). "Les Fonctionnaires." In Maurice Duverger, ed., *Partis politiques et classes sociales en France*, pp. 109–154. Paris: Armand Colin.

Cazorla, José (1992). *Del clientelismo tradicional al clientelismo de partido: Evolución y características*. Working Paper no. 55. Barcelona: Institut de Ciències Polítiques i Socials.

Cazorla, José (1994). *El clientelismo de partido en España ante la opinión pública: El medio rural, la administración y las empresas*. Working Paper no. 86. Barcelona: Institut de Ciències Polítiques i Socials.

Cazorla, José (1995). "El clientelismo de partido en la España de hoy: Una disfunción de la democrazia." *Revista de Estudios Políticos*, no. 87: 35–51.

Cazorla, José, Miguel Jerez, and Juan Montabes (1997). "Analysis of Political Clientelism." Paper prepared for Workshop on "Clientelist Politics and Interest Intermediation in Southern Europe," ECPR Joint Sessions, Bern.

Cazzola, Franco (1976). "I pilastri del regime: Gli Enti pubblici di sicurezza sociale." *Rassegna Italiana di Sociologia* 17, no. 3: 421–447.

Chagnollaud, Dominique (1991). *Le premier des ordres: Les hauts fonctionnaires XVIIIe–XXe siècle.* Paris: Fayard.

Chapman, Brian (1955). *L'administration Locale en France.* Paris: Armand Colin.

Charlot, Jean (1983). *Le Gaullisme d'opposition, 1946–1958.* Paris: Fayard.

Chester, Norman (1981). *The English Administrative System, 1780–1870.* Oxford: Clarendon Press.

Chiarini, Roberto (1985). "Dalla mobilitazione industriale alla riconversione produttiva: Relazioni sociali e dinamiche politiche a Brescia nel 1919." In Paolo Corsini and Gianfranco Porta, eds., *Aspetti della società bresciana tra le due guerre,* pp. 3–34. Brescia: Micheletti.

Christie, Ian R. (1970). "British Newspapers in the Later Georgian Age." In Ian R. Christie, *Myth and Reality in Eighteenth Century British Politics, and Other Papers.* London: Macmillan.

Chubb, Judith (1982). *Patronage, Power and Poverty in Southern Italy.* Cambridge: Cambridge University Press.

Cingari, Gaetano (1988). *Reggio Calabria.* Bari: Laterza.

Ciranna, Giuseppe (1958). "Partiti ed elezioni in Basilicata nel secondo dopoguerra (III)." *Nord e Sud* 5, no. 41 (April): 80–110.

Clapham, Christopher, ed. (1982). *Private Patronage and Public Power: Political Clientelism in the Modern State.* New York: St. Martin's Press.

Clark, J. C. D. (1985). *English Society, 1688–1832: Ideology, Social Structure and Political Practice during the Ancien Regime.* Cambridge: Cambridge University Press.

Clark, Martin (1984). *Modern Italy, 1871–1982.* New York: Longman.

Cohen, Emmeline W. (1941). *The Growth of the British Civil Service, 1780–1939.* London: Allen & Unwin.

Cohen, Stephen S., and Peter A. Gourevitch, eds. (1982). *France in the Troubled World Economy.* London: Butterworth Scientific.

Crispi, Francesco (n.d.). *Scritti e discorsi politici, 1849–1890.* 2nd ed. Torino: Roux e Viarengo.

Daalder, Hans (1981). "Consociationalism, Center and Periphery in the Netherlands." In P. Torsvik, ed., *Mobilization, Center-Periphery Structures and Nation-Building: A Volume in Commemoration of Stein Rokkan,* pp. 181–240. Bergen: Universitetsforlaget.

De Jong, Jacob J. (1985). *Met goed fatsoen: De elite in een Hollandse stad 1700–1780.* Dieren: De Bataafsche Leeuw.

De Juana, Jesus, Julio de Prada, and Raúl Soutela (1995). "Transición política y élites políticas: El nacimiento de Coalición Galega en Ourense." In Javier Tusell et al., eds., *Historia de la transición y consolidación democrática en España 1975–86,* vol. 1, pp. 475–496. Madrid: UNED/UAM.

Bibliography

De Riquer i Permanyer, Borja (1995). "Social and Economic Change in a Climate of Political Immobilism." In Helen Graham and Jo Labanyi, eds., *Spanish Cultural Studies: An Introduction*, pp. 259–271. Oxford: Oxford University Press.

de Tarr, Francis (1961). *The French Radical Party*. London: Oxford University Press.

De Vries, Jan, and Ad van der Woude (1995). *Nederland 1500–1815: De eerste ronde van moderne economische groei*. Amsterdam: Balans.

Delgado Sotillos, Irene (1997). *El comportamiento electoral municipal español, 1979–1995*. Madrid: Centro de Investigaciones Sociológicas.

Della Porta, Donatella, and Yves Mény, eds. (1997). *Democracy and Corruption in Europe*. London: Pinter.

Demarchi, Franco (1967). "Espansione e tendenze della burocrazia pubblica." *Rassegna Italiana di Sociologia* 8, no. 3 (July/Sept.): 383–411.

Demertzis, Nikos (1994). "Η επιλεκτική παράδοση της Ελληνικής πολιτικής κουλτούρας σήμερα." In Demertzis, ed., *Η Ελληνική πολιτική κουλτούρα σήμερα*. Athens: Odysseas.

Diamandouros, Nikiforos (1984). "Η εγκαθίδρυση του κοινοβουλευτισμού στην Ελλάδα και η λειτουργία του κατά τον 19ο αιώνα." In D. G. Tsaousis, ed., *Όψεις της Ελληνικής κοινωνίας του 19ου αιώνα*. Athens: Estia.

Diamant, Alfred (1957). "The French Administrative System: The Republic Passes but the Administration Remains." In William J. Siffin, ed., *Toward the Comparative Study of Public Administration*, pp. 182–218. Bloomington: Indiana University Press.

Díaz Nosty, Bernardo (1977). *Radiografía de las nuevas Cortes*. Madrid: Sedmay.

Dijksterhuis, Roelof (1984). *Spoorwegtracering en stedebouw in Nederland: Historische analyze van een wisselwerking, de eerste eeuw: 1840–1940*. N.P.: Proefschrift Technische Hogeschool Delft.

Duijvendak, Maarten G. J. (1990). *Rooms, rijk of regentesk: Elitevorming en machtsverhoudingen in oostelijk Noord-Brabant, circa 1810–1914*. 's-Hertogenbosch: Het Noordbrabants Genootschap.

Eggertsson, Dagur (1999). *Steingrimur Hermannsson. Aevisaga II*. Reykjavik Vaka-Helgafell.

Ehrmann, Henry (1957). *Organized Business in France*. Princeton: Princeton University Press.

Einaudi, Mario, Maurice Byé, and Ernesto Rossi (1955). *Nationalization in France and Italy*. Ithaca: Cornell University Press.

Eisenstadt, Shmuel, and René Lemarchand, eds. (1981). *Political Clientelism, Patronage and Development*. Beverly Hills, Calif.: Sage.

Eisenstadt, Shmuel, and Luis Roniger (1980). "Patron-Client Relations as a Model of Structuring Social Exchanges." *Comparative Studies in Society and History* 22, no. 1: 42–77.

Eisenstadt, Shmuel, and Luis Roniger (1984). *Patrons, Clients and Friends*. Cambridge: Cambridge University Press.

Emiliani, Vittorio (1975). *L'Italia mangiata*. Torino: Einaudi.

Englund, Peter (1993). "Om klienter och deras patroner." In Stellan Dahlgren, Anders Florén, and Åsa Karlsson, eds., *Makt och vardag*, pp. 86–97. Stockholm: Atlantis.

Ertman, Thomas (1997). *Birth of the Leviathan: Building States and Regimes in Medieval and Early Modern Europe*. Cambridge: Cambridge University Press.

Esping-Andersen, Gösta (1990). *Three Worlds of Welfare Capitalism*. Cambridge: Polity.

Evans, Eric J. (1983). *The Forging of the Modern State: Early Industrial Britain, 1783–1870*. London: Longman.

Falivena, Aldo (1957). "Un confronto col Delta Padano." *Nord e Sud* 4, no. 31 (July): 109–128.

Fantozzi, Pietro (1993). *Politica, clientela e regolazione sociale: Il Mezzogiorno nella questione politica italiana*. Rubbettino: Soveria Mannelli.

Farelo Lopes, Fernando (1997). "Partisanship and Political Clientelism in Portugal (1983–1993)." *South European Politics and Society* 2, no. 3: 27–51.

Fayol, André (1952). "L'Inspection Generales des Finances." In La Documentation Française, *L'organisation gouvernementale, administrative et judiciaire de la France*, pp. 167–168. Paris: La Documentation Française.

Finer, Samuel E. (1952). "Patronage and the Public Service: Jeffersonian Democracy and the British Tradition." *Public Administration* 30 (Winter): 329–360.

Fiorina, Morris P. (1981). *Retrospective Voting in American National Elections*. New Haven: Yale University Press.

Foord, Archibald S. (1947). "The Waning of the Influence of the Crown." *English Historical Review* 62: 484–507.

Fox, Jonathan (1994). "The Difficult Transition from Clientelism to Citizenship: Lessons from Mexico." *World Politics* 46, no. 2: 151–184.

Franchetti, Leopoldo (1992). *Condizioni politiche e amministrative della Sicilia*. Rome: Meridiana.

Frohnert, Pär (1993). *Kronans skatter och bondens bröd*. Stockholm: Nerenius och Santérus förlag.

Fuks-Mansfeld, Renate G. (1995). "Moeizame aanpassing (1840–1870)." In Johan C. H. Blom, Renate G. Fuks-Mansfeld, and Ivo Schoeffer, eds., *Geschiedenis van de joden in Nederland*, pp. 207–246. Amsterdam: Balans.

Gaïti, Brigitte (1987). "Les 'Modernisateurs' dans l'administration d'après guerre: Histoire de la formation d'un groupe." Unpublished Mémoire DEA, Cycle Superieur d'Histoire du XXᵉ Siècle, Institut d'Études Politiques de Paris.

Galant, Henry C. (1955). *Histoire politique de la sécurité sociale française, 1945–1952*. Paris: Armand Colin.

Galli, Giorgio, and Alfonso Prandi (1970). *Patterns of Political Participation in Italy*. New Haven: Yale University Press.

Gambetta, Diego (1993). *The Sicilian Mafia: The Business of Private Protection*. Cambridge: Harvard University Press.

Gans, Herbert J. ([1962], 1982). *The Urban Villagers*. New York: The Free Press.

Gash, Norman (1979). *Aristocracy and People: Britain 1815–1865*. London: Arnold.

Gash, Norman (1986). *Pillars of Government and Other Essays on State and Society, circa 1770–1880*. London: Macmillan.

Gellner, Ernst, and James Waterbury, eds. (1977). *Patrons and Clients in Mediterranean Societies*. London: Duckworth.

Bibliography

Gerth, H. H., and C. Wright Mills, eds. (1948). *From Max Weber*. London: Routledge, Kegan & Paul.

Gillespie, Richard (1989). *The Spanish Socialist Party: A History of Factionalism*. Oxford: Clarendon Press.

Gillespie, Richard (1994). "The Resurgence of Factionalism in the Spanish Socialist Workers' Party." In David S. Bell and Eric Shaw, eds., *Conflict and Cohesion in Western European Social Democratic Parties*, pp. 50–69. London: Pinter.

Gilson, Etienne (1948). *Notre démocratie*. Paris: Société d'Editions Républicains Populaires.

Ginsborg, Paul (1989). *Storia d'Italia dal dopoguerra a oggi: Società e politica, 1943–1988*. Torino: Einaudi.

González Calbet, Teresa (1986). "La Destrucción del Sistema Político de la Restauración: El Golpe de Septiembre de 1923." In José L. García Delgado, ed., *La crisis de la restauración: España entre la primera guerra mundial y la Segunda República*. Madrid: Siglo Veintiuno Editores.

González Encinar, José J. (1982). *Galicia: Sistema de partidos y comportamiento electoral 1976–81*. Madrid: Akal Editor.

Graziano, Luigi (1976). "A Conceptual Framework for the Study of Clientelistic Behavior." *European Journal or Political Research* 4: 149–174.

Graziano, Luigi (1980). *Clientelismo e sistema politico: Il caso dell'Italia*. Milano: Angeli.

Gribaudi, Gabriella, and Luigi Musella (1998). "Il processo alla clientela: Il caso di Napoli nelle inchieste giudiziarie degli anni Novanta." *Quaderni Storici* 33, no. 1: 115–142.

Grimsson, Olafur R. (1976). "The Icelandic Power Structure 1800–2000." *Scandinavian Political Studies* 11: 9–33.

Grugel, Jean, and Tim Rees (1997). *Franco's Spain*. London: Arnold.

Güneş-Ayata, Ayşe (1994). "Clientelism: Pre-modern, Modern, Post-modern." In Luis Roniger and Ayşe Güneş-Ayata, eds., *Democracy, Clientelism and Civil Society*, pp. 19–28. Boulder, Colo.: Lynne Rienner.

Gunther, Richard (1980). *Public Policy in a No-Party State: Spanish Planning and Budgeting in the Twilight of the Franquist Era*. Berkeley: University of California Press.

Gunther, Richard (1991). *The Dynamics of Electoral Competition in a Modern Society: Models of Spanish Voting Behavior, 1979 and 1982*. Barcelona: ICPS Working Paper no. 28.

Gunther, Richard (1992). "Spain: The Very Model of the Modern Elite Settlement." In Richard Gunther and John Higley, eds., *Elites and Democratic Consolidation in Latin America and Southern Europe*, pp. 38–80. New York: Cambridge University Press.

Gunther, Richard (1996). *Spanish Public Policy: From Dictatorship to Democracy*. Estudio/Working Paper No. 84. Barcelona: Institut de Ciencies Politiques.

Gunther, Richard, Giacomo Sani, and Goldie Shabad (1986). *Spain After Franco: The Emergence of a Competitive Party System*. Berkeley: University of California Press.

Guttridge, George H. (1963). *English Whiggism and the American Revolution.* Berkeley: University of California Press.

Guttsman, W. L. (1968). *The British Political Elite.* 3rd rev. ed. London: MacGibbon.

Hall, Peter A. (1986). *Governing the Economy: The Politics of State Intervention in Britain and France.* Oxford: Oxford University Press.

Hanham, H. J., ed. (1969). *The Nineteenth Century Constitution 1815–1914: Documents and Commentary.* London: Cambridge University Press.

Hardarson, Olafur Th. (1995). *Parties and Voters in Iceland.* Reykjavik: Social Science Research Institute.

Harling, Philip (1996). *The Waning of "Old Corruption": The Politics of Economical Reform in Britain, 1779–1846.* Oxford: Clarendon Press.

Heckscher, Gunnar (1958). *Svensk statsförvaltning i arbete.* Stockholm: SNS.

Helmfrid, Staffan (1961). "The Storskifte, Enskifte and Laga Skifte in Sweden: General Features." *Geografiska Annaler* 18: 114–129.

Hernández Bravo de Laguna, Juan, and Augustín Millares Cantero (1995). "Los partidos de centro-derecha en la transición canaria: Subestatalidad e insularismo." In Javier Tusell et al., eds., *Historia de la transición y consolidación democrática en España 1975–86,* vol. 1, pp. 89–100. Madrid: UNED/UAM.

Higgins, Michael (1982). "The Limits of Clientelism: Towards an Assessment of Irish Politics." In Christopher Clapham, ed., *Private Patronage and Public Power: Political Clientelism in the Modern State,* pp. 114–141. London: Pinter.

Hildebrand, George H. (1965). *Growth and Structure in the Economy of Modern Italy.* Cambridge: Harvard University Press.

Holmes, Geoffrey (1982). *Augustan England: Professions, State and Society, 1680–1730.* London: Allen & Unwin.

Hooper, John (1995). *The New Spaniards.* London: Penguin.

Hopkin, Jonathan (1997a). "Clientelism and Party Organization in Italy and Spain: A Comparative Analysis." Paper prepared for Workshop on "Clientelist Politics and Interest Intermediation in Southern Europe," ECPR Joint Sessions, Bern.

Hopkin, Jonathan (1997b). "Political Parties, Political Corruption and the Economic Theory of Democracy." *Crime, Law and Social Change* 27, nos. 3–4: 255–274.

Hopkin, Jonathan (1999). *Party Formation and Democratic Transition in Spain: The Creation and Collapse of the Union of the Democratic Centre.* Basingstoke: Macmillan.

Hopkin, Jonathan, and Caterina Paolucci (1999). "New Parties and the Business Firm Model of Party Organization: Cases from Italy and Spain." *European Journal of Political Research* 35, no. 3: 307–339.

Institut National de la Statistique et des Études Économiques. (1967). *Resumé retrospectif 1966.* Paris: INSEE.

Irving, R. E. M. (1973). *Christian Democracy in France.* London: Allen & Unwin.

Israel, Jonathan I. (1998). *The Dutch Republic: Its Rise, Greatness, and Fall, 1477–1806,* Oxford: Oxford University Press.

Bibliography

Istituto Centrale di Statistica e Ministero dell'Interno (1946). *Statistica delle elezioni amministrative dell'anno 1946 per la ricostituzione del consiglio comunali*. Roma: Istituto Poligrafico dello Stato.

Istituto Centrale di Statistica e Ministero dell'Interno (1953). *Annuario Statistico Italiano, 1952*. Roma: Istituto Poligrafico dello Stato.

Izard, Georges (1937). "Le Parlement et les Professions." *Europe Nouvelle* 20: 738.

Jáuregui, Fernando (1987). *La derecha después de Fraga*. Madrid: Ediciones El País.

Johansson, Roine (1992). *Vid byråkratins gränser: Om handlingsfrihetens organisatoriska begränsningar i klientrelaterat arbete*. Lund: Arkiv.

Jupp, Peter (1998). *British Politics on the Eve of Reform: The Duke of Wellington's Administration, 1828–1830*. London: Macmillan.

Katz, Richard, and Peter Mair (1995). "Changing Models of Party Organization and Party Democracy: The Emergence of the Cartel Party." *Party Politics* 1, no. 1: 5–28.

Kaufman, Robert (1974). "The Patron-Client Concept and Macro-Politics: Prospects and Problems." *Comparative Studies in Society and History* 16, no. 3: 284–308.

Keating, Michael (1998). *The New Regionalism in Western Europe: Territorial Restructuring and Political Change*. Cheltenham, U.K.: Edward Elgar.

Keir, David L. (1934). "Economical Reform, 1779–87." *Law Quarterly Review* 50: 368–851.

Kesselman, Mark. (1967). *The Ambiguous Consensus: A Study of Local Government in France*. New York: Alfred A. Knopf.

Kitschelt, Herbert (2000). "Linkages Between Citizens and Politicians in Democratic Polities." *Comparative Political Studies* 33, no. 6/7: 845–879.

Kooijmans, Luuc (1985). *Onder regenten: De elite in een Hollandse stad: Hoorn 1700–1780*. Amsterdam: De Bataafsche Leeuw.

Komito, Lee (1984). "Irish Clientelism: A Reappraisal." *Economic and Social Review*. 15, no. 3: 173–194.

Korovkin, Michael A. (1988). "Exploitation, Cooperation, Collusion: An Enquiry into Patronage." *Archives Européennes de Sociologie* 29: 105–126.

Korpi, Walter (1983). *The Democratic Class Struggle*. London: Routledge & Kegan.

Kossmann, Ernst H. (1978). *The Low Countries 1780–1940*. Oxford: Clarendon Press.

Kristinsson, Gunnar H. (1996). "Parties, States and Patronage." *West European Politics* 19, no. 3: 433–457.

Kristinsson, Gunnar H. (1999). *Ur digrum sjodi*. Reykjavik: Social Science Research Institute.

Kristjansson, Svanur (1994). *Fra flokksraedi til personustjornmala*. Reykjavik: Social Science Research Institute.

Kubler, George (1962). *The Shape of Time: Remarks on the History of Things*. New Haven: Yale University Press.

Lalumière, Pierre (1959). *L'Inspection des Finances*. Paris: Presses Universitaires de France.

Landé, Carl (1961). "Networks and Groups in Southeast Asia: Some Observations on the Group Theory of Politics." *American Political Science Review* 67: 103–127.

Landé, Carl (1977). "The Dyadic Basis of Clientelism." In Steffen Schmidt et al., eds., *Friends, Followers and Factions*, pp. xiii–xxxv. *A Reader in Political Clientelism*. Berkeley: University of California Press.

Langford, Paul (1991). *Public Life and the Propertied Englishman, 1689–1798*. Oxford: Clarendon Press.

LaPalombara, Joseph (1964). *Interest Groups in Italian Politics*. Princeton: Princeton University Press.

LaPalombara, Joseph (1988). *Democrazia all'italiana*. Milan: Mondadori.

Laroque, Pierre (1952). "La Sécurité Sociale." In La Documentation Française, *L'Organisation gouvernementale, administrative et judiciare de la France*, pp. 146–152. Paris: La Documentation Francaise.

Leenders, Jos M. M. (1991). *Benauwde verdraagzaamheid, hachelijk fatsoen: Families, standen en kerken te Hoorn in het midden van de negentiende eeuw*. The Hague: Stichting Hollandse Historische Reeks.

Legendre, Pierre (1968). *Histoire de l'administration de 1750 à nos jours*. Paris: Presses Universitaires de France.

Letamendia, Pierre (1975). *"Le M.R.P."* Ph.D. thesis, Université de Bordeaux I.

Levy, Jonah (1999). *Tocqueville's Revenge: State, Society, and Economy in Contemporary France*. Cambridge: Harvard University Press.

Levy, Marion J. ([1966], 1996). *Modernization and the Structure of Societies*, vols. 1 and 2. New Brunswick: Transaction Publishers.

Lijphart, Arend (1968). *The Politics of Accommodation: Pluralism and Democracy in the Netherlands*. Berkeley: University of California Press.

Lindqvist, Rafael (1990). *Från folkrörelse till välfärdsbyråkrati: Det svenska sjukförsäkringssystemets utveckling, 1900–1990*. Lund: Arkiv.

Linz, Juan (1967). "The Party System of Spain: Past and Future." In Seymour M. Lipset and Stein Rokkan, eds., *Party Systems and Voter Alignments: Cross-National Perspectives*, pp. 197–282. New York: The Free Press.

Linz, Juan (1981). "A Century of Politics and Interests in Spain." In Suzanne Berger, ed., *Organizing Interests in Western Europe: Pluralism, Corporatism, and the Transformation of Politics*, pp. 365–415. Cambridge: Cambridge University Press.

Linz, Juan, and José Ramón Montero eds. (1984) *Crisis y cambio: Partidos y electores en la España de los años 80*. Madrid: Centro de Estudios Constitucionales.

Lipset, Seymour M., and Stein Rokkan (1967). "Introduction." In Seymour M. Lipset and Stein Rokkan, eds., *Party Systems and Voter Alignments: Cross National Perspectives*, pp. 1–69. New York: The Free Press.

Locke, Richard M., and Kathleen Thelen (1995). "Apples and Oranges Revisited: Contextualized Comparisons and the Study of Comparative Labor Politics." *Politics and Society*, no. 23: 337–367.

Loubère, Leo A. (1974). *Radicalism in Mediterranean France: Its Rise and Decline, 1848–1914*. Albany: State University of New York Press.

Lowi, Theodore (1979). *The End of Liberalism*. 2nd ed. New York: W. W. Norton & Company.

Lyrintzis, Christos (1984). "Political Parties in Post-Junta Greece: A Case of 'Bureaucratic Clientelism'?" *West European Politics* 7, no. 2: 99–118.

Mann, Michael (1988). *States, War and Capitalism*. Oxford: Basil Blackwell.

Bibliography

Mann, Michael (1993). *The Sources of Social Power*, vol. 2: *The Rise of Classes and Nation-States, 1760–1914*. Cambridge: Cambridge University Press.

March, James (1978). "Bounded Rationality, Ambiguity and the Engineering of Choice." *Bell Journal of Economics* 9, no. 2: 587–608.

Márquez Cruz, Guillermo (1992). *Movilidad política y lealtad partidistica en Andalucía*. Madrid: Centro de Investigaciones Sociológicas.

Martín de Pozuelo, Eduardo, et al. (1994). *Guía de la corrupción*. Barcelona: Plaza y Janés.

Mastropaolo, Alfio (1996). *La Repubblica dei destini incrociati: Saggio su cinquant'anni di democrazia in Italia*. Florence: La Nuova Italia.

Mavrogordatos, George Th. (1997). "From Traditional Clientelism to Machine Politics: The Impact of PASOK Populism in Greece." *South European Society & Politics* 2, no. 3: 1–26.

Mazower, Mark (1998). *Dark Continent: Europe's Twentieth Century*. London: Allen Lane, Penguin Press.

McCord, Norman (1991). *British History, 1815–1906*. Oxford: Oxford University Press.

McDonough, Peter, et al. (1981). "The Spanish Public in Political Transition." *British Journal of Political Science* 11, no. 1: 49–79.

McDonough, Peter, et al. (1984). "Authority and Association: Spanish Democracy in Comparative Perspective." *Journal of Politics* 46, no. 2: 652–688.

Melis, Guido (1980). *Burocrazia e socialismo nell'Italia liberale: Alle origini dell'organizzazione sindacale del pubblico impiego (1900–1922)*. Bologna: Il Mulino.

Melis, Guido (1996). *Storia dell'amministrazione italiana 1861–1993*. Bologna: Il Mulino.

Mellbourn, Anders (1979). *Byråkratins ansikten*. Stockholm: Liber Förlag.

Mershon, Carol (1996). "The Costs of Coalition: Coalition Theories and Italian Governments." *American Political Science Review* 90, no. 3 (Sept.): 534–554.

Merton, Robert (1968). *Social Theory and Social Structure*. New York: Free Press.

Miller, William (1905). *Greek Life in Town and Country*. London: George Newnes.

Montassier, Valérie-Anne (1980). *Les années d'après-guerre, 1944–1949*. Paris: Fayard.

Moore, Barrington Jr. (1978). *Injustice*. London: McMillan.

Moss, David (1995). "Patronage Revisited: The Dynamics of Information and Reputation." *Journal of Modern Italian Studies* 1, no. 1: 58–93.

Mouvement Républicain Populaire ([1946a]). *La nationalisation*. Paris: Imprimeries Parisiennes Réunies.

Mouvement Républicain Populaire ([1946b]). *Les grandes options de la politique économique*. Paris: Marcel Dodeman.

Mouzelis, Nicos (1986). *Politics in the Semi-Periphery: Early Parliamentarism and Late Industrialization in the Balcans and Latin America*. London: Macmillan.

Müller, Wolfgang (1989). "Patry Patronage in Austria: Theoretical Considerations and Empirical Findings." In Anton Pelinka and Fritz Plasser, eds., *The Austrian Party System*, pp. 327–356. Boulder, Colo.: Westview Press.

Nadal, Jacques (1952). "Les Finances Locales." In La Documentation Française, *L'Organisation gouvernementale, administrative et judiciare de la France*, pp. 111–116. Paris: La Documentation Francaise.

Namier, Lewis B., and John Brooke (1964). *The House of Commons, 1754–90.* 3 vols. London: Secker & Warburg.

Nilsson, Sven A. (1990). *De stora krigens tid.* Stockholm: Almqvist & Wiksell International.

Nilsson, Torbjörn (1997). *Liberalismen och 1800-talets ämbetsmannastat: Fiender eller allierade.* Stockholm: SCORE, Rapportserie 1997: 6.

Nilsson, Torbjörn (1999). "Ämbetsmannen som kapitalist: En okänd 1800-talshistoria." *Scandia*, no. 1: 71–96.

Novick, Peter (1968). *The Resistance versus Vichy: The Purge of Collaborators in Liberated France.* New York: Columbia University Press.

Núñez Seijas, Xosé-Manoel (1995). "Nacionalismos y regionalismos ante la formación y consolidación del Estado autonómico español (1975–1995): Una interpretación." In Javier Tusell et al., eds., *Historia de la transición y consolidación democrática en España*, vol. 1, pp. 427–456. Madrid: UNED/UAM.

O'Gorman, Frank (1967). *The Whig Party and the French Revolution.* London: Macmillan.

O'Gorman, Frank (1975). *The Rise of Party in England: The Rockingham Whigs, 1760–1782.* London: Allen & Unwin.

O'Gorman, Frank (1989). *Voters, Patrons and Parties: The Unreformed Electoral System of Hanoverian England, 1734–1832.* Oxford: Clarendon Press.

Olson, Mancur (1971). *The Logic of Collective Action.* Cambridge: Harvard University Press.

Pahl, R. E. (1968). "The Rural-Urban Continuum." In R. E. Pahl, ed., *Readings in Urban Sociology*, pp. 263–297. Oxford: Pergamon Press.

Paine, Thomas (1791). *Rights of Man.* London: Printed for J. S. Jordan.

Panebianco, Angelo. (1982). *Modelli di partito: Organizzazione e potere nei partiti politici.* Bologna: Il Mulino.

Papadopoulos, Yannis (1997). "Transformations of Party Clientelism in Southern Europe in a Phase of Democratic Consolidation." *Swiss Political Science Review* 2, no. 4: 81–89.

Papakostas, Apostolis (1995). *Arbetarklassen i organisationernas värld: En jämförande studie av fackföreningarnas sociala och historiska förutsättningar i Sverige och Grekland.* Stockholm: Almqvist & Wiksell International

Papakostas, Apostolis (1997). "Staten: Sociologiska perspektiv." *Sociologisk Forskning*, no. 3: 25–45.

Parris, Henry (1969). *Constitutional Bureaucracy.* London: Allen & Unwin.

Pérez Díaz, Victor (1993). *The Return of Civil Society: The Emergence of Democratic Spain.* Cambridge, Mass.: Harvard University Press.

Petropulos, John (1985). Πολιτική και συγκρότηση κράτους στο Ελληνικό βασίλειο. Athens: MIETE.

Piattoni, Simona (1996). "Local Political Classes and Economic Development: The Cases of Abruzzo and Puglia in the 1970s and 1980s." Ph.D. dissertation, Massachusetts Institute of Technology.

Bibliography

Piattoni, Simona (1998). "'Virtuous Clientelism': The Southern Question Resolved?" In Jane Schneider, ed., *Italy's "Southern Question": Orientalism in One Country*, pp. 225–244. Oxford: Berg.

Pizanias, Petros (1993). *Οι φτωχοί των πόλεων*. Athens: Themelio.

Pizzorno, Alessandro (1974). "I ceti medi nei meccanismi del consenso." In Fabio L. Cavazza and Stephen R. Graubard, eds., *Il caso italiano*, vol. 1: 67–98. Milan: Garzanti.

Pizzorno, Alessandro (1981). "Interests and parties in pluralism." In Suzanne Berger, ed., *Organizing Interests in Western Europe*, pp. 247–284. Cambridge: Cambridge University Press.

Pizzorno, Alessandro (1992). "La corruzione nel sistema politico." In Donatella Della Porta, *Lo scambio occulto: Casi di corruzione politica in Italia*, pp. 13–74. Bologna: Il Mulino.

Pizzorno, Alessandro (1994). *Le radici della politica assoluta e altri saggi*. Milan: Feltrinelli.

Pizzorno, Alessandro (1996). "Vecchio e nuovo nella transizione italiana." In Nicola Negri and Loredana Sciolla, eds., *Il paese dei paradossi: Le basi sociali della politica in Italia*, pp. 253–285. Rome: La Nuova Italia Scientifica.

Poggi, Gianfranco (1990). *The State: Its Nature, Development and Prospects*. Cambridge: Polity Press.

Porras Nadales, Antonio (1985). *Geografía electoral de Andalucía*. Madrid: Centro de Investigaciones Sociológicas.

Porter, Roy (1982). *English Society in the Eighteenth Century*. Harmondsworth: Penguin.

Posner, Michael V., and Stuart J. Woolf (1967). *Italian Public Enterprise*. Cambridge, Mass.: Harvard University Press.

Prak, Maarten R. (1985). *Gezeten burgers: De elite in een Hollandse stad, Leiden 1700–1780*. Dieren: De Bataafsche Leeuw.

Preston, Paul ed. (1993). *Revolution and War in Spain, 1931–39*. 2nd ed. London: Routledge.

Prieto-Lacaci, Rafael (1992). "Asociaciones Voluntarias." In Salustiano del Campo, ed., *Tendencias Sociales en España 1960–90*, vol. 1: pp. 200–232. Bilbao: Fundación BBV.

Prieur, Christian (1957). "La campagne électorale dans l'Aveyron." In Maurice Duverger, François Goguel, and Jean Touchard, eds., *Les Élections du 2 Janvier 1956*, pp. 322–352. Paris: Armand Colin.

Przeworski, Adam, and John Sprague (1986). *Paper Stones: A History of Electoral Socialism*. Chicago: University of Chicago Press.

Psychogios, Dimitris (1987). *Προίκες, φόροι, σταφίδα και ψωμί*. Athens: EKKE.

Puech, Louis (1922). *Essai sur la candidature officielle en France depuis 1851*. Montpellier: Mende.

Putnam, Robert D. (1993). *Making Democracy Work: Civic Traditions in Modern Italy*. Princeton: Princeton University Press.

Ramírez Jiménez, Manuel (1969). *Los grupos de presión en la Segunda República española*. Madrid: Editorial Tecnos.

Ramírez Jiménez, Manuel (1981). "La Segunda República: Una visión de su régimen político." *Arbor* 426/427: 27–36.

Randeraad, Nico (1994). "Ambtenaren in Nederland (1815–1915)." *Bijdragen en Mededelingen betreffende de Geschiedenis der Nederlanden* 109: 209–236.

Randeraad, Nico (1998a). "Faces of Centralization: Prefects in Italy and Commissioners of the King in the Netherlands in the Second Half of the Nineteenth Century." In Nico Randeraad, ed., *Mediators between State and Society*, pp. 87–109. Hilversum: Verloren.

Randeraad, Nico (1998b). "Gemeenten tussen wet en werkelijkheid." In Nicolaas C. F. van Sas and Henk te Velde, eds., *De eeuw van de Grondwet: Grondwet en politiek in Nederland, 1798–1917*, pp. 246–265. Deventer: Kluwer.

Randeraad, Nico (2000). "Het geplooide land." In Johan C. H. Blom and Jaap Talsma, eds., *De verzuiling voorbij: Godsdienst, stand en natie in de lange negentiende eeuw*. Amsterdam: Het Spinhuis.

Randeraad, Nico, and Dirk J. Wolffram (1998). "De Nederlandse bestuurscultuur in historisch perspectief." In Frank Hendriks and Theo A. J. Toonen, eds., *Schikken en plooien: De stroperige staat bij nader inzien*, pp. 35–49. Assen: Van Gorcum.

Richards, Mike (1995). " 'Terror and Progress': Industrialization, Modernity and the Making of Francoism." In Helen Graham and Jo Labanyi, eds., *Spanish Cultural Studies: An Introduction*. Oxford: Oxford University Press.

Rioux, Jean-Pierre (1987). *The Fourth Republic, 1944–1958*. Translated by Godfrey Rogers. Cambridge: Cambridge University Press.

Ritcheson, Charles R. (1954). *British Politics and the American Revolution*. Norman: University of Oklahoma Press.

Rokkan, Stein (1966). "Numerical Democracy and Corporate Pluralism." In Robert Dahl, ed., *Political Opposition in Western Democracies*. New Haven: Yale University Press.

Romero-Maura, Joaquín (1977). "Caciquismo as a Political System." In Ernst Gellner and John Waterbury, eds., *Patrons and Clients*, pp. 40–65. London: Duckworth & Co.

Roniger, Luis (1981). "Clientelism and Patron-Client Relations: A Bibliography." In Shmuel E. Eisenstadt and René Lemarchand, eds., *Political Clientelism, Patronage and Development*, pp. 297–330. Beverly Hills, Calif.: Sage.

Roniger, Luis (1983). "Modern Patron-Client Relations and Historical Clientelism: Some Clues from Ancient Republican Rome." *Archives Européennes de Sociologie* 24: 63–95.

Roniger, Luis (1988). "La fiducia: Un concetto fragile, una non meno fragile realtà." *Rassegna Italiana di Sociologia* 29, no. 3: 383–402.

Roniger, Luis (1990). *Hierarchy and Trust in Modern Mexico and Brazil*. New York: Praeger.

Roniger, Luis (1994). "The Comparative Study of Clientelism and the Changing Nature of Civil Society in the Contemporary World." In Luis Roniger and Ayşe Güneş-Ayata, eds., *Democracy, Clientelism and Civil Society*, pp. 1–19. Boulder, Colo.: Lynne-Rienner.

Bibliography

Roniger, Luis, and Ayşe Güneş-Ayata, eds. (1994). *Democracy, Clientelism and Civil Society.* Boulder, Colo.: Lynne Reiner.

Roseveare, Henry (1973). *The Treasury, 1660–1870: The Foundations of Control.* London: Allen & Unwin.

Rossi-Doria, Manlio (1963). *Rapporto sulla Federconsorzi.* Bari: Laterza.

Rotelli, Ettore, ed. (1981). *Tendenze di amminstrazione locale nel dopoguerra.* Bologna: Il Mulino.

Rothstein, Bo (1996). *The Social Democratic State.* Pittsburgh: Pittsburgh University Press.

Rothstein, Bo (1998). "State Building and Capitalism: The Rise of the Swedish Bureaucracy." *Scandinavian Political Studies* 21, no. 4: 287–306.

Rousso, Henri (1991). *The Vichy Syndrome: History and Memory in France since 1944.* Trans. Arthur Goldhammer. Cambridge: Harvard University Press.

Rubinstein, William D. (1983). "The End of Old Corruption in Britain, 1780–1860." *Past and Present* 101: 55–86.

Sabetti, Filippo (1984). *Political Authority in a Sicilian Village.* New Brunswick: Rutgers University Press.

Saraceno, Pasquale (1972). "La disoccupazione italiana è dovuta a ragioni strutturali." In Augusto Graziani, ed., *L'economia italiana: 1945–1970*, pp. 100–103. Bologna: Il Mulino.

Sartori, Giovanni (1970). "Concept Misformation in Comparative Politics." *American Political Science Review* 64, no. 4: 1033–1053.

Sartori, Giovanni (1976). *Parties and Party Systems: A Framework for Political Analysis.* Cambridge: Cambridge University Press.

Sartori, Giovanni (1984). *Social Science Concepts: A Systematic Analysis.* Beverly Hills, Calif.: Sage.

Sastre García, Cayo (1997). "La transición política en España: Una sociedad desmovilizada." *Revista Española de Investigaciones Sociológicas*, no. 80: 33–68.

Scarrow, Susan (1994). "The 'Paradox of Enrolment': Assessing the Costs and Benefits of Party Memberships." *European Journal of Political Research* 25, no. 1: 41–60.

Schama, Simon (1992). *Patriots and Liberators: Revolution in the Netherlands, 1780–1813.* London: Fontana.

Schattschneider, Elmer E. (1960). *The Semi-Sovereign People: A Realist View of Democracy in America.* New York: Holt, Rinehart & Winston.

Schmidt, Steffen, et al., eds. (1977). *Friends, Followers and Factions: A Reader in Political Clientelism.* Berkeley: University of California Press.

Schmitter, Philippe (1974). "Still the Century of Corporatism?" In Frederick B. Pike and Thomas Strich, eds., *The New Corporatism: Social-Political Structures in the Iberian World*, pp. 85–131. Notre Dame: University of Notre Dame Press.

Schneider, Jane, and Peter Schneider (1989). *Classi sociali, economia e politica in Sicilia.* Rubbettino: Soveria Mannelli.

Scoppola, Pietro (1977). *La Proposta Politica di De Gasperi.* Bologna: Il Mulino.

Scott, James (1977). "Patronage or Exploitation?" In Ernst Gellner and James Waterbury, eds., *Patrons and Clients in Mediterranean Societies*, pp. 21–40. London: Duckworth.

Sharp, Walter Rice (1931). *The French Civil Service: Bureaucracy in Transition*. New York: Macmillan.

Shefter, Martin (1977). "Party and Patronage: Germany, England, and Italy." *Politics & Society* 7: 403–451.

Shefter, Martin (1994). *Political Parties and the State: The American Historical Experience*. Princeton: Princeton University Press.

Shubert, Adrian (1990). *A Social History of Modern Spain*. London: Unwin Hyman.

Silberman, Bernard (1993). *Cages of Reason: The Rise of the Rational State in France, Japan, the United States and Great Britain*. Chicago: University of Chicago Press.

Silverman, Sydel (1977a). "Patronage and Community-Nation Relationships in Central Italy." In Steffan Schmidt et al., eds., *Friends, Followers, and Factions: A Reader in Political Clientelism*, pp. 293–304. Berkeley: University of California Press.

Silverman, Sydel (1977b). "Clientelism as Myth." In Ernst Gellner and James Waterbury, eds., *Patrons and Clients in Mediterranean Societies*, pp. 7–20. London: Duckworth.

Simmel, George ([1902–3], 1950). "The Metropolis and Social Life." In Kurt Wolf, ed., *The Sociology of Georg Simmel*, pp. 409–424. New York: Free Press.

Siwek-Pouydesseau, Jeanne (1989). *Le syndicalisme des fonctionnaires jusqu'à la guerre froide*. Lille: Presses Universitaires de Lille.

Socialisme and Democratie. Maandblad van de Partij van de Arbeid (1957).

Sombart, Werner ([1906], 1976). *Why Is There No Socialism in the United States?* New York: M. E. Sharpe, Inc.

Sotiropoulos, Dimitri (1996). *Populism and Bureaucracy: The Case of Greece under PASOK, 1981–1989*. Notre Dame: University of Notre Dame Press.

Stinchcombe, Arthur (1965). "Social Structure and Organizations." In James March, ed., *Handbook of Organizations*, pp. 142–193. Chicago: Rand McNally.

Stoetzel, Jean, and Pierre Hassner (1957). "Résultats d'un sondage dans le premier secteur de la Seine" In Maurice Duverger, François Goguel, and Jean Touchard, eds., *Les elections du 2 janvier 1956*, pp. 199–248. Paris: Armand Colin.

Suleiman, Ezra N. (1974). *Politics, Power, and Bureaucracy in France: The Administrative Elite*. Princeton: Princeton University Press.

Sylos Labini, Paolo (1975). *Saggio sulle classi sociali*. Bari: Laterza.

Tarrow, Sidney (1967). *Peasant Communism in Southern Italy*. New Haven: Yale University Press.

Tarrow, Sidney (1972). *Partito comunista e contadini nel Mezzogiorno*. Turin: Einaudi.

Tarrow, Sidney (1977). *Between Center and Periphery: Grassroots Politicians in Italy and France*. New Haven: Yale University Press.

Tarrow, Sidney (1990). "Maintaining Hegemony in Italy: 'The softer they rise, the slower they fall!'" In T. J. Pempel, ed., *Uncommon Democracies: The One-Party Dominant Regimes*, pp. 306–332. Ithaca: Cornell University Press.

Theobald, Robin (1992). "The Decline of Patron-Client Relations in Developed Societies." *Archives Européennes de Sociologie* 33: 183–191.

Therborn, Göran (1978). *What Does the Ruling Class Do When It Rules?* London: Verso.

Therborn, Göran (1989). *Byråkrati och borgarklass i Sverige.* Lund: Arkiv.

Thompson, Edward P. (1963). *The Making of the English Working Class.* London: Gollancz.

Thörnberg, E. H. (1912). "Folkrörelser och samhällsklasser i Sverige." *Svensk Tidskrift* 2: 77–90.

Tilly, Charles (1984). *Big Structures, Large Processes, Huge Comparisons.* New York: Russell Sage Foundation.

Tilly, Charles (1990a). *Coercion, Capital and European States.* Cambridge: Blackwell.

Tilly, Charles (1990b). "Transplanted Networks." In Virginia Yans-Mclaughlin, ed., *Immigration Reconsidered*, pp. 79–95. Oxford: Oxford University Press.

Tilly, Charles (1998). *Durable Inequality.* Berkeley: University of California Press.

Tilton, Timothy (1974). "The Social Origins of Liberal Democracy: The Swedish Case." *American Political Science Review* 68, no. 2: 561–571.

"The Tragedy of Diana." (1997). *The Economist*, September 6.

Trice, Thomas G. (1974). "Spanish Liberalism in Crisis: A Study of the Liberal Party during Spain's Parliamentary Crisis." Ph.D. dissertation, University of Wisconsin.

Trigilia, Carlo (1992). *Sviluppo senza autonomia: Effetti perversi delle politiche nel Mezzogiorno.* Bologna: Il Mulino.

Tsoucalas, Constantin (1978). "On the Problem of Political Clientalism in Greece in the Nineteenth Century." *Journal of Hellenic Diaspora* 5, no. 1: 1–17.

Tusell Gómez, Xavier (1976). "The Functioning of the Cacique System in Andalusia, 1890–1931." In Stanley Payne, ed., *Politics and Society in Twentieth-Century Spain*, pp. 1–28. New York: New Viewpoints.

Van Braam, Aris (1957). *Ambtenaren en bureaucratie in Nederland.* Zeist: De Haan.

Van der Voort, René H. (1994). *Overheidsbeleid en overheidsfinanciën in Nederland 1850–1913.* Amsterdam: Proefschrift Vrije Universiteit.

Van IJsselmuiden, Pieter G. (1988). *Binnenlandse Zaken en het ontstaan van de moderne bureaucratie in Nederland 1813–1940.* Kampen: Kok.

Van Sas, Nicolaas C. F. (1981). "Het politieke bestel onder Koning Willem I." *Documentatieblad Werkgroep 18ᵉ eeuw*, no. 49–50: 110–133.

Van Tijn, Theo (1965). *Twintig jaren Amsterdam: De maatschappelijke ontwikkeling van de hoofdstad van de jaren '50 der vorige eeuw tot 1876.* Amsterdam: Scheltema en Holkema.

Van Vugt, Joseph P. A. (1980). "De verzuiling van het lager onderwijs in Limburg, 1860–1940." In *Jaarboek van het Katholiek Documentatiecentrum* 10: 17–60.

Varela, Santiago (1982). "Los Partidos Políticos en la Segunda República." *Cuenta y Razón* 5: 63–76.

Velain, Serge, and Corinne Nadin (1990). *Les Leaders de la Démocratie Chrétienne dans le Morbihan sous la IVᵉ République.* Vannes: École de droit et des sciences économiques, DEUG II.

Verdier, Daniel (1995). "The Politics of Public Aid to Private Industry: The Role of Policy Networks." *Comparative Political Studies* 28, no. 1: 3–42.

Verhoeven, Theodora H. G. (1994). *Ter vorming van verstand en hart. Lager onderwijs in oostelijk Noord-Brabant, ca. 1770–1920*. Hilversum: Verloren.

Vinen, Richard (1995). *Bourgeois Politics in France, 1945–1951*. Cambridge: Cambridge University Press.

Vitali, Rocco (1996). "Politique locale et cliéntelisme: Analyse du cas tessinois." *Swiss Political Science Review* 2, no. 3: 47–68.

Von Platen, Magnus, ed. (1988). *Klient och patron*. Stockholm: Natur och Kultur.

Wade, John (1820). *The Black Book; or, Corruption Unmasked*. London: J. Fairburn.

Wade, John (1826(?)). *Appendix to the Black Book*. London: J. Fairburn.

Wade, John (1832). *The Extraordinary Black Book*. London: Effinghan Wilson

Waline, Marcel (1958). "Les résistances techniques de l'administration au pouvoir politique." In Gaston Berger et al., *Politique et Technique*, pp. 159–179. Paris: Presses Universitaires de France.

Walston, James (1981). "Electoral Politics in Southern Calabria." *Contemporary Crises* 5, no. 4: 417–445.

Walston, James (1988). *The Mafia and Clientelism: Roads to Rome in Post-War Calabria*. London: Routledge.

Walzer, Michael (1992). "The Civil Society Argument." In Chantal Mouffe, ed., *Dimensions of Radical Democracy*, pp. 89–107. London: Verso.

Warner, Carolyn M. (1994). "Priests, Patronage and Politicians." Ph.D. dissertation, Harvard University.

Warner, Carolyn M. (1997). "Political Parties and the Opportunity Costs of Patronage." *Party Politics* 3 (Oct.): 533–548.

Warner, Carolyn M. (1998). "Getting Out the Vote with Patronage and Threat: Constructing the French and Italian Christian Democratic Parties, 1944–1958." *Journal of Interdisciplinary History* 28, no. 4 (Spring): 553–582.

Warner, Carolyn M. (2000). *Confessions of an Interest Group: The Catholic Church and Political Parties in Europe*. Princeton: Princeton University Press.

Waterbury, John (1977). "An Attempt to Put Patrons and Clients in Their Place." In Ernst Gellner and James Waterbury, eds., *Patrons and Clients in Mediterranean Societies*, pp. 329–342. London: Duckworth.

Weil, Georges-Denis (1895). *Les Élections législatives depuis 1789: Histoire de la législation et des moeurs*. Paris: Germer Ballière.

Weingrod, Alex (1968). "Patrons, Patronage and Political Parties." *Comparative Studies in Society and History* 7, no. 3: 377–400.

White, Caroline (1980). *Patrons and Partisans: A Study of Politics in Two Southern Italian Comuni*. Cambridge: Cambridge University Press.

White, Harrison C. (1970). *Chains of Opportunity*. Cambridge: Harvard University Press.

Williams, Philip M. (1964). *Crisis and Compromise: Politics in the Fourth Republic*. Hamden, Conn.: Archon Books.

Winberg, Christer (1977). *Folkökning och proletarisering*. Lund: Bo Cavefors Bokförlag.

Wintle, Michael J. (1987). *Pillars of Piety: Religion in the Netherlands in the Nineteenth Century*. Hull: Hull University Press.

Bibliography

Wirth, Louis (1938). "Urbanism as a Way of Life." *American Journal of Sociology* 44, no. 1: 1–24.

Wolffram, Dirk J. (1993). *Bezwaarden en verlichten: Verzuiling in een Gelderse provinciestad, Harderwijk 1850–1925*. Amsterdam: Het Spinhuis.

Wood, Ellen M. (1995). *Democracy against Capitalism: Reviewing Historical Materialism*. Cambridge: Cambridge University Press.

Woolf, Stuart J. (1991). *A History of Italy 1700–1860: The Social Constraints of Political Change*. London and New York: Routledge.

Worst, Ids J. H. (1992). "Koning Willem I: Het begin van 'ons grondwettig volksbestaan.'" In Coen A. Tamse and Els Witte, eds., *Staats- en natievorming in Willem I's Koninkrijk (1815–1830)*, pp. 56–75. Brussel: VUB Press.

Wright, Gordon (1953). "Catholics and Peasantry in France." *Political Science Quarterly* 68, no. 4: 526–551.

Wright, Gordon (1964). *Rural Revolution in France*. Stanford: Stanford University Press.

Wright, Vincent (1991). "Representative Bureaucracy: Some Introductory Comments." In Vincent Wright, ed., *The Representativity of Public Administration: Cahier d'Histoire de l'Administration no. 3*, pp. 5–15. Brussels: Institut International des Sciences Administratives.

Wright, William (1971). "Comparative Party Models: Rational-Efficient and Party-Democracy." In William Wright, ed., *A Comparative Study of Party Organization*, pp. 17–54. Columbus: Charles E. Merrill.

Wylie, Laurence (1964). *Village in the Vaucluse: An Account of Life in a French Village*. Rev. ed. New York: Harper Colophon.

Yates, William Ross (1958). "Power, Principle, and the Doctrine of the Mouvement Republicain Populaire." *Americain Political Science Review* 52, no. 2: 419–436.

Zeldin, Theodore (1973). *France 1848–1945*, vol. 1. London: Oxford University Press.

Zolberg, Aristide (1986). "How Many Exceptionalisms?" In Ira Katznelson and Aristide Zolberg, eds., *Working-Class Formation*, pp. 397–455. Princeton: Princeton University Press.

Zuckerman, Alan S. (1979). *The Politics of Faction: Christian Democratic Rule in Italy*. New Haven: Yale University Press.

Index